Witches Mill – Isle of Mann

French name (moe – neek)

META-PSYCHOMETRY:
Key to
Power and Abundance

META-PSYCHOMETRY:
Key to
Power and Abundance

Gavin Frost
and
Yvonne Frost

PARKER PUBLISHING COMPANY, INC.
West Nyack, N.Y.

Library of Congress Cataloging in Publication Data

Frost, Gavin.
   Meta-psychometry.

   1. Success. 2. Occult sciences. I. Frost,
Yvonne, joint author. II. Title.
BJ1611.2.F73   131'.32   77-10432
ISBN 0-13-578583-9

Blessed be all those who seek

Also by the Authors

The Magic Power of Witchcraft

Nothing in life is to be feared . . .
It is only to be understood.

—Madame Marie Curie

A Special Note: In recent years, the Federally recognized non-profit Church and School of Wicca (that is, of Witchcraft) has taught over 12,000 people to be Witches: to use their powers, especially their psychometric powers, to help themselves and others toward better lives. There are presently Witchcraft churches in several states and foreign countries. Their members are "new Witches," practicing neither black nor white Witchcraft but using these powers as their own consciences guide them.

You should become aware of what your power can do for you and for others so that you can decide whether to join the friendly ranks of the Witches or learn how to remain free of their influence. Serious inquirers may write the authors at the School of Wicca, Box 1502, New Bern, North Carolina 28560.

HOW THIS BOOK WILL CHANGE YOUR LIFE

Do you sometimes feel that the world is against you? That, given just a little extra luck, you would be as good as anyone else? Do you know successful people, apparently no more intelligent than you are, who take it easy while you work hard?

How many people do you know whose luck changed when they bought a lucky charm?

If you want and need that extra edge on the world, that extra bit of luck, Meta-Psychometry can give it to you, and this book is for you. The gambler and his lucky piece, the child and her rabbit's foot, and the Christian and his cross, all unknowingly use Meta-Psychometry to help themselves in their lives.

With the aid of this book, you can consciously direct and use the same astral forces they do; but because you will know what you are doing, you will be able to be infinitely more effective in your efforts, and you will gain miraculous results that earlier you might have called magical.

Meta-Psychometry is not magic. As this book clearly points out for the first time, Meta-Psychometry is the application of well-known natural laws to daily situations. Follow the simple methods and techniques outlined herein and you will gain sure-fire results, amazing results that will literally cost you little money and only a few moments of your time each day. With Meta-Psychometry, anything you want can be brought within your grasp—health, happiness, power, wealth: you name it, and it can be yours.

TWENTY-FIVE WAYS THIS BOOK WILL HELP YOU

Here are just twenty-five of the ways this book will help you to achieve your goals.

EASY-TO-USE TABLES AND GUIDES

Throughout this book, you will find numerous tables and illustrations to help you logically develop your innate talents and to guide you in gaining your desires. For instance, Chapter 1 alone has five illustrative guides to aid you in your work.

In addition to all these guides, an Appendix lists the best available sources of materials and help that we have found. This short listing is the distillation of our years of work in the field. The people are highly recommended; all are personally known to us.

Thus, in this one book, you have in your hands all the information you need to use your God-given abilities in gaining all your desires.

JOEL S GOES TO WASHINGTON

Dr. Loy S is a well-known occultist who lives near Amarillo, Texas. One evening while talking to the local sheriff, Dr. Loy showed Joel that by gently rubbing his finger across the outer cellophane wrapper of a cigarette package, the finger could actually pick up the line of demarcation between one color and another. As Dr. Loy put it afterward, "It was a real revelation to Joel that he had a sense which he didn't realize was there. All the rest of the evening he sat at the kitchen table testing himself with the cigarette package." From this simple beginning, Joel developed a good Meta-Psychometric ability. He found he could sense when a car was carrying stolen property, and soon he was known throughout the state as a brilliant detective. It was not long before he was being promoted over the heads of more senior men.

Joel was invited to head up a drug squad at a south Texas border town; very soon his squad was seizing more contraband than the teams at the more major border crossings. When drug traffickers realized that it was very difficult to get past Joel's post, the traffic through his area dwindled to almost nothing. In fact, we are told, it became a joke in Mexico to send the unwanted amateur smugglers through Joel's post with a shipment so they would be picked up and gotten out of the hair of the professional drug runners. Of course, Joel's success resulted in several promotions and eventually the offer of a senior position in Washington. So, from a back-country sheriff, Joel almost abruptly became a Washington executive through his use of the power of Meta-Psychometry.

PROVE IT FOR YOURSELF TODAY

You can emulate Joel's success; you, too, can prove to yourself right now that it is possible to do it the same way Dr. Loy showed Joel. The simplest and easiest thing to test yourself with is a cellophane-wrapped package of cigarettes. If you don't have a pack handy, take a piece of plastic film wrap and place it on a boldly colored book jacket. Pick a quiet time when you won't be disturbed; lean back in your chair; relax with your eyes closed. Very gently pass the pad of your index finger across the film wrap or the cellophane of the cigarette package. After a little practice, you will find you can detect the line of demarcation between two colors. You are using the receptors in your fingertip to pick up psychometrically the different emanations from two different colors. Scientists call this ability "dermal vision," and they are very excited about exploring this field to help those unfortunate people who have vision problems.

From this first simple step in psychometry, just as Joel did, you can develop your ability into its Meta-Psychometric state.

To develop your ability fully, you need to experience a wide variety of feelings. You may have an acquaintance who feels her house is "unfriendly." Go with her to her home and see whether you pick up the same impression. Every little experiment you conduct enables you to add to your store of knowledge of the way you react to various emotional feelings that are impressed into buildings and places. As the great Olympic runner started in earliest childhood with a few toddling steps, so you, by being able to detect color differences with your fingertip, are exercising the toddling psychic muscles which, when developed, will allow you to become a gold medal winner in the occult race of life.

PSYCHOMETRY AND YOUR ENERGY BANK

Literally all objects absorb psychic and emotional energy. Police forces all over the world make use of famed psychics like Bevy Jaegers and Peter Hurkos to "read" the events which have happened in a crime area. The many hundreds of successes that these people have had in solving previously insoluble crimes show how real the science of psychometry is.

Emotional energy is real energy. Everyone puts out emotional energy. It is stored and accumulated in objects, just as electricity is stored in your car's battery. Not only can you impress an object with your emotional energy; you can also withdraw some of that energy in time of need from what we call astral energy banks. Suppose someone has been discussing whether or not you should get a promotion. By using the methods in this book, and by visiting the scene of the argument, you can find out the outcome. Since everyone, no matter how unsuspecting, is affected by the vibrations of an area, you can improve your chances of winning that promotion if you impress your boss's desk, for instance, with thoughts of how efficient you, the candidate, are.

MR. SEITO AND HO TEI

A simple example of such an energy accumulator or astral energy bank is the little Ho Tei figurine, the "Laughing Buddha" that many Japanese families keep in their homes.

Mr. K. Seito is a Tokyo businessman. Every evening upon his arrival home he pats his Ho Tei statuette on its smiling head and rubs its big round tummy. Now Japanese businesses are conducted in much more of a family-like manner than any American organization would dream of doing. If an employee makes a faux pas, he is not fired; instead (and very discouraging it is to a Japanese businessman, too) he suffers "loss of face." This day, Seito-San had really lost face; he had let a Chinese mainland competitor know of one of his firm's manufacturing processes.

Seito-San was really very despondent and his wife could tell that drastic measures were needed to pull him out of his depression. Though he was too westernized to consider hara kiri, as he sat before a picture of his ancestors, his obvious depression meant many weeks of misery for himself and the family. Mrs. Seito went out and brought the family's Ho Tei into the room where Seito-San sat. Then she boiled her largest pot full of water. She carried that boiling pot into the room and poured it over the poor little laughing Buddha. This sudden change in temperature released all the happy energy that Seito-San and his family had stored in the Ho Tei; and with this vast amount of happy energy in the room, Seito-San was unable to maintain his despondent attitude.

Mrs. Seito had used the family's astral energy bank or accumulator of energy to change her husband's attitude. You, too, can use your astral energy banks in this way. This book will teach you how to store energy and release it to change the attitudes of other people to you and to your ideas.

CHOOSING YOUR ASTRAL ENERGY BANK

As you work with these natural energy patterns, you will find that objects of certain types accumulate corresponding types of energy. The type of energy accumulated is dependent on many factors: the color and surface texture of the object, the material the object is made from, and whether or not the object has for the beholder any emotional tie. For instance: If you had a beautiful ivory image of the goddess Diana, it would be difficult for you to store in it any great amount of perverted hate-energy. Obviously, if the goddess has been in a room where a crime was committed, she might have some amount of such energy imprinted into her. In general, however, a beautiful object works best at storing positive, loving thoughts; whereas negative objects such as a hard-lined red cross should be used to store thoughts of enmity, blood, and destruction. For almost everyone, at the sight of a cross —especially a red cross—thinks immediately of accidents, terror, and perhaps even of crucifixion.

Throughout this entire book, we shall give you very careful guidelines so you can select for yourself the astral energy bank most appropriate to your purpose. This choice of the right power object is one of the keys in turning normal everyday psychometry into Meta-Psychometry. Too many people merely spin their wheels and dissipate their energies in trying to store astral energy simply because they have chosen the wrong type of object. You cannot store dollars in your car's lead acid electrical accumulator; you store dollars in a bank. Conversely, you cannot store electricity in a bank vault; you store it in your car's accumulator. Sadly, many otherwise competent occultists seem to make this basic error again and again. This book will put you far ahead of such people, for after reading it you will be fully competent to select at a moment's notice the right astral energy bank for your purpose.

NOBODY IS IMMUNE TO META-PSYCHOMETRY

Every day people write to us asking for help; they feel they are being damaged by hexes, by curses, and even by vibes from places in which they live. You yourself know that certain places feel friendly but others feel hostile; some places you feel at home in, and others you want to leave promptly. This book will tell you both how to avoid being affected by these energy forms and how to sense them more readily. Too many people learn to sense feelings but are unable to resist their influence. Thus, as we teach you how to sense impressed emotions, we must also tell you how to become impervious to their influence; otherwise, your life could become a misery, since almost every place has some negative feelings associated with it. Imagine entering a room and being affected by all the emotions that have ever been experienced there. This book will tell you how to avoid such problems.

Just as you are affected by these low-level emotions, so others also are unwittingly affected by them. So when you know a certain place affects people negatively, you can get your enemies to go there more often so that they are dragged down. Conversely, if a friend needs a boost, you can take him to a place that has positive vibes; this will give him that needed energy to face the future. It is, of course, just a short step from taking people to places of varied emotions to your charging jewelry with the emotions that you intend the person to feel, and giving the jewelry to him. Ever afterward, his life will be affected by the thoughtform you put into your energy bank. Through these techniques, your life can be dramatically changed when you learn to direct the awesome astral powers with Meta-Psychometry.

Gavin and Yvonne Frost

CONTENTS

7 Heal Yourself with Medi-Psychometry (cont.)

*Does It to Herself • Other People's Vibrations Can Be
Dangerous • Mavis Gets a Bonus • Protect Yourself with
Meta-Psychometric Techniques • Your Complete Meta-Psychometric
Healing Procedure*

8 Healing Others with Medi-Psychometry • 144

*The Whole World Seems to Be Sick • The Buddhist Doctor Amazes the
Hospital • Start Developing Your Ability Today • You, Too, Can
Medi-Psychometrize Others • Healing is Both Psychic and
Somatic • Frances R Moves to Health • Psychic Energy Deficiencies
Cause Illness • Letters and Photos Don't Tell the Whole
Story • George's Daughters Were Not Possessed • Medi-Psychometry
Changes Dis-Ease to Ease • Shake the Feathers and Rattle the
Gourds • Edwin Regains His Potency • You are the Plus Factor in
Healing • Miracles Do Happen • Bob's Arm Straightened
Itself • Your Standard Medi-Psychometric Healing Ritual • Your
Complete Medi-Psychometry Healing Guide*

9 Use Meta-Psychometry to Gain Your Ideal Mate • 163

*Sex Isn't Everything • It May Not Be Your Fault • Heather Quickly
Outgrows Her Lover • Identifying Your Twin Soul • Reading Beyond
the First Year • Color Yourself Sexy • Doug and the Vocalist • Getting
to Home Plate • Coupling is the Ultimate Psychic Link • Casey Never
Knew He Had Been Dumped • Make Them Want to Leave • Your
Complete Meta-Psychometric Guide to Mating*

10 Use Maga-Psychometry to Dominate Others • 179

*Some People Need to Be Directed • Lummy and His
Motorcycle • Protecting Others From Themselves with
Maga-Psychometry • Your Psychic Time-Bomb • The Customer is
Always Right • Grannie Makes the Mechanic Back Down • A Lesson
from Grannie • Store Your Confidence and Use It • Always a
Bridesmaid • You Can Get Your Own Way with
Maga-Psychometry • "I Was a Teen-Age Loser" • Kelly Changes
Course • You, Too, Can Beat the Establishment • Your Complete
Maga-Psychometric Guide to Dominance*

11 Tapping the Universal Gold Mine with Mida-Psychometry • 194

*Linking Yourself to the Money Thoughtform • Health and Wealth Can
Be Yours • Mida-Psychometry, Fabled Gold Maker • Money Makes
Money • Olive and the Silver Dollars • Your Guide to Money*

SWITCH ON YOUR META-PSYCHOMETRIC ABILITY

FIRST STEPS

Psychometry is the science of reading the emanations from objects and from people. The art of Meta-Psychometry is your use of emanations from people and objects to gain all you could possibly desire. This chapter will show you how you can learn to read psychometrically the emanations from inanimate objects, just as many psychics like Bevy Jaegers and Peter Hurkos can lead the police to a criminal through the emanations from inanimate objects left at the scene of a crime.

You, too, can learn to read and use these emanations. Every single object that you handle has its own radiation or emanation pattern. We are sure you have had jewelry given to you that felt "good." We are also sure you have been in places that felt comfortable and friendly, but in other places that felt hostile and dangerous. The reason the jewelry and the place felt friendly or hostile is because you were picking up the radiation pattern from inanimate objects, the jewelry or the building—even the very ground on which you were standing. You were doing exactly the same thing that Hurkos does: you were psychometrizing your surroundings.

We will show you the simple steps you can take to enhance your inborn ability to psychometrize your surroundings; and, further, we will give you the methods by which you can turn this psychometry into Meta-Psychometry, the ability to use the radiation as your key to awesome power. Once we have given you this key, and once you have grasped it and made it unlock your desires for the first time, you will realize how simple it is to apply Meta-Psychometry to your daily life. Never again need you lack material, psychic, or sexual fulfillment.

ANNA K OVERCOMES BLINDNESS

We told you in the introduction how Joel S was amazed and then enthralled by the power he found in his fingertips to detect color differences, and how this ability led him to a senior position in the Customs Service in Washington, D.C. In our files we have countless examples of people whose first noticeable psychometric talent was the ability to differentiate among colors. Such differentiation is the easiest talent for most people to develop.

Anna K is a lady, now in her nineties, whose sight failed her some twenty years ago. Even though she learned to read Braille, she had never thought of extending her fingertip sensitivity to the detection of color or to the direct reading of printed pages without the secondary step of having to go through the Braille alphabet. Perhaps because of her deficiency in vision, Anna was interested in every aspect of the occult world and especially in psychometry. We were introduced to her after one of our lectures on Witchcraft, and found her to be a charming, interesting woman who had had many psychic and occult experiences. In the course of our conversation, we showed her the cigarette-package demonstration. Much to her surprise, she could immediately detect the color differences of the lettering across the package through the cellophane. Next, we asked her whether she could tell which package of the two was predominantly green and which was predominantly red. Again, imagine her surprise when she was immediately able to tell which was which.

Having previously seen sightless people do similar things, we were not as surprised as Anna was, and we felt that such an alert, outgoing person would continue her experiments now that she had been shown the first step. This she did, and soon she was able to detect sixteen different color shades, identifying them with her fingertips. From this tentative start, she explored various aspects of Meta-Psychometry and learned to help herself in many ways. Now she can "see" things which she had thought for twenty years were beyond her capability.

It is true, of course, that sightless people have to develop their remaining senses more than do those with the gift of vision; thus sightless people have more drive to explore those remaining senses to their fullest. However, time and time again we have proven that sighted people likewise can develop a sixth and perhaps a seventh sense. It is just like the baseball pitcher who would be unable to perform if he didn't practice; so in order to develop your psychometric ability, you must practice. The first exercise we give you is one that you will use as a foundation for nearly all your psychometric work in this book: it is your Basic Fingertip Detector.

DEVELOPING YOUR FINGERTIP COLOR DETECTOR

From a glossy magazine, select a picture which has in it patches of red, green, and yellow. Cut small pieces of four different colors from this picture. Place them into a linen bag which is big enough so that you can get your hand inside it. Now feel each piece of paper between your thumb and fingertip down in the linen bag, and attempt to detect which color is which. It may take you several sessions of practice before you are able to get the right color every time, but this practice will pay off handsomely in your future efforts at psychometry; so keep at it.

The following four secrets will help you immensely in your ability to detect the color differences.

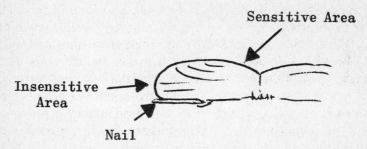

Figure 1-1
Fingertip Sensitivity

1. Look in Figure 1-1. It shows the most sensitive area of your fingertip to use psychometry. Notice that it is not the tip of the finger but the lower portion of the pad. It is this area against which you should press the pieces of colored paper in your practice sessions.

2. You will find that your various fingers have differing levels of sensitivity. Normally the most sensitive is your longest finger; but if your fingers are of about the same length, you will find they all have approximately the same level of sensitivity.

3. Power flows out of your hands, especially out of the palms. Later, you will learn how to impress your emotions on an object. For now, though, it is most important that while you are trying to read an object (that is, to receive emanations from it), you avoid imprinting that object with your own thoughts. For instance if you pick up a piece of paper in your linen bag practice and think very strongly, "This one is the red piece," you may impress on that piece of paper red-emanations to such an extent that it will always feel red to you from them on. This impressed-emanation problem will diminish if you use your secondary* hand in your psychometric work. Remember, too, that if you are consistently guessing, for example, that the yellow piece of paper is red, you have perhaps accidentally impressed red emanations on it. To avoid this sort of confusion, you should use new, fresh scraps of paper after every four or five trial sessions.

4. You are more sensitive to receiving information through your fingertips when you are in a condition that we call "homeostasis." To gain this state, you should:

a. Adjust the room temperature to the level at which you are most comfortable.

b. Work after a light, satisfying meal rather than after a heavy meal.

c. Be emotionally at rest. There is no point in trying this test if you are being pushed into it by someone else or if you are angry or sexually uptight, because all of these things will tend to disguise the results that you should get from your own fingertips.

d. Arrange your body to be unbound. If, for instance, you have on your wrist a bracelet heavily laden with past emotions, the very weak emanations from the variously colored pieces of paper will never get past your wrist to your head. They will instead be totally absorbed in the emotional output of the bracelet. The same is true of such things as wedding rings or in fact any binding on the body. Women should be particularly aware that metal

---

*Throughout this book, we will use the terms "dominant" and "secondary" with regard to your hands. If you are right-handed, your dominant hand is the right hand; if you are left-handed, your dominant hand is the left one.

hair-fasteners can totally disrupt their efforts at psychometry, and they should remove all such objects.

It will take you only a few moments to arrange yourself so that you can try this color-detector test. Once you have learned how to detect the four different colored paper scraps, you will be using the same technique to do such things as psychometrize the name of the stock that will gain the most for you in the market, or which companion will be the most enjoyable on a date. Practice and learn. Learn how easy it really is.

YOU CAN ALSO DETECT HEAT AND COLD

Dr. Louise Rhine, who worked in association with her husband at the famous ESP Lab of Duke University, invented the following test. This was designed both as a test of psychometry and as a test of the skill called psychokinesis, which is very similar to Meta-Psychometry. Psychokinesis is the extension of psychometry to making both inanimate objects and living beings do your bidding.

Dr. Rhine started with twelve ball bearings, simple steel balls you can buy at any auto-parts store. She heated six of them on a gas stove till they were red-hot. Then she allowed them to cool. This gave her six ball bearings that were white-steel-colored and six ball bearings that had a bluish tinge caused by their having been heated. Next, she placed all twelve in a rubber squeeze ball off the top of a syringe. She placed a glass tube into the ball instead of the syringe as shown in Figure 1–2. The test was run as follows: Each subject was asked to shake up the rubber ball with the tube pointing upward, then slowly to tip the ball bearings out of the glass tube. The subject was to try to concentrate on making all six of one color ball bearing come out together.

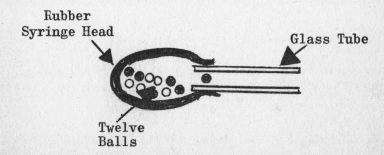

Figure 1-2

Dr. Rhine's Ball Experiment

Several subjects in Dr. Rhine's experiments were able to make all the heated ball bearings come out first and all the unheated ball bearings come out second. This is a very difficult undertaking, for not only was the subject required to psychometrize and identify which balls had been heated, but he was to make sure, by Meta-Psychometric means, that the balls were sufficiently "pushed" to come out in a given sequence. Yet, some of the students at Duke University were able to demonstrate this ability. How much easier it is then for you merely to get twelve quarter-inch ball bearings from the auto-parts store, and wash them in surgical alcohol; then heat six until red-hot on your gas stove, allow them to cool, place them in your linen test bag, and draw them out one at a time. On their very first trial, many people are able to draw out five similar balls in succession. If you have completed the fingertip color development work that we have recommended, you should be able to draw out six identical balls on your first or second trial.

JOHN DECLINES THE HOUSE FOR SALE

John G is a writer and part-time newspaper reporter who lives in western Texas. He had been interested in psychometry for many years, especially in Sybil Leek's work with Hans Holzer on haunted houses. Thus, when John was looking for a house to live in, in Houston, and was offered a tremendous bargain, he wondered if it was haunted. He decided to spend a night in it and find out.

That first night he spent there was near new moon; though he had various feelings of uneasiness, he could not pin down any specific problem area or ghostly phenomenon. He called us and explained his situation, "Look, we have to get out of the place we're living in within a couple of weeks because they're going to bulldoze it for the new freeway. I know I should wait till full moon and have another sitting, but this is a fantastic old house at a real bargain price."

Our first thought was that John's difficulty was purely on the mundane level, that perhaps there was something wrong with the title on the house or some legal entanglement with the survey. For hard-headed realtors don't usually lower prices for such intangibles as ghosts. In fact, nowadays a tame ghost seems to be a selling point in favor of a house rather than a detraction from its value.

John checked with the lawyers, talked to the title company, and did all the things a suspicious buyer can do; yet he could not come up with any logical reason for the very low price on the property. A mutual friend of ours, Leonard A, happened to be planning a trip through

Houston. Because of John's timing squeeze, I asked him to go look at the house with John; but Leonard, too, could find nothing wrong with the house. John was all ready to pay the $4,000 deposit on it when something prompted me to call him on the phone and tell him to get the original deeds (*not* a copy) and let Leonard psychometrize them.

This request for original deeds seemed to cause some furor in Houston, but, after a little haggling, John got the documents into Leonard's hands. Leonard immediately said, "They feel bad. They don't feel right." In due course he was able to identify the particular deed, three owners back, that felt "wrong" to him. A visit to the county courthouse proved there had been a little forgery and hanky-panky in the deed, which rendered it worthless as a legal document. The forger had sold the house cheaply in order to move it quickly, and the present owner, who probably knew something of the deal, was now attempting to pass the house along to another sucker so as to get his own money out. Sensibly, John declined to purchase the house. Since he was interested, though, he followed the case, and less than a year later learned that the property was being repossessed by the defrauded family members. Court action over the matter is still in process at the time of this writing.

If the house had been listed at full market value, John might never have become suspicious; even if his suspicions had been aroused, without Leonard's psychometrizing ability, John probably would have lost a considerable amount of money on the deal, and would have incurred the added upset of having to move his family twice.

YOUR SHIRT-BUTTON ABILITY DEVELOPER

To do this test, you will need the help of a trustworthy friend. He should not be present, though, when you actually do the test. Go to your local five-and-dime store and purchase 12 identical pearl shirt buttons, a piece of black silk fabric about a foot square, the same size cloth in white silk, a paperback book on Satanism or some other very negative book, a book of light-hearted cartoons (perhaps a Peanuts book or something of that nature), and a package of plain white envelopes. Place six of the buttons in the negative book and wrap the book in the black cloth; put the other six buttons in the light-hearted book and wrap it in the white cloth. In the Western world, of course, black is "evil" and white is "good"; and what you are trying to do is impress on the sets of buttons negative and positive emanations.

Keep the buttons wrapped up in their books for a week. Then

have your friend take the buttons out one at a time and place them in individually numbered envelopes, making a record for himself of which are the "evil" button-envelope combinations and which are the "good" combinations. He should then return all the envelopes to you. After he has departed, and when all the conditions of homeostasis (page 25) are fulfilled, you are to psychometrize the envelope-button combinations and list the numbers which you feel are "bad" and those which you think are "good."

In tests of this nature, it is standard practice to run four or five trials on yourself, then to pick from your impressions the three envelope numbers that occur most frequently in your "bad" set and the three envelope numbers which occur most often in your "good" set. Making a table of impressions like that shown in Figure 1–3 is a help in this work. When you have run the several trials, call your friend and get the key to the envelope numbers, which will tell you which are actually good and which are bad.

One of two things should happen: You will get a majority right or a majority wrong. Don't worry. What we call "negative psychometry" often occurs. It is as though you have a switch in your head which has turned you the wrong way around. To you, something which feels psychometrically "hot" will feel psychometrically "cold" to most psychics. But, as soon as you have completed this good-button, bad-button test, you will know which way your switch is set, and all you have to do is let it work for you.

If we ourselves are driving down an unfamiliar road and Gavin quickly asks a question of Yvonne like, "Is the nearest gas station right or left?" she typically replies—without thinking—"Right," and Gavin typically turns left. We have learned that she has just such a psychometric reversal in her own head. If you allow her time to think, she will tell you the correct direction because she will have allowed for the reversal in herself; but if you force her into an immediate reply, she will give you the reverse answer. So when you analyze the results of your self-test, which should look like Figure 1–3, you will know how well your ability is developing and whether your switch is set to full-ahead or to reverse.

If you get totally random results in this test, we suggest that you ask another friend to try it with you because your first friend may be putting you on. This, we can assure you, is far more probable than your having such a poor psychometric ability that you get a wholly random score.

All right, you can now distinguish between "good" and "bad."

Envelope Number	Trial Number					Correct Reading	Score
	1	2	3	4	5		
1							
2							
3							
4							
5							
6							
7							
8							
9							
10							
11							
12							

Figure 1–3

Trial Table, "Good" and "Bad" Envelopes

Instruction: Black in the upper line for "good" and the lower line for "bad" reading. In the illustration, the reader would use line 2 as a "good" selection, but would throw out line 3 as inconclusive.

The next time you go to buy something, perhaps something that has a warranty on it, you can ascertain whether the warranty is any good —or, indeed, whether the item itself is any good. In general, however, if it is some object that you have really set your heart on, for instance that new, gleaming Razzle-Dazzle 250 TN from Detroit, your other emotions will obscure your psychometric ability. So, if it is possible, have identical Razzle-Dazzles side by side to pick from, so you can avoid that new-car emotional excitement that can cause you to invest in the proverbial lemon.

COLOR YOUR LIFE "GOOD"

You have learned the feeling that tells you "good" and the one that means "bad." Now stop for just a moment and think about the clothes you are presently wearing. Do they all have good feelings, or are some of them so-so, or perhaps some of them actually feel negative? This has little to do with the physical colors of the garments, but more to do with the psychic emanations of the clothes. It is true that psychics talk about the colors of emanations, and if you look at Table 1–1 you will see the colors that psychics traditionally tend to equate with various emotions. If you are wearing a light-yellow sweater, this sweater will

Emotional Tie	Color
Purity	White
Death	Black
Anger	Red
Coolness	Blue
Life	Green

Table 1–1

Colors and Emotions in the Western World

tend to put out emanations of light-hearted, good, "sunny" feelings. But, if you wore this same sweater when something very negative happened to you, the sweater may not be putting out just its natural, light-hearted emanations; it may be emitting emanations from the negative happening as well. The sweater may also bear negative feelings imprinted into it before you ever bought it. Let us say that it is a factory second, or that the seamstress who made it was in a vile mood as it lay in her hands. Any of these things will tend to color the sweater psychically so that it will influence yourself and everyone you meet.

Perhaps you are wearing a nice sexy pair of jeans which should be putting out good green sexual emanations that will attract the opposite sex. But what if you broke up with your former lover in a very emotional scene on that last date—in those jeans—or you had to reject the advances of some unattractive and aggressive person? Then, the psychic color of the jeans will not be what you might wish. In such a case, although you may have a perfect color combination on the physical plane, your psychic color emanations could be horrible; thus, everyone you meet would be turned off by your clothing, even though they might not know why they are being turned off.

Everyone has psychometric ability. Even though they never develop it or put it to use, still almost everyone you meet will tell you they have met people they disliked at first glance or that they have been to some place that really turned them off. They are merely verbalizing what they have picked up with their subconscious psychometric ability.

Now, you can take your first real step in Meta-Psychometry. Lay out your clothing on the bed and psychometrically feel the various garments for good and bad feelings, using the same feelings that you developed when you psychometrically analyzed your shirt-button-envelope combinations. Your first step into Meta-Psychometry is to psychometrize and wear only those clothes that will make you look good—that is, the clothes that will give you good psychic color. Usually there is no need to throw away clothing that has very negative emanations. It has been found by such noted psychics as Peter Hurkos that if you send a negatively radiating garment to the cleaners twice in a row, the emanations are cleaned off it and are no longer at such a level of intensity that they can affect either you or your acquaintances.

Until you can get your clothes shaped up, or replaced in the case of those that have physical flaws (for obviously no amount of cleaning will remove the emanations from a suit that has badly woven fabric), wear only those garments that feel good. Your world will suddenly become brighter as people feel more friendly toward you.

CECILIA CHANGES COURSE

Gracie B is a secretary for the North Carolina Telephone Company. She is a 28-year-old divorcee with two children; her ex-husband has skipped out of state, and pays her neither alimony nor child support. Her well-paying secretarial position with the telphone company is very important to her because, even with such a job, she is only just able to make ends meet by doing such things as making her own clothes and getting some food stamps from the local family services offices.

Gracie is not the brightest secretary in the world, as she herself will readily admit; but she has been with the telephone company since leaving school and has risen to the top of her secretarial grade. Somehow or other, shorthand eluded her, so she has not been eligible for further promotion. We should say that recently we have been able to help her learn shorthand with Meta-Psychometry, and now she is approaching eligibility for the promotion. (See also "Alex T Gets His Doctorate," p. 38.)

Gracie's best friend, Cecilia, was promoted to supervisor of the secretarial pool working for the manager of the business office, an ingratiating and attractive man named Bruce. Now Gracie felt that, because Cecilia had been such a close friend, her job worries were really over, provided, of course, that she kept up a reasonable performance. Imagine Gracie's surprise, then, when a couple of weeks after taking the job, Cecilia turned into a veritable bitch. Before she knew what had happened, Gracie had accumulated two of the dreaded disciplinary warnings. Since she had never received even one in her entire previous work life, she was terribly upset, especially since she knew that one more would mean at least a demotion if not dismissal.

Gracie tried unsuccessfully to talk with Cecilia. She even talked with Cecilia's ex-boyfriend—"ex" only since Cecilia's promotion. The boyfriend told Gracie that, even before she showed him the door, Cecilia had confided to him that, since she had been promoted, she didn't understand what was happening to her. She could watch her own change of personality, but she was helpless to change herself back.

Gracie was a student of the School of Wicca. She wrote to us and asked whether Cecilia had been hexed or what on earth was happening. Our immediate response was, "Sometimes people react that way when given authority but if you can send us a photo of Cecilia before and after her promotion . . ."

It took Gracie a little time to get that photo of Cecilia after her promotion for Gracie was living in fear of her livelihood and dared risk nothing. Finally, she got the two photos. Although the second photo showed some signs of hypertension, there were none of the regular authoritarian "bitchy" symptoms or emanations from it. We told Gracie to wear as much in the way of orange and earthtone clothing as she could manage, to calm her hypertensive boss. Further, we suggested that Gracie spend some time in Cecilia's office and in her apartment meditating—with Cecilia absent.

A fortunate Providence smiled on us at this time, for Cecilia contracted the flu, which turned into pneumonia, and she was briefly hospitalized for intensive care. During her absence, a capable, elderly executive secretary from another branch was brought in to replace her. This woman, too, although previously calm and competent, began to play the role of the virago as soon as she took over Cecilia's desk.

Just before this older woman reported for her fill-in assignment, Gracie was able to meditate in Cecilia's office for a few moments. She wrote us that she wouldn't meditate in that room again if her life depended on it, for it was full of very negative thoughtforms and feelings. Almost as soon as she sat down quietly to feel the area, she was assailed by terrible doubts, depression, and a feeling that everyone was whispering about her behind her back. We knew then that Cecilia's problems were not self-induced, but were in fact being induced by emotions that had been imprinted in the office earlier by its previous occupant, Minette. She, it turned out, had been having a very hot and heavy, but necessarily secret, emotional love affair with charming Bruce, Cecilia's new supervisor.

In this case, most fortunately, we were acquainted with the manager of another branch of the telephone company who knew Bruce, Minette, various other high-level employees, and all the respective spouses. A meeting was arranged. We started things off by telling Bruce that the supervisory problems he was experiencing were traceable to the office itself, and that he should repaint it and, if possible, get a new desk, secretarial chair, and filing cabinets for his secretary. Of couse, Bruce spurned this as just laughable; he assumed we were a bunch of interloping freaks trying to tell him how to run his office. Clearly we would get nowhere pussy-footing around; so in order to jolt him out of his sneering complacent attitude, we laid it on the line:

"Look Bruce, we know darn well that you and Minette spent a lot of time in bed together, and that she, poor thing, was scared out of her wits lest your wife or the District Manager should find out. Those are the vibrations that are giving the girls trouble. Now, dammit, for the sake of Cecilia and Gracie and the temporary transfer, you either fix that office or we'll blow the gaff on you."

It wasn't long till Bruce admitted he could find the money in his budget to refurbish the "poisoned" office. Cecilia returned from the hospital to find that her problems had ended; today she is an extremely capable and popular supervisor. Gracie is looking forward to passing the shorthand examination and becoming an executive secretary.

THE DESK-CALENDAR HEX

If you have a boss whose ways you dislike, you can probably make adjustments in that boss's surroundings so he can change course just as Cecilia did. Or, if you wish, you can, in your own life, manufacture a situation like the one that caused Cecilia so great a problem; or you can switch things around and manufacture a pleasant situation. It is absolutely true that if you think negative thoughts, you will attract negative things to yourself. So be very careful when you decide that you wish to hex somebody rather than help them.

Let us say that you have had a good relationship with your boss for a matter of years, but suddenly this relationship has turned to the proverbial horseapples. What can you do about it? Well, first set your own house in order. Make sure that you are not antagonizing your boss (whether physically or psychically) by wearing or carrying with you something that puts out very negative emanations. If your colors are psychically good, see then whether you can figure out what is wrong with your boss. The easiest way to do this is to spend some time in his office. Attempt to find out whether some object in the office may be either putting out negative vibrations, as in Cecilia's case, or perhaps absorbing too much of a given type of energy. For absorbers of energy, or what we call psychic vampires, will cause depression in people just as quickly as will something which is putting out negative energy. In other words, psychic energy can flow in two directions: it can flow from an object into a person, or from a person it can be drawn into the object.

If a complete redoing of the office is not feasible, the solution to either of these problems of energy flow is to add compensating energy to the office environment. This is done by taking some object and charging it up with your own energy. Perhaps an object is transmitting a great deal of hypertensive blue-turquoise energy into the office. This is often the case with a telephone, an object you cannot really move or work on. To balance this undesirable blue-turquoise energy, look at the color table of energy balance shown in Table 1–2. You notice that

Excess "Color" Detected	Balance Color	Body Location for Changing
White	Black	Back of Head
Black	White	Breast
Red	Turquoise	Genitalia
Blue	Yellow	Heart
Green	Violet	Feet
Yellow	Blue	Thighs
Violet	Green	Lower Back
Turquoise	Red	Neck

Table 1–2

Detected Excessive "Color" and Its Balance

opposite blue you have yellow, and opposite turquoise is red. What you need to do, then, is to put orange energy into some object in the office. In this case, let us say you select the desk calendar. It is charged in this manner:

Buy an orange candle and a length of orange fabric. When you have these things, take the desk calendar home with you. At midnight, place the desk calendar on the orange cloth and light the orange candle near it. Remove all your clothing from your body and remove all rings, jewelry, hairpins, and body bindings so that you are totally unbound. While the candle burns, lift the calendar pad on its cloth and hold it to the base of your throat, just above the breast. Concentrate on the candle and think orange thoughts. Think of marigolds, of jack-o-lanterns, of fragrant juicy oranges, of anything that is attractive, loving, and orange. Hold this position for perhaps five minutes. Then wrap the calendar pad in the orange cloth, extinguish the candle flame by clapping your hands together on it, and go to bed. Take the calendar pad with you to the office in the morning and place it back on the boss's desk. It will now be emanating the low level of orange power that will compensate for the blue-turquoise power you detected in this specific office.

This is a basic Meta-Psychometric procedure. You have used your developed psychometric gift to sense the problem, and you have corrected the problem by adding something which will balance the undesirable radiation in the office.

If the problem is of another sort, perhaps an object absorbing too much turquoise energy, you could still use the same object, the desk calendar, for the solution to this problem as well, different though it is. In this case you would hold the calendar pad against the genitalia and think in terms of warm, earthy things. The calendar pad would then supply the office absorber with the necessary energy, and the boss in this case would be able to regain his or her sexual balance.

Now that you have this psychometric ability, you should use it in every situation you go into. Before you rent that new apartment, check it out. If you feel the emanations are unbalanced, can you balance them with your Meta-Psychometric skills? If it feels like a big problem, don't rent the place. Is that new boss really as nice as he seems? Check him out! Just swipe a piece of his note paper and psychometrize it in the privacy of your home.

META-PSYCHOMETRIZING CARS:
A MATTER OF LIFE AND DEATH

Just as you psychometrized your boss's office, so should you always psychometrize any car you ride in, preferably before the car is in motion, but at least some time during your proximity to the vehicle. You can save yourself from getting into hassles with a belligerent date, for instance, by reading any negative emanations from the car. Moreover, if the car has had frequent close shaves in traffic, you obviously don't want to ride in it. If it is important to you that you do ride in the car, however, then you can use Meta-Psychometry to balance the car's emanations in just the same way as you did for your boss' office. We have found that the easiest way to do this is to Meta-Psychometrically charge a new set of seatcovers for the car. You can buy them, of course, in the appropriate color. This gives you a leg up on getting the car's emanations balanced.

Every single object, either because of its natural color or because emanations have been impressed on it, transmits some psychic force.

Books, of course, transmit the power of the thoughts that are within them, especially if they have previously been read and understood.

ALEX GETS HIS DOCTORATE WITH META-PSYCHOMETRY[1]

Alex T had been told in his grade school years that he had a very low IQ. Today, with many scholastic achievements to his credit including a doctorate in music, you might say that he hides his low IQ pretty successfully. It may be that this early false evaluation of his IQ biased Alex's attitude through high school; Whatever the cause, it is true that he had to repeat his sophomore year.

Fortunately, Alex came from a family that dabbled in the occult; so, witnessing Alex's concern when he failed that year and was separated from his friends, his older brother suggested to him, "Hey, why don't you try reading your textbooks, then sleeping with them under your pillow? It really helped me." From the day he started doing it, Alex's grades magically improved. He was absorbing information from those books while he slept, and was able scholastically to disprove his critical teachers' poor opinion of him. From then on, he outshone the other members of all his classes.

A similar case is that of Frances F,[2] who always had difficulty in earning those extra-high grades she wanted so badly. She developed her psychometric fingertip ability so that (especially in multiple-choice questions) she could detect the right answer merely by running her fingertip over the possible choices.

Frances' case seems to us to be purely the development of psychometric ability; whereas Alex's is definitely a Meta-Psychometric procedure. For, knowing his deficiencies, his brother suggested an appropriate energy transmitter, the textbooks in this incident, to improve Alex's grades. While at rest, Alex was able to get sufficient detail from his textbooks to be able to answer accurately detailed technical questions. You, too, can use Alex's or Frances' system. All it takes is the time to try it; for once you have done it, you will be convinced that it will work for you, too.

YOU HAVE THE TALENT

Countless examples convince us that everyone has some psychometric ability. You can either develop your ability in yourself or

---

[1] As documented in the Newsletter, October 1976, of the National Speakers' and Psychics' Association
[2] Ibid.

let it go to waste. We, of course, strongly recommend that you develop it and that you then follow through by developing your ability to change the world and your environment to the way you want it by using Meta-Psychometry: either to balance your environment and that of your friends, or to unbalance it in a direction that will be advantageous to you.

If you doubt that you have any ability, try the simple color-scrap test. If you don't have enough ability to make this work, try putting a previously read book or a second-hand book under your pillow for a couple of nights. This should be a book which you have not read and know nothing about. Now, after the few nights of sleeping with it under your pillow, read it and see whether you don't know ahead of time how it is going to come out. In nine cases out of ten, you will have a lot more than just an inkling as to the convolutions of the book's plot and of the motivations of the characters in the book.

You must also keep in mind that everyone is affected by Meta-Psychometric emanations. Whether they like it or not, people exposed to negative emanations become negative; when exposed to positive emanations, they become positive. Most people are also extremely responsive to much finer gradations than just positive and negative. For instance, they will get turned on sexually for no demonstrable reason in a certain environment. With your ability and with the aid of Table 1-2, you can make this happen at will by adding to people's environment the Meta-Psychometric emanations that will affect them in the manner you wish.

The emanations are all around you all the time. Go for a drive with your lover and look at the autumn-colored trees. As soon as you get home, you both will want to go to bed and make love. The vivid colors of nature have Meta-Psychometrically affected you. Now, as you read the rest of this book, all you have to do to grasp that key of power which we promised you is to apply a few simple rules to Meta-Psychometrically affect your surroundings. The first step, of course, will be for you to learn how to detect or psychometrize your own surroundings and every animate and inanimate object with which you come into contact.

YOUR COMPLETE META-PSYCHOMETRIC TRAINING GUIDE

Table 1-2 gives you the information you need, both to balance and to unbalance anyone's environment Meta-Psychometrically. Thus you have a key to power. But in order to place an object in someone's environment that is emitting the correct radiation for your purpose, you must first be able to psychometrize that object and the environment in question.

Training yourself to psychometrize objects is a very simple procedure:

1. Establish the conditions we advised in the paragraph entitled "Fingertip Color Detector." Learn to differentiate consistently among pieces of colored paper. When you have done this, carry on and learn to distinguish between good and evil with your shirt-button development aid.

2. In a specific case you may want to differentiate perhaps between platonic love and romantic love. The two would be very closely allied in any psychometric analysis that you would do. Type on a plain sheet of paper the words "platonic love" six times and "romantic love" six times. Cut these out so you have twelve separate slips of paper. Place all twelve slips in twelve separate envelopes, shuffle them as you would a deck of cards, and psychometrically sort them into two stacks. The one stack, of course, will be "platonic love" and the other will be "romantic love." Now, question yourself as to how you did it. What emanation from the envelopes containing "romantic love" was it that gave you the clue? It is this emanation that you want to employ in your Meta-Psychometric work.

3. Now, find an object that has the same emanation as the "romantic love" envelopes; or you must impress on some object like a desk calendar the emanations that you felt in the "romantic love" envelopes, being careful not to impress the same emanations you got from the "platonic love" envelopes. Incidentally, we have learned that certain objects such as gems, dried flowers, or a silk handkerchief emanate "romantic love" vibrations at a much higher level than "platonic love" vibrations: you might want to introduce objects of this kind secretely into the environment of your target person.

In summary, Meta-Psychometry makes use of the emotional emanations that are necessary to balance or unbalance an environment. It is your psychometric ability that will tell you (a) what is needed, and (b) when an object has the emanations you need for your Meta-Psychometric purposes.

We have been talking generally about the very elementary psychometry of objects. We did mention Anna K, the sightless woman who learned to read with her fingertips, and also Sybil Leek's work with haunted houses wherein Sybil is able to sense not just the difference between good and bad, or heat and cold, or one color and another, but a complete story, in some cases together with actual dates and names of the participants.

By carefully working with your own psychometric ability, you, too, will develop these more advanced and subtle capabilities. Then you will be able to take more accurate Meta-Psychometric corrective measures so that your life will be improved. It is purely a matter of practice and attention to the fine detail of the emanations you receive. It is not a matter of your IQ or your educational level, nor does it seem to be a matter of your genetic heritage, though we have found that Amerindian and Oriental people have higher untrained capabilities than the average Caucasian Christian. We really believe that everyone can do it. It is just a matter of overcoming all those negative admonitions you received; both from establishment religious leaders who say "you mustn't" and from scientists who say "you can't."

USE META-PSYCHOMETRY TO KNOW WHAT OTHERS THINK

PEOPLE RADIATE, TOO

You learned in Chapter 1 that objects radiate emanations which can affect people. In "The Desk Calendar Hex," you learned that you could Meta-Psychometrically impress emanations into objects that could later be retransmitted to gain your desired end. Inherent in this concept is the fact that people truly are fantastically powerful emanators of emotion. From current research, we know that the radiation of human bodies can be accurately measured; in fact, the Russians have demonstrated that your emanations can be sensed at distances of up to 3,000 miles. This means that a human being radiates more power than most radio stations. In American scientific circles, this power emanated by living creatures is generally called "bioplasmic energy," and many interesting experiments are presently being conducted into its possibilities. Recently, for instance, Dr. Olga Worrall, a noted healer, was able to affect instruments at the University of Atlanta from more than 600 miles.

These emanations also become stored in any object near a person who is involved in an emotional situation. It is these stored emanations, as well as the direct emanations from a person you are talking with, that you will learn in this chapter to analyze and to use.

In any Meta-Psychometric procedure, the first move must be to analyze the existing patterns of emanation; then you can change those patterns to your own advantage. Since most of your work will consist of attempts to influence people, it is most important that you first learn how to analyze the emanation patterns from people. In occult circles, this radiation pattern is called the "aura," and occultists tend to think of it in terms of various colors. In your personal work you may not detect these radiation patterns as colored emanations; instead you may detect them with your sense of hearing or of smell. Any one of your senses may be the predominant means through which your mind detects the patterns. So you should remember when you are analyzing people to pay attention to all of your senses; for it may be that a sense other than psychic "sight" will be your best method of perception. Because well over 80 percent of people do psychometrize with "second sight," we shall, in this book, generally refer to "color" of emanations; but always remember that "color" could also mean "sound," "smell," "feel," or "taste."

DAL GETS HIS PROMOTION

Dal J, a railroad ticket clerk in New Orleans, had a weakness for gambling. Apart from this weakness, he was a model husband. In their modest home, Dal and Junie and the twins lived comfortably if not luxuriously. But Dal was never satisfied with this just-adequate level of living; he was always working on his beloved "system" for making it big at the racetrack. His training was totally in mathematics, so his system was not based on any psychic technique, and it completely ignored Lady Luck. His friend at work, Fred M, also had a "system," but Fred's system was entirely based on picking the ponies psychometrically.

Dal and Fred were friendly rivals—sometimes one would buy the victory drinks, sometimes the other. One day, Fred made a big killing by using his technique, known at the track as "rollup." He used rollup psychometrically to pick three successive winners; his winnings from the earlier horse got plowed back in as the betting money for subsequent races. Altogether, Fred made enough that day to pay off his house and his car, and to take a vacation in Mexico.

At first, Dal was very happy for his friend's luck, but he eventually became rather frustrated; Fred constantly prodded him about how the occult was beating science one more time. Dal determined that he, too, was going to win big; so he secretly took out a second mortgage on his home—for $5,000—and promptly lost it at the track using his system. The payoff on this second mortgage was only a matter of $65 a month extra; but that $65 really was more than the budget could stand, especially when one of the twins fell down and broke off a front tooth, adding another $300 dental bill to the already overstrained budget. Dal began to look for a second job, but times were tough and nothing was available.

Just as things were getting really desperate, Dal learned that his boss was being promoted, and that he, Dal, would have at least a chance of getting the boss' vacated position. He went to work with all his scientific training to analyze what would be required in the new job, signed up for a supervisory course at the local college, read several books on railroading, and did all the things that his calculating, scientific mind indicated were rational steps in the right direction. After several interviews and a written examination, he was one of three finalists for the position.

Now, his friend Fred suggested to him that he should "psych out" the situation and the people on the board who were going to interview him for this much-needed promotion and higher salary. Dal had long since ceased laughing at Fred's hunches and his psychometric ability, so he asked him for guidance in approaching the decisive interview. Fred gave him the following simple advice:

"Before you go to the interview, get as thoroughly relaxed as you can. When any one of the board asks you a question, especially a personal question, take a moment to consider the underlying meaning and implications of the question, and try to 'feel' the radiations from the questioner that go with the spoken question.

"Many times, you will find that the spoken question isn't exactly what the guy is asking you. The unverbalized question is the one you should answer first. Then, answer the spoken question as best you can."

Dal followed Fred's advice and, as it turned out, he was easily able to outshine his rivals for the promotion. What he was doing was a Meta-Psychometric procedure. He was psychometrically picking up the real question and fulfilling the questioner's need by answering this implied question as well as the spoken one.

YOUR GUIDE TO PSYCHOMETRIZING PEOPLE

When you first attempt to psychometrize someone, you may be put off by such things as the brightly colored clothes that person is wearing, as these bright colors will overwhelm the lower-level psychic radiations. Also, as we said in Chapter 1, a person's clothes may be transmitting emotional emanations that they have picked up in earlier wearings. One way to "read" a person more accurately is to actually touch him physically. If he is wearing rings and bracelets, though, touching his fingers is useless. You must get to the real person, which means touching him on the wrist or above any bracelet he may be wearing. You can do this, as a doctor does, by pretending to take his pulse. A possible opening might be, "Gee, you don't look well; let me take your pulse," or some other pretext such as, "I am practicing for a first-aid class; would you let me take your pulse?" Of course you are not actually interested in taking the pulse, but just in establishing the physical contact that you need to overcome the confusing emanations from his clothing and jewelry.

Once you have this physical contact, you can use the same sensations that you developed in Chapter 1 to read the person's emanation pattern. If you have time, you can also obtain a great deal more information about him by following the word-association technique of a psychologist and by just blithely talking about the subject which you are trying to check the person out for. If you are looking for a mate, you might talk about sexual matters. If you are thinking in terms of working for this person, you might choose to talk about office discipline or some other work-related topic.

As you do this, you should notice a subtle change in the person's radiation pattern: this will tell you how he is really and truly reacting to your words. If you suddenly get an upsurge of hypertensive green radiation when you talk about sex, you should obviously be very wary of establishing a liaison with him, for this is not the type of radiation that you are seeking. If, on the other hand, when you talk of sex you get an increase in bright yellow loving emanations, this is a person with whom it is probably worth while to intensify your friendship.

If physical contact with the person you are analyzing is not possible, you can simply watch for radiation patterns around the head of that person, where such patterns will be less distorted by the confusing emanations from jewelry and clothes. While you are sitting in a restaurant, even before you attempt to start a conversation with that delightful person who just came in, take a moment to study the emanation pattern. See whether he is balanced. If he is not, in your first conversation it would be wise to interject something that will balance the pattern of your prospect; for this balancing is psychically welcomed and much appreciated by the receiver; thus you are assured of a warm reception from your target person.

FINDING OUT WHAT HAPPENED

Have you ever wondered what someone is saying about you when you are not there? Is he being positive, or negative? And if he is talking negatively about you behind your back, what can you do to make those conversations more positive?

The answer, of course, is that most of the time people are so wound up with themselves that they don't bother to talk about anyone else in private conversations. When they do talk about a third person, usually it is because something heavily emotional is going on. Because the situation is emotional, the room in which the conversation is held will pick up and hold these emotional emanations; for when people are emotional, they transmit more energy than when they are in a state of calm. If you can gain access to an office where you suspect you have been discussed, you can tell by psychometrizing the room whether the outcome of that conversation was positive or negative. Similarly, objects that have been at the scene of high emotion pick up and store these emotions. This is the reason why various psychics can help police authorities by giving them a description of people who were at the scene of a crime. For crimes are very emotion-laden events, and it is these emotions which impress objects at the scene.

BEVY AND THE BULLET

Bevy Jaegers, the noted St. Louis psychic, operates a psychic detective squad whose members give their time to help the police and other authorities solve criminal cases and mysteries.[1] Although we had known Bevy for many years, we never thought that we would have to use her abilities in our personal lives. It happened, though, that on one Hallowe'en night we were soundly asleep in bed (as all good Witches should be), when a group of ruffians poured six shots into our home, smashing a kitchen window in the process. Anyone standing at the kitchen sink would have been instantly killed by their fusillade. Although we recovered several bullets from the walls and from the kitchen cabinets, still the sheriff had so little to go on that the case was essentially closed before it was ever opened. Our own concern was whether or not the people who had fired the shots were out to get Witches or whether it was just a Hallowe'en prank, just the icing on an evening of trick-or-treating.

---

[1]See Appendix.

We tried unsuccessfully to psychometrize the bullets. The problem was that we were so emotionally uptight and involved in the caper, that we could not have read black from white with the aid of those particular bullets. We took the bullets to Bevy; she was able to assure us that it was just a bunch of teen-agers out to spook the Witches, rather than Fundamentalists taking Jehovah's vengeance into their own hands. This assurance was comforting in itself, of course, but not really enough to set our minds at rest. Bevy continued to sit pensively holding the bullets in her left (secondary) hand; she gave us a detailed description of the 1973 blue Chevrolet farm truck that the kids had been driving; she gave a description of the boy who had actually fired the shots, and told us that the boys came from a town some thirty miles north of us in Missouri, and had gotten liquored up prior to their escapade against the Witches.

Later, we were able to visit the dance hall they frequented (which, it turned out, is rather notorious for its wild crowd), and we talked to some of the youngsters, who confirmed Bevy's reading in every detail. After we discussed our religious beliefs with some of the youngsters, they assured us that with this new understanding of what Witchcraft was all about, they certainly would not bother us again. In fact a couple of them showed enough interest to sign up for our course in the Old Religion.[2]

FOLLOWING THE ASTRAL PATH

Employing her developed sensitivity, Bevy was able to psychometrize the bullets, traveling backward along the bullets' path to sense the person who was holding the gun at the time of the shots as well as the truck that he rode in and the direction from whence the truck had come. If she had been pushed, she probably could have traced those bullets right back to their original manufacturer. Natives of Hawaii say that this path which Bevy traced is the "aka thread" of the bullet. We express it as the "psychic link" that is in all things; that once an object has been touched or handled by someone, it will always retain some memory of that person unless it is washed clean of emanations. Let us say you wish to trace backward the astral path of an object and find out, for instance, what its owner was thinking about when he got rid of it. Sit with the object in the palm of your secondary hand. Concentrate on it, as you were taught in Chapter 1, to read the present state of the object. What emanations is it now giving off?

Now, imagine a clock running backward; take the object back in

---

[2]See Appendix.

time to where you want to read the person who was handling it. You may be surprised to find that, after a little practice, you can in fact read the impressed emanations from time past; you can continue to reel time back until the emanations become too faint for you to pick up. Again with Bevy, we have been able to read back in time details of the long-distant past from such objects as bones found in an archaeological dig. Recently, in a top-level archaeological conference, two papers were presented which combined physical facts of the dig with psychic readings of objects found. The papers received much serious attention, presaging wider acceptance of psychometry as a science.

You, too, can read back personal dramas of people who have handled an object, especially when intense emotions were experienced in connection with the object. Do you want to know what Grandma was really like, instead of all those nice pious things Mother says about her? Get out the old family album and psychometrize it. You may learn that Grandma wasn't exactly pure white all the way through as she has been presented to you. We ourselves believe that Yvonne's paternal grandmother rests more peacefully now that we have learned what a blithe minx she really was, and what high old times she had in her youth. It's fun, it's easy, and it can really help you in your life. If you don't try it, the loss is yours alone.

EAVESDROPPERS MAY LOSE

You might not want to know that Grandpa was a horse-thieving rascal, or that he was a fire-and-brimstone fundamentalist preacher, or a salty dog, or whatever. For better or for worse, the knowledge may radically alter the whole concept of your family. But we think that having this kind of information about your family can be very healthful emotionally, particularly when you wish to analyze your own emotional reactions to a situation.

It often happens that the peeping tom or the telephone eavesdropper hears or sees things which cause him pain and anguish. There is no real difference between physical and psychic eavesdropping, though you can more easily arrange for a psychic eavesdropping device called a "bug" to be in your target person's environment than you can get a telephone bugged.

You may learn from eavesdropping through your psychic bug that your best friend has what seems to be a very negative opinion of you. This may actually be a temporary situation, but these emanations are impressed on your psychic bug and you may read them for more than they really are. Therefore, we recommend that you eavesdrop only in cases where you really have a need to know the true state of affairs. If you just want entertainment, watch TV. Don't waste the effort and risk the possible pain in using a psychic bug.

BEULAH SELLS HER BOOK

Beulah M is a housewife from Wilmington, North Carolina. She writes children's stories aimed specifically at the black children's market. Since she didn't depend on this writing for her income, she was able to craft small stories beautifully, spending a lot of time getting them into what she considered to be good English so that her books would be usable by schools and libraries. But she was completely unable to sell these polished stories. She got reject-slip after reject-slip, and was becoming more and more discouraged; this discouragement began to affect both her health and her family relationships. Her husband, normally an easy-going fellow, found that Beulah was less responsive to his needs, and he consequently embarked on an affair with one of the women at his office. Learning of this, Beulah became even more depressed, and finally went to a psychiatrist who happened to be a friend of ours. She asked him what to do to sell her books—not, you will notice, what to do to straighten out her life.

After a few sessions, Dr. Legg asked us to come in and listen to Beulah's story. Plainly she had totally wrapped herself up in the obsession that her writing had to sell. She showed us a sheaf of rejection slips—all courteously worded—from various publishers. When we tried to suggest that her stories were on altogether too high a level to appeal to the youngsters and that no publisher would consider them seriously, she became distraught, saying, "But these rejection slips are so friendly they really mean I should go on. They don't say 'do it differently' or 'change the English.' " We tried to tell her that publishers are very courteous people who very rarely suggest changes in manuscripts until after a contract is signed with the author. Dr. Legg later told us that the conference had done very little good because Beulah was not able to accept what she looked upon as an opinion from a couple of negative know-nothings.

We suggested to Dr. Legg, "Look. She's a keenly sensitive person. I'll bet she's got pretty good psychometric ability. Why don't we see whether she can tell the difference between good and bad? If she can, have her psychometrize some of those rejection slips."

This advice was the magical key to Beulah's dilemma. She became quite interested in psychometry and found that she was indeed able to read the underlying meaning of several of the rejection slips. This underlying meaning bore out our evaluation of the situation.

Beulah's next step smacked of genius. She extended her psychometry into Meta-Psychometry by reading the reviewers' thoughts from each returned manuscript. She was sensitive enough to be able actually to psychometrize each manuscript page and pick up the reviewer's reaction to her work page by page. This is something that we ourselves have not been able to do; we are too emotionally involved in our work to read the reviewers' emotions.

Beulah rewrote her book with the unknowing aid of two top-flight reviewers; on its resubmission to one of the smaller presses, she was able to get it accepted without further amendments. However, she found, as many authors do, that writing is one of the poorest paid occupations in the world; so she lost interest in the work after just the one success. Her home life has now returned to normal; when we lost touch with her, she was busy teaching disabled children. In this work, she was actively employing her psychometric abilities to reach past the communication barrier of deaf-mute children, and to aid in medical diagnostic work of those children whose health problems resisted the standard approach.

THE ULTIMATE BUG

Nowadays, everyone enjoys reading detective stories and learning how terribly clever spies are at planting listening devices in the most unusual places. To us, this whole thing is really very trivial, because any object in an office can be used to read out events and conversations that have transpired in that office; the same is true, of course, in the case of residential rooms. The following secret steps will increase your chances of getting accurate information from such a psychic bug.

1. Either select some insignificant object in the office that can be exactly duplicated, like the desk calendar holder; or give the occupant of the office some decoration or trinket or gadget that you can buy in duplicate. This should be some device that will be left either on the desk or close to the conversation center of the office. Ideally this gift object should be of heavy metal like lead and should have an intricately worked form. If a metal object is not possible, you could try for a stone statuette; depending on the temperament of your target person, you might think in terms of something like Rodin's "Thinker" or a Venus statuette.

Before you place this new ornament in the office that you want to bug, or before you switch the duplicate for the object already there, you must clean it of its previous, emotion-laden imprints. This is best done by bringing some water to a brisk boil on the stove and adding two tablespoons of sea salt per cup of water. Dunk the object in the water, making sure that it is completely submerged, and boil it for three minutes. Then quickly take the object out of the water with your secondary hand, and place it in your deep freeze or in the freezer compartment of your refrigerator. Leave it there for about two hours. Now, sit quietly and psychometrize the object. If it still has residual emotions in it, repeat the treatment. After a maximum of three treatments, you will find that the object is psychically clean. Even though there may be a very minor background emanation remaining, still this is of so low a level that it will be easy to read any new emotions and conversations occurring in the office near your bug.

2. When you have decided that a particularly important meeting took place, replace the object you are using with its twin that you have kept in reserve, and which you have also psychically cleansed. Now, in the leisure of your home, you can read what the psychic bug has to tell you about goings-on in the office—or in any other place that you care to install a psychic bug. Suspicious people can look forever for this type of device, but they will be totally unable to detect anything. Only a psychic detective would be able to pinpoint the leak in the security system.

THE MORE EMOTIONAL THE SUBJECT, THE EASIER IT IS

A person puts out emanations in proportion to the intensity of the emotion he is feeling. Thus, if there is a quiet, business-like discussion going on, you will have some difficulty in psychometrizing the nature of the conversation, no matter how good your psychic bug may be. On the other hand, if your own mate is involved in a hot and heavy love affair, or if the boss is about to fire you, you will be able to pick this up with great ease from your psychic bug. Since you are most interested in situations that raise emotion (for these are the ones which are going to affect you most dramatically), psychic bugs work out very well for your needs. When the discussion is emotional, you will pick it up from your psychic bug and will be forewarned of any problem you are going to have. It is up to you, then, to convert this warning into Meta-Psychometric action.

KIT SAVES HIS MARRIAGE

Kit W, a rising young executive in an occult-oriented Los Angeles book publishing firm, became very suspicious of his wife Sherry. She was supposedly attending several evening courses, yet she never brought home any books, nor did she study at odd moments as most students seem to find necessary. Also, Kit thought, Sherry was smoking and drinking more than usual. He had been reared according to rather rigid Christian fundamentalist beliefs in a home broken up by his mother's heavy drinking; yet he had managed to reconcile these rigid teachings with the occult matters treated in books published by his firm.

As Sherry's drinking increased, he became more and more worried that his own home was going to break up and that he was going to relive his childhood horror experiences. Because he was a real Christian, he wanted to believe everything Sherry told him. But because of his familiarity with occult practices and because of his extreme agitation, he took a step that under normal circumstances would have been foreign to him. That was, he psychically bugged Sherry. He gave her a new charm bracelet, a duplicate of which he kept locked away at his office.

The very first reading he took from the psychic bug confirmed his worst suspicions. Sherry was heavily involved with another man. As far as Kit could tell, she had not taken the Ultimate Step and had not yet been unfaithful to their marriage. Kit's psychometric ability was rather well-developed: he could detect some elements of fear, and even horror, mixed in with the heavily sexual emanations. This naturally puzzled him. He could understand why Sherry would be fearful of his finding out about her affair, but what was this horror that he was picking up?

Kit wisely decided against immediately casting Sherry aside without further investigation of the situation. After all, there were at stake fifteen years of a good marriage, as well as three precious children. Deep in despair, he managed to hide his feelings from her. That night he once again exchanged the charm bracelet that he had just retrieved, he found that this time it was giving no sexual emanations, indicating that Sherry had (at least in this period of time) been faithful to him. But it was giving out the same horror feelings that he had previously detected; and now that the heavy sexual emanations were not in the bracelet, he could also read blackmail and even the name of the person who was his wife's secret partner. Now Kit was really confused. The man involved was at least ten years older than Sherry and was not particularly attractive. In fact, Kit had the impression that Sherry considered him somewhat slimy and loathsome. Why was straight-arrow Sherry seeing someone whom she didn't even like?

Kit was now narrowing in on the key to the problem, and was glad that he had refrained from accusing Sherry of infidelity; for now he felt that there was some hidden, underlying secret that was forcing her reluctantly into this affair. That night he got up enough courage to approach her, and holding her tenderly in his arms he broached the subject of her boyfriend. Once she understood that he knew of her revulsion for the man she was seeing, and that he wished to know why she was still continuing their meetings, feeling as he knew she did about the man, she broke down and told him everything.

When Sherry had been in high school, her blackmailer had gotten her and her girlfriend hooked on heavy drugs. Sherry had been present to witness Pam's overdosing and death. Her supplier had gotten her away before the police arrived. The shock of Pam's death had caused Sherry to stop taking drugs cold. After a few months of living in terror lest the police and her parents find out, she had forgotten the incident until she met her ex-dope supplier at a company office party. He was, as Kit well knew, the sales manager of the die-casting firm where Sherry worked. He had told Sherry that if she didn't yield to his desires, he would not only inform the police, thus ruining her marriage, but he would also destroy Kit's career in his publishing firm.

Kit and Sherry were still presented with something of a problem: that was, how to disarm the blackmailer. Never having been involved in a situation of this type before, Kit asked our advice. He thought perhaps we could hex the blackmailer, or make him move out of town. After considering the matter for a time, we decided that the punishment should fit the crime. We told Sherry how to charge the blackmailer's desk calendar so as to make him impotent. She followed our instructions. We are happy to say that not only did he become impotent, but the fact of his impotence was whispered around the office to such an extent that he had to leave his job. As far as we know, he is still impotent; we feel this is a fitting reward for his previous destructive acts.

PSYCHO-BANKS FOR LISTENING TO OTHERS

Kit was able to interchange the charm bracelets and use them as a psychic bug. Then, using the knowledge thus gained, he took the Meta-Psychometric step of using his knowledge to defeat his opponent. We have suggested that a desk calendar pad-holder can be used in like manner as a psychic energy transmitter. Normally a desk calendar, unless it is cleaned, has so many emotional emanations imprinted on it that it is difficult to use it as a listening device.

The situation where you want to listen to a conversation often arises at a moment's notice; moreover you will often find you get into a series of events that make it impossible to go out and buy some fancy ornament that you can use as a psychic bug. In such a case, the best possible psychic bug you can use in the office situation is the silver wrapping paper from a cigarette pack or from a candy bar. Crumple it up with your secondary hand, but do not entirely crush it. Then, as you are leaving the office, throw it into the boss's ashtray. The convolutions of the foil make ideal psychic energy traps, and the presence of a crumpled-up piece of foil in the ashtray tends to be completely over-looked by anyone in the office. Of course, you must show good sense and care in recovering the foil, but this is usually easy to accomplish. Most foil, right from its high-temperature forming process, has not been touched by human hands until it gets into the package; thus, although you may read high-temperature emanations and impressions of machinery, the foil rarely has any human emotional emanations. Since it is so "clean" psychically, it is an ideal form of instant psychic bug.

YOUR META-PSYCHOMETRIC DECODER

One disadvantage you may face with a psychic bug is that it can become impressed with a very emotional scene that has little or no interest to you. The boss may be having an affair with the secretary and the psychic bug may pick up heavy sexual emanations which would tend to cover up the lower-level conversational emanations that you are trying to read.

The way to handle this problem is to Meta-Psychometrically remove the high-level emanations and then read the lower-level back-ground. To do this, exactly gauge the emotional color of the high-level emanations and then place your psychic bug in a lightbox, constructed as shown in Figure 2–1, having first adjusted the light-box so that its output exactly cancels your psychic bug's imprinted color. You will see that the light-box has three different colored filters in it: red, green, and blue. You will also notice that there are three dimmer controls, one for each colored bulb. Between the bulbs and the psychometry

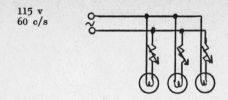

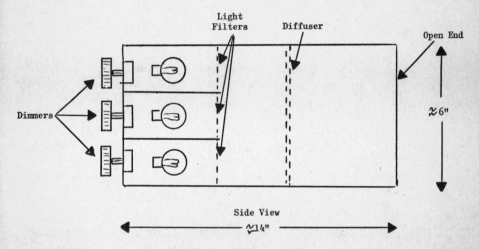

Figure 2-1

Meta-Psychometric Elimination Light-Box

chamber there are two sheets of glass. This is to prevent your being confused by heat from the bulbs coming through to the chamber.

Hold your charged psychic bug in your secondary hand and read the high-level emanations. Then adjust the color in the light-box chamber to be precisely the reverse of this emanation. Do this by placing a small piece of white card in the chamber and by adjusting the chamber in accordance with the color balance chart in Table 1–2. Now, place your psychic bug in the chamber; every ten minutes or so, take it out and re-psychometrize it. You will find that the level of emanations which you are trying to remove is lowering. You may also find that you have not adjusted the color in the chamber exactly or correctly, but you can easily make a minor adjustment at this time. Continue the process of exposing the bug and re-adjusting your Meta-Psychometric elimination chamber until you have removed from the bug the irrele-

vant emanations. Now you will be able to read the lower-level emanations that are of interest to you.

YOUR COMPLETE META-PSYCHOMETRIC EAVESDROPPER'S GUIDE

Psychic eavesdropping is one of the easiest, yet the least detecta-
ble, means to gain information and serenity in your life. All you have to
do is place some inconspicuous object in the area of interest, then later
retrieve it or exchange it for a similar object, and read out what you
want to know. The secrets of success in picking a psychic bug are these:

1. Depend on metals, especially heavy metals with convoluted
surfaces, as the easiest substances to read. They also seem to absorb
more information than any other material. Closely following the metals
in usefulness are objects of stone with rough-textured surfaces.

2. Before you start your experiments, psychically clean any object that you plan to use as a psychic bug, being careful to remove all
previous irrelevant emanations. Often it is best to have two similar
objects which can be exchanged so that you have ample time to
psychometrize and cleanse the bug.

3. Avoid using vividly colored objects, as the color may confuse
you in your work.

4. When you are analyzing your bug, remember to remove any
high-level irrelevant information with your light-box before looking for
the finely detailed information that you need.

5. Lastly, don't be surprised at what you hear. Remember two
things: you wouldn't be listening if you thought they were going to be
nice to you; and some of the information on the bug may not refer
specifically to you.

3

WARD OFF EVIL
BY META-PSYCHOMETRIZING
YOUR SURROUNDINGS

EVERYONE IS AFFECTED BY PSYCHIC EMANATIONS

As you develop your psychometric ability, you will become more and more aware of the feelings which emanate from objects in your environment. Meta-Psychometry will help you adjust your environment so as to give you more serenity by reducing the effect of these background emanations. This will be especially valuable during this time when you are working at the development of your latent psychometric ability.

Everyone, no matter how psychically blank he may believe himself to be, is affected by psychic emanations. Ask anyone you meet who has spent time just sitting in an old stone church whether or not that time didn't make him feel calmer. Go yourself and try it. After a few moments of quiet sitting, you will feel your tensions drain away; you will automatically become more serene. On the other hand, if you want to recharge yourself, go to the local football stadium (when no game is scheduled) and sit in one of the team dugouts. You will feel your tensions build and your heartbeat speed up. Merely by sitting there and absorbing the emotions from the very walls and benches of the area, you can extend this "high" as long as you like.

DIAMOND'S EMANATIONS LEAVE A TRAIL OF DEATH

Almost every minute of the day that it's open, there is a crowd around one special display case in the Smithsonian Institute. The hushed crowd is looking at a violet-blue stone of destiny, one that, if the legends are true, has brought death and sorrow to countless men and women. That violet-blue stone is the infamous Hope Diamond. Its history is well worth repeating to show how ill luck can follow an object from hand to hand and from decade to decade.

No one really knows who first owned the diamond from which the Hope was cut; but it seems likely that the last of the great moguls, Aurangzeb, sold it to a French adventurer, Tavernier, in about 1660. Aurangzeb was famous for the iron claw he wore on his right hand, a claw he used to disembowel his enemies in a leisurely manner. The claw earned him the sobriquet "The Grasper." Aurangzeb the Grasper is reputed to have worn the diamond in his turban at hundreds of disemboweling sessions.

After he purchased the diamond, Tavernier died in dreadful agony in the snows of Russia, where his partially eaten body was recovered from the drifts in 1668. The subsequent history of the diamond is well documented.

Louis XIV	died of smallpox
Louis XVI And Marie Antoinette	died on the guillotine
Queen Marie Luisa	died in childbirth
Henry Hope	died intestate
Hope's nephew	died a pauper after his wife deserted him

The Hope now changed hands more rapidly, for its growing reputation preceded it. That reputation was strengthened when a Follies star, wearing the stone for a single night on a reckless bet, was killed by her lover. A Greek merchant who bought it fell from a cliff with all his family—to their deaths. Just a few days after the Sultan of Turkey purchased it, his entire country rebelled. Finally it came into the possession of Mrs. Edward McLean, who loved the diamond so much that she would not part with it. While it was hers, first her son, then her daughter died; and her husband went mad and died in a mental hospital. When Mrs. McLean herself died, the diamond was purchased by Harry Winston, who mailed it to the Smithsonian, where he hoped it would no longer be able to cast its evil influence.

The horror of the Grasper's terrible acts may have worn off by now, weakening the curse of the Hope Diamond; or perhaps it is as strong as ever, pent up in that velvet display case.

If the Hope Diamond were the only such "stone of destiny," you might laugh it off as only gossip; but there are many others which bring with them good luck or bad. Since diamonds of great value are usually owned only by ruthless and grasping men—men who will stop at nothing to enlarge their power—it is no wonder that they become impregnated with such baleful influences.

PSYCHOMETRIZE YOUR SURROUNDINGS FOR SERENITY

Just as the Hope Diamond puts out its very heavy negative emanations, so there may be something in your own surroundings that is causing you a problem. The successive owners of the Hope naturally came to consider themselves hexed or to have had the evil eye put on them; and thousands of people write to us every year with just such beliefs about themselves. In most of these cases, no one has gone to the trouble of hexing them or casting the evil eye on them. They have, instead, brought into their own lives something with extremely negative emanations, probably without realizing the fact.

You learned in Chapter 1 that objects can be imprinted with emanations. And you can do it to yourself! Perhaps you have had a tragic love affair, yet you have retained in your apartment mementos of that affair. These mementos are impressed with all the negativity that went into the tragedy. They will still emanate into your environment those old bitter thoughtforms of sorrow, disappointment, and all the rest of it. On the other hand, maybe you have recently purchased a Mexican stool with a natural leather seat. Very often we find that leather carries with it all of the fear and horror that the animal experienced at the moment of its slaughter. When you have an object right there under your nose that is silently radiating emotions of blood and terror, can you wonder that sometimes you have dreams of horror and death?

Maybe you feel an unaccustomed sadness. In 1976 many people wrote to us saying that they had terrible feelings of nostalgia and sadness, and a wish to recapture past lives. Many of these people, it later transpired, had purchased antiques during America's Bicentennial celebration; and of course these antiques put out radiations that would induce feelings of sadness and nostalgia and longing. Think of how many people have died near that 200-year-old clothing chest.

Think of how many love affairs and emotional scenes occurred in front of that charming 18th Century dressing table.

Your problem is: How to clean up thse undesirable influences from your own environment. Only when this is done can you live a more serene life—and, moreover, do your psychometry without having your subconscious receptors confused by local radiated thoughtforms.

First, then, you must locate in your own dwelling the major contributors to your disquiet. Look first for natural animal emitters and attempt to pinpoint the "color" of their emanations. Now, place these harmful (for harmful they truly are) objects under the appropriate balancing light which you have set up from the light-box shown in Figure 2–1. Here is the easiest way to set up this balancing light. After you have decided on the "color" the object is emitting, look up its balancing color in Table 1–2 and adjust the three controls of your light-box so that the box emits the color your need. Place the object in the color balance you have chosen. After fiften minutes' exposure, re-psychometrize it. If it needs more exposure, give it another fifteen minutes, then recheck your results. Continue the exposure-check procedure until you are satisfied that the object is truly cleansed and in good balance.

It may take days or even weeks to get all the harmful sinister emanations out of your environment. You may even find that the very walls of your dwelling are imprinted with emanations that need to be corrected with the appropriate light treatment. Be persistent, and be careful; for you obviously don't want to impress on the walls, or on any other object, thoughtforms of further imbalance. The trick lies in your alternation of exposure to light-box rays and re-psychometrizing to see how much effect your cleansing procedure is having.

Eventually you will find that you have achieved a pleasantly balanced environment, and you will be happily surprised at how much more restful your entire life will become when you have completed the cleansing process we have recommended.

If you prefer to buy a light-box complete, rather than the less expensive procedure of constructing your own, the Appendix lists the name and address of a company that sells such light-boxes.

Some experimenters report that flashing lights work better than a steady glow. If you wish, you may connect a Christmas-tree light flasher in series with the box.

CONTROLLING THE COMFORT LEVEL OF OTHER PEOPLE

When your friends become aware of your psychometric ability and your growing expertise in occult matters, many of them will come to you with their problems, afraid that in some way they have been hexed or psychically attacked. You can do a tremendous amount of good by helping them clean up their surroundings just as you cleaned up your own. We suggest that when you do this, you avoid taking your light-box or other equipment to their residence. The clean-up procedure is so simple that many people find it difficult to accept the idea that you have in fact removed harmful emanations through the disappointingly simple technique they will witness. You should, instead, identify the offending objects and take them away with you, keeping them for a time while you expose them to the radiation from your light-box.

Every coin has two sides. If you have some deadly rival, you can negatively affect him by placing some harmful or hateful radiations in his environment.

When you are attempting to cleanse areas of undesirable thoughtforms, you will occasionally find that you have not been successful using the light-box and the appropriate rituals. There are two possible reasons for this lack of success.

1. Someone may be beaming thoughtforms at you from outside. Later in this chapter we will tell you how to protect yourself from such radiation.

2. Perhaps more commonly, you may be working with an object to which a spirit has attached itself. At one time, Yvonne Frost had an antique wedding ring which couldn't be cleaned psychometrically. We found that the elderly lady who previously owned the ring still came to see it from time to time. She had been so emotionally attached to it, that her spirit was unable to progress in its upward path because she frequently came back to see what was happening with her ring.

In order to alleviate a problem of this sort, you must learn how to talk to the clinging spirit. The teaching of that procedure, though not at all difficult, is outside the scope of this book and we suggest you get assistance from a local occultist, or (better) take the School of Wicca's correspondence course and learn for yourself how to communicate with the spirits. We do not recommend an exorcising procedure. Exorcism banishes the spirit into the outer shades, cutting it adrift from its natural progression and from its accustomed haunts.

JEANNIE WAS ALWAYS HIGH

Jeannie T is a pleasant blond woman approaching her thirtieth birthday. She lives in a prestigious lakefront subdivision near St. Louis. Her husband, whom we call Tab, had been a relatively calm and conscientious salesman for a local manufacturer of electrical equipment. His boss came to me one day to tell me that good old Tab was falling apart at the seams. Since we were in a tight competition with another firm on some equipment, the manager was considering replacing Tab in his job. Before doing so, he wanted me to talk with Tab to see whether I could find out what was wrong with this normally reliable worker.

Tab and I had a few drinks together. He told me that Jeannie was driving him berserk. "Over the past few months she has gotten so 'up' and so jumpy and over-full of life that I just can't keep up with her. Not only that, but she seems to be burning herself out." Tab and I discussed Jeannie for over an hour. Tab was convinced that she was not having an affair, nor was there anything he could pin down as being wrong with the marriage.

Yvonne visited Jeannie and talked to her independently woman to woman. She, too, was unable to find any mundane explanation for Jeannie's high energy level. She did say that Jeannie had become a shadow of her former self and that she seemed unable to sit still for a moment. Yvonne reported that even during the coffee-and-donuts woman-to-woman talk, Jeannie was constantly jumping out of her chair and fidgeting around the kitchen, making even Yvonne edgy. Of course, we wondered about all the things any competent psychic would. Was the house haunted? Was somebody affecting Jeannie from a distance? Et cetera, et cetera.

With the cooperation of both Tab and Jeannie, we continued our investigation of their home. We spent hour upon hour trying to check out various objects in the house. During this time, Tab had to go on a business trip; and one night when Gavin was in Jeannie's bedroom and Yvonne was working in the kitchen, Jeannie approached Gavin with an X-rated proposition. If Yvonne had not been in the house, Gavin might have been quite tempted, since Jeannie was, after all, a very attractive lady.

Gavin talked the proposition over with Jeannie, and finally learned that part of her current problem was that she was constantly "turned on" and had almost become a semi-nymphomaniac. Because she had had no previous history of excessive sex drive, Gavin asked her about her diet and whether her other body functions such as her menstrual cycle had shown any changes. Jeannie said no, she was (so far as she knew) still eating the same foods that she always had, and her physical health seemed to be normal.

Jeannie had taken the trouble to put on a negligee before proposing her X-rated activity. Now, for the first time, Gavin could see that she wore a silver medallion on her bosom. Tab had brought it to her from Mexico; it depicted a rather erotic scene, so she had been wearing it *under* her outer garmets. Since no one had mentioned it in conversation, we had not been aware of its existence. Gavin asked her to take off the medallion so he could psychometrize it; for having noticed the naughty scene depicted on it, he had a feeling that it was somehow connected with her problem. She handed it to him, and he almost dropped it; to his advanced sensibilities, it felt like a white-hot, green energy furnace. He asked Jeannie if he could take it away with him, so as to work on it in a quiet environment. She agreed.

Gavin found what he might have expected: shortly after its construction, the amulet had gotten saturated with thoughtforms of raunchy, animalistic sex. These thoughtforms had caused Jeannie to be constantly turned on and had indirectly caused poor Tab his problem. We took that medallion away with us; we rebalanced it with an amber light treatment and returned it to her. She still wears it daily, knowing now that it can bring her only the better sort of sexual influence. With the calming of their domestic life, Tab was able to get his feet back on the ground and to bring in the contract his manager had been so worried about.

OVERBALANCE YOUR ADVERSARY
WITH META-PSYCHOMETRY

You can affect your friends (or your enemies) positively or negatively by introducing into their immediate environment objects that unbalance the local radiation patterns. When you psychometrize the person whom you wish to affect, you will usually detect one unbalanced energy level. If this is a friend, you would want to give him a gift, such as a piece of jewelry, saturated with thoughtforms that will balance this unbalanced condition. If it is an enemy, you would wish to give him a gift saturated with thoughtforms that would tend to reinforce the unbalanced condition. You should not give him a gift saturated with such things as indiscriminate hate, for this is far too general a thoughtform to affect him.

If someone you want to affect negatively has, say, a low level of sexual drive, and you think it would be fun to turn him into the office Casanova overnight, you have a hard job ahead of you: not only will you have to bring his naturally low level up to normal, but you will have to add even more sexual emanations to turn him into a slavering animal. Instead, since this person has a negative sexual balance, you can effectively utilize this imbalance and add to it. In this way, you push the scale even further in the direction of its imbalance, tipping it clear over into antisexual bigotry.

DEKE GETS THE CONTRACT

Deke V was a salesman of muffler equipment in the southeastern U.S. His main competitor was Stanley L, whose muffler equipment was almost identical to Deke's and was, if anything, priced a shade lower. Though their rivalry had been friendly, it was driving Deke to drink because he just couldn't seem to close many sales recently in competition with Stanley. The make-or-break situation came when a well-capitalized division of a large corporation decided that, if mufflers were the profit-makers the corporation had heard, it, too, would get into the business. This would mean an initial order of at least ten major muffler production machines with follow-up orders for many more. Deke wanted their order.

In his life as a salesman, Deke had spent many solitary hours on the road; he had filled some of those hours by learning to psychometrize the motel rooms he had stayed in. Very early in the development of his ability, he had found that by taking even minimum precautions, such as moving a negatively radiating lamp into the bathroom for the night, he could get a better night's sleep than if he simply ignored emanations from the room's furnishings. Occasionally he had gone so far as to change his room for one with better feelings.

The competition with Stanley over the initial corporate order for muffler equipment was getting down to the short strokes, and Deke felt that he had a really good chance on this one. But he knew that if he stopped concentrating even for a moment, he could lose the contract and probably his cozy area franchise as well. He and his wife spent hours game-playing what Stanley would do to win that contract. Through friends, word had come back to Deke that Stanley was really going to go after this one, because he knew that if he got it, his competition with Deke would be over, leaving Stanley free to sell muffler equipment at his leisure in the whole southeastern United States.

Deke had become pretty good buddies with the corporate purchasing officer; he, too, told Deke that his offer must be as good as he could possibly make it to overcome Stanley's bid. Though he did not actually let Deke see Stanley's bid price, he did show him the rest of Stanley's proposal. Holding the document in his hands, Deke was able to pick up from it fundamentalist Christian emanations of almost fanatical intensity. He wondered whether these were Stanley's feelings or perhaps had come from the secretary who had typed the proposal. He thought he knew Stanley rather well, yet he had not been aware of any heavy religious commitment on Stanley's part.

Over lunch with the purchasing agent, Deke casually brought the conversation around to religion. The purchasing agent groaned. "God darn it, Deke, not you too! I had enough of that yesterday from Stanley." Deke promptly veered off—but now he had a glimmer of new hope; for Deke knew that if he could push Stanley further over into his religious zeal, he stood a chance of making his fanaticism show through to an even more disagreeable extent. That, he knew, would set up sufficient negative reaction in the purchasing agent to assure Deke of the contract.

How could he introduce into Stanley's environment something that would tip the balance toward Deke? He knew that in the following weekend both he and Stanley would be attending an automotive show in the local arena, and it was from this that he got his idea. For one of the tailpipe manufacturers was a close friend of his and had left Deke samples of the literature he would be handing out during the show. That following Sunday, Deke took some of this literature to a revival meeting. When a woman a couple of seats away from him went through the born-again experience, he quietly laid the literature under her seat, then recovered it after the service. With the cooperation of his friend, it was these same sheets that were given to Stanley when he collected his updated tailpipe information from the booth at the auto parts show.

The next time Deke saw the corporate purchasing agent, he was pleased to receive a far warmer welcome than he had previously gotten:

"Deke, old buddy, it looks like you're gonna get the contract. That Stanley must have flipped his wig. He's so psyched up with religion that he can't seem to concentrate on business. When he was in the office yesterday, everything was going fine until I asked him for some new tailpipe prices; then all he could talk about was being born again. Man, that gets old in a hurry when you're trying to conduct a business meeting."

Well, Deke got the contract. Stanley still does very well in competition with Deke because the pages saturated with revival energy ended up in the wastebasket and were replaced with updated literature. Their removal meant that Stanley regained his balance and was able again to function as a salesman.

BASIC META-PSYCHOMETRIC CHARGING

In Chapters 4 and 5, we will tell you how to make psycho-stores that transmit so much energy as to be irresistible. In most cases, you don't need to go through long elaborate procedures in producing these high-intensity psycho-stores. In his work against Stanley, Deke just used the born-again woman's energy impressed on a few sheets of paper to push Stanley over the edge of rationality.

You, too, can make use of emotional situations to impress thoughtforms on your psycho-stores. Obviously, a thoughtform of raw hungry lust could be impressed by having the psycho-store close by when a lusty sexual encounter occurs; a rage thoughtform could easily be generated by yourself thinking of the last time that you were frustrated and enraged, for instance, by an expired warranty or by a questionable act of Congress. All you need do is hold the chosen psycho-store in your dominant hand while allowing your feeling of rage to build up, and the psycho-store will pick up sufficient energy to thoroughly disturb a person who is naturally prone to temper tantrums.

If you are good at visualizing things and summoning high emotions, you can impress many subtle variations of emotion on your psycho-stores. You can, for instance, visualize yourself in a setting of affluence and luxury, and impress this onto the psycho-store. You can imagine yourself being very cool and calm, perhaps while you are resting in a tepid bath, and impress these emotions onto a psycho-store to bring calmness to one who has a fiery temper.

When you have done your best to impress an emotional thoughtform onto a psycho-store, let it rest and soak for perhaps an hour, wrapped in a plain white cloth of linen or cotton. Now, take it in your secondary hand and read out the emanations you have actually impressed upon it, as opposed to the emanations you intended to impress. Occasionally, you may find that you haven't quite got it right, and you will need to cleanse the psycho-store in boiling water and start over. After a few practice efforts, though, you will find that in less than five minutes you can dramatically change the radiation and emanation pattern of almost any object.

CHANGING THE PSYCHIC COMFORT LEVEL IN A ROOM

You are now equipped to change the psychic feelings of an entire room. You can either introduce a psycho-store to balance the room, or you can add or remove those objects which are actively causing influences. In fact, you can ring the changes on a room so that sometimes it feels friendly and other times it feels hostile. Since color is universally associated with psychic feelings, even a subtle change in the paint color balance in a room will greatly affect the comfort of you and your friends while you are in that room. Every time you make a change, you should spend a few days living with the new psychic balance before you embark on a further change. As we said before in the discussion of psychic bugs, when you erase or balance the high-level emanations, the lower-level emanations become more conspicuous. Because you spend so many hours a day in your home environment, even the lowest level of unbalance will affect you eventually. Given time, the most minute feelings will make themselves apparent. Naturally you cannot entirely prevent emotional incidents from occuring in a given room; but after any emotional incident you have a choice of either eradicating the impressed emotional thoughtforms or balancing them with a new psycho-store.

One way that people have attempted to keep their lives balanced is to impress on a room high levels of all the emotional experiences they can think of. Thus, they hope that the low levels will not be apparent, being masked by the more vivid "colors" of the deliberately impressed emanations. Though it is true that high levels of impressed thoughtforms tend to cancel one another out, some people find it very difficult to live in an emotionally saturated environment. Thus, we recommend that you try to get the psychic color of your room first balanced and then shifted slightly over into the light-yellow emotional area.

SLEEPLESS KATIE GETS FIRED

Katie W was an electronics technician who worked for Western Electric in southern California, assembling switchboard equipment. This is a job that requires constant attention to fine detail, one on which you cannot afford to be slipshod. Katie consistently earned bonuses for her excellent work; one day she decided that she could afford to move to a new and more expensive apartment. She knew from the start that her basic wages would not cover her rent there; the frequent bonuses were a basic premise of her move. Soon after moving in, though, she found that she was getting fewer and fewer bonuses because she could not seem to get to sleep at night.

Katie's lover, who is also a friend of ours, attempted to help Katie by psychometrizing her apartment. He could find nothing wrong with it; certainly there were no big psychic generators that would account for her staying awake at night. So sure were they that the change of apartment was the problem, that both Katie and Bill had gone directly to the psychometrizing of the place without checking out the more mundane possibilities of health problems associated with a glandular or other condition.

When Bill wrote to us about the situation, we immediately told him to have Katie get a complete physical. She cooperated, but the doctors could find nothing wrong with her; her sleepless nights continued. Using the prescribed barbiturates, she was able to sleep, but they slowed her reactions down so badly, that her work deteriorated still further. Finally, her work got so bad that she was fired from her high-paying job. This naturally meant that she had to give up the new luxury apartment.

She moved in with her mother—which to Katie was a real letdown. As soon as she got "home" and slept in her old bed again, though, she found she had no problem getting to sleep and remaining sound asleep all night long. Very soon, she felt so well that she called her ex-boss and asked for another chance at her former job. Quite willingly he allowed her to come in for a test, which she passed with flying colors. Now, more than ever, Bill was firmly convinced that there was something in that luxury apartment, either an entity or a psycho-store of negative emotion, that had caused Katie her insomnia. Apart from his concern for her health, Bill, too, wanted to get Katie away from her mother's watchful eye.

When we were next in California, Bill arranged for us to visit with the new resident of the apartment to see whether we could pick up any emanations. We spent some time in the bedroom of the apartment, but we were unable to identify any specific problem. Through Bill's persistent efforts, and with some unexpected juggling of our own schedule, we were finally able to meet Katie, who turned out to be a beautiful

Piscean person. In fact, at first meeting, she was radiating tremendous amounts of lavender Piscean energy.

"Do you have a foot problem?" was Yvonne's first question.

"Yes," Katie nodded. "I've worn corrective shoes for years."

"What color is your bedroom?" was the next question.

"Lavender and white."

This told us that Katie's difficulty was caused by purely mundane factors. Her slightly malformed feet caused her to radiate lavender energy in amounts harmful to her health. In the lavender-painted bedroom of her mother's home, she was able to recharge herself. Though it was attractive, the beige bedroom of the high-priced apartment was the wrong color to act as a battery for her. When she lacked the lavender battery, the deficiency manifested itself as insomnia. In Chapter 8, you will see insomnia mentioned as one of the group of health problems associated with the lavender of Piscean influence.

Bill had assumed her problem could simply be written off as one of the drawbacks of being a Pisces. We told Katie that she did not have to endure insomnia as long as she always kept one lavender room in her home. She must have arranged this, because we have not heard from her since our California visit.

A LITTLE ENERGY IS ALL THAT IS NEEDED

In our examples, we have stressed the fact that many successful efforts are the result of relatively low energy emanations from such things as the walls of the room. In Katie's case, you saw how she was affected by a change in the color of ther bedroom.

Major changes can happen, too, when people simply re-orient their beds with respect to the magnetic field of the earth itself. Now you would not normally think that the earth's field is a decisive influence in your life. Anyone who has used a magnetic compass knows how delicately balanced the needle must be in order to even detect the field; yet Professor Jose Feola at the University of Minnesota has consistently been able to demonstrate that test subjects are able to detect fields whose strength is as little as one-tenth that of the earth's field. In dowsing experiments, psychic Ron Warmoth has demonstrated an ability to detect oil and mineral deposits whose effect on the earth's magnetic field was imperceptible to the most sensitive instruments of professional geologists.

Other people—many of them—have reported that they are able to pick up the telephone before it rings; tests have shown that such

people are somehow able to detect the presence of the minute electrical currents in the telephone circuit before the bell actually starts
ringing. This proves once more that a human being is far more sensitive
than you have been led to believe. This is not some big psychic or
occult thing; it is a fact of life—a fact that has all too long been ignored
by giant firms which string more and more electrical wires and heavy
current-carrying cables around us, let alone the highly secret but
potent radiation from antennas of airports and defense installations.

Only a minute amount of energy is required to change your
environment—for the better, or for the worse. Tests with animals near
overhead cables and with convalescent nursing homes have indicated
that people and animals are affected adversely by most man-made
electrical radiation patterns. In these tests it has been shown that cattle
often preferred to starve themselves rather than graze under overhead
cables, and that convalescent patients would go to great effort to get
their rooms changed away from those rooms that had heavy electrical
currents flowing through them. Neither the cattle nor the patients
knew why they felt uncomfortable or why they wanted to move; but we
would caution you to make sure that your man-made and earth-
induced magnetic and electrical fields are minimized, especially in
your living and sleeping quarters. When you have psychically balanced
everything, and still a problem persists, it may be that a very mundane
electrical cable is the source of your discomfort.

PROTECTING YOURSELF AGAINST
NEGATIVE THOUGHTS

Once you have quieted your psychic and mundane electrical
environment, you should regularly check to see whether changes have
occurred in that environment. If a power company has run a new cable
near your home, for instance, you may have to move; for oftentimes a
private individual does not swing enough weight to undo as drastic a
change as this would be.

What if everything seems quiet and calm in your environment,
yet you are still having a streak of bad luck and feel as if you are
continuously hexed? Well, it may be that you are! In any case, the
precautions to overcome a hex of this sort are elementary and easily
accomplished. In the arcane world of the ancient grimoire we find that
to defeat a hex, you should place around you coffin nails and horseshoes with their open ends outward. Psychic emanations behave like
some sort of magnetic wave, and electromagnetic waves are affected by
disturbance in the earth's magnetic field. This is especially true of the

very low levels of emanation that we are dealing with in these phenomena.

You want to be sure that you are absolutely free from a hex? All you have to do is arrange a ring of protection at least around your bed, and, if possible, around your whole house.

YOUR PSYCHOMETRIC RING OF PROTECTION

Any ferrous metal object such as a used coffin nail or a horseshoe, if lying in the earth's magnetic field, will disturb that field when it is first placed in position.

In time past, iron nails were quite rare. So, if a Witch was asked for help in the arranging of a ring of protection, she would often recommend gathering some old nails, perhaps from a church yard; for in those days of hand labor, most other nails were too expensive for poor folk. Nowadays a Witch will take a handful of nails and bend them in two directions (See Figure 3–1).

Figure 3-1

Nail Bent to Disturb
Electromagnetic Field

You, too, can go to your local hardware store and buy some nails, then bend them as shown in the figure. Bent nails have a greater disturbing effect on the earth's field, naturally, than do straight nails. If nails are too expensive, take an old coffee can and cut strips from it ¼ inch wide. Twist these strips into as many convolutions as possible. For the ring of protection to be constructed around your bed, place either the nails or the convoluted metal strips around your bed, under the carpet. As you place them, reinforce their protection with a positive high-energy thoughtform. Such a thoughtform can be built by chanting a rhyme like this one:

"Here within dwells protection for me.
As I will, so mote it be."

Once this protective ring is formed, nothing from outside can harm you. Provided you are careful to psychometrize the objects within your ring of protection, you cannot be hexed. There is the possibility that possession may have occurred before the construction of your ring; or there may be an independent entity following you around; it takes a qualified occult expert to help you with a problem of this sort. An expert is listed in the Appendix. Please don't expect him to spend a lot of time with you working on your problem without adequate compensation. Like you, he, too, has to live and eat, as much as he would like to help all comers free of charge.

It is best to form your ring of protection at the time of the new moon; and you should remember to change the position of every metal object in the ring on each successive new moon so that the objects will continue to cause what is called a magnetic anomaly; this anomaly or disturbance disturbs and nullifies any incoming negative radiation patterns. Magnetic material lying in the earth's field, given enough time, rearranges its molecular structure so that it is aligned with the field and no longer distorts the waves of energy.

YOUR META-PSYCHOMETRIC SERENITY GUIDE

Below are listed the steps you should take to gain serenity and to live in a psychically neutral or quiet environment.

1. Analyze your surroundings psychometrically and find out precisely which objects are putting out hateful or disturbing emanations. Take these articles and neutralize their effect with the aid of a light-box, or by adding a balancing psycho-store of your own making to the environment.

2. Make sure that your environment includes no heavy electrical or magnetic field patterns caused by cabling or by radar equipment in your neighborhood. If these undesirable things do exist, then moving is probably your only adequate solution to the problem.

3. Make sure that you are sleeping with your head to the north. Note that some homosexual persons find more quiet sleep with their heads to the east. Regrettably, we have no idea why this is true.

4. If you have made sure that your environment is as psychically quiet as you can make it, and you still are having problems that can be ascribed only to external psychic emanations, then either you are being hexed externally or you have an entity following you around. To eliminate the possibility of a hex, surround yourself with your Meta-Psychometric ring of protection. If problems still persist even after this step, contact the skilled exorcist listed in the Appendix.

4

FILLING YOUR ASTRAL ENERGY STORE WITH META-PSYCHOMETRIC MIRACLE POWER

GET YOURSELF INTO SHAPE PSYCHICALLY, MENTALLY, AND PHYSICALLY

The procedures we outlined in earlier chapters required a minimum of effort and psychic balance. Now, as you approach more advanced Meta-Psychometric procedures, you should be sure you are prepared to face these challenges. You need to be in near-perfect physical, mental, and psychic (or "astral") balance before you can attempt to make things happen.

The best comparison we can give you is that of an athlete who plans to run an Olympic race. If he entered that race without strenuous preparation, obviously he would fail; and probably the abruptness and fierceness of his competing would do his body irreparable damage. The athlete knows he must train himself for a matter of months if he is to be able to participate in such a fierce competition.

Not only does the athlete have to train his body, but he also has to get the right mental attitude in order to reach the pitch required to win an Olympic race. A chess master playing in a world tournament competition has to pay attention to his physical health, but this is not as important as his mental acuity. He must, while being careful to remain in good health, train his mind to the world championship pitch of acuity. In your case, you are going into the Meta-Psychometry Olympics; therefore, you must be sure that (1) you are in good health; (2) your mental acuity is adequate; and (3) you train yourself to the Olympic standard of Meta-Psychometric ability.

Today, you may have problems—through no fault of your own—or you may have allowed your psychic astral batteries to lie idle, to become unbalanced or run-down. In this chapter, we shall first discuss the recharging of your astral batteries and then go on to rebalancing them with the aid of energy stored in mascots or psycho-stores.

In starting off, though, ask yourself honestly: Are you in good physical shape? If you are, fine; roll up your sleeves and begin. If you are not, we would recommend that you go to a good clinic for a thorough physical, and that you get into good physical shape before you ever embark on a program of psychic development. Likewise, if you are feeling mentally dull, you should attempt to sharpen up your mind by taking a few college courses in a favorite subject, in competition with the youngsters.

ASTRAL ENERGY IS ALL AROUND YOU

Just as this planet is unceasingly bombarded with light from the sun and with reflected light from the moon, so it is also bombarded with invisible radiation that you can use in your daily life. Stand facing eastward, as shown in Figure 4–1, your head slightly back and your arms extended, with your right palm up and your left palm down. Wait for a moment; feel the energy flow into your upturned palm and out of your downturned palm. Now, quickly turn each hand over so that your left palm is facing upward and your right palm downward. Can you feel the change? Do it again; this time more quickly. Some skeptics might say that you are feeling nothing more than a temperature difference of the blood in your palms; but you can adequately demonstrate to yourself that this is not true by turning your hands quickly. If, indeed, you felt just a temperature difference, it could not occur instantaneously as does the energy flow feeling.

If it is late at night or if you are very tired, you will not feel these energy flows as readily as when you are on top of the world. Also, your sensitivity to the energy flow will be lowerd if you have rings on your fingers or a closed bracelet around your wrist. So take off those rings and bangles before you try the Star Position.

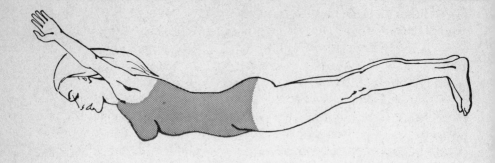

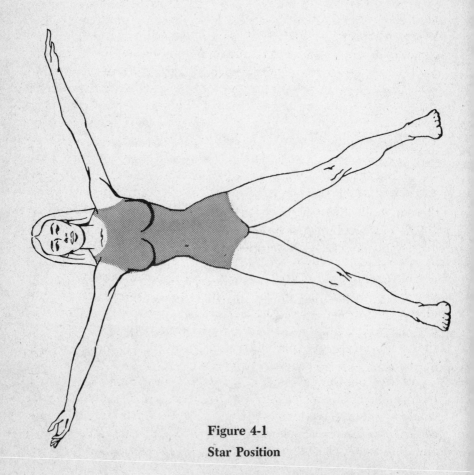

Figure 4-1
Star Position

This power you are feeling is astral energy, the energy that you will use to recharge your astral batteries or to get yourself back into good balance. Once you are fully charged, it is the energy that you will be able to put out to make things happen in accordance with your will.

JANICE RECHARGES HERSELF

In the summer vacations between her college years, Janice M took a job as a cave guide in the limestone area of south central Missouri. In this job, she worked deep underground for most of the daylight hours. After the first couple of weeks of this work, she found she was becoming terribly lethargic and felt a dread of going to work. She felt there was something evil in the cave that was sapping her strength.

Nevertheless, she persisted in her job; but she noticed more and more that things were just not going well with her. She asked her boss, Wade, whether anyone else had mentioned trouble of this sort in connection with the underground work. He replied that it occurred quite regularly and that she would find that regular sexual relations would help her overcome the problem. In a burst of generosity he suggested himself as the perfect partner. Janice was pretty much turned off at this proposal, because Wade was a rather slimy character, and she was committed to her Edwin, whom she had dated all through high school.

Janice had gone to a great deal of trouble convincing both Edwin and her rather narrow small-town parents that she could safely venture out on her own to get a job, so she was loath to admit defeat. Her life's circumstances and her health continued to deteriorate—and Wade's insistence that he should help her did nothing to lighten her load.

Coincidence (if coincidence it was) intervened in Janice's life when Yvonne and I visited the cave. Janice was one of the very few people to recognize us from our publicity photographs. Before we went down into the cave with another guide, Janice took Yvonne to one side and asked her to see whether she could feel anything "bad" down there. Yvonne does not particularly like caves anyway, so Gavin got the job of doing the psychometric checkout.

Over coffee and donuts with Janice after the tour, Gavin told her that he could feel nothing at all untoward, but, in order to be sure, we would have to spend a lot more time in the cave; that was, unless Janice could pinpoint some specific spot where problems occurred. She admitted that it was not any particular area; it was just that as soon as she went underground, she felt hexed, and she constantly felt as if Wade or the cave or something was sapping her energy.

Again, the thing that Christians call "coincidence" and we call the Natural Law played a hand: Wade himself came to join us for coffee. This allowed us to psychometrize his energy patterns. Apart from some minor imbalances caused by his being sexually frustrated (this told us clearly that he had not been successful with his offers of assistance to the tour guides), we could find nothing wrong with him. He certainly did not seem to be some big psychic vampire sucking energy out of his victims.

Gavin arranged with Wade for Janice to have the rest of the day off. We accompanied her back to her basement apartment. First, we psychometrized Janice; we found that her level of astral energy was shockingly low. Next, we cross-questioned her about such things as her diet. We learned that she ate very poorly from a psychic point of view, getting very few "live" or green foods and relying instead on the junk foods served in the cave park's snack bar. We told her these things:

1. She should recharge herself at a sunrise service (see Page 79).

2. At least twice a day on her breaks from her cave tours, she should use the recharging method outlined in the paragraph below.

3. She should eat at least one large green salad each day.

A couple of weeks later, we got a letter from Janice saying that our instructions had worked; she no longer felt any dread of going into the cave; in fact, she quite welcomed the contact with the tourists. Moreover, she wrote, she had summoned sufficient courage to approach the district supervisor and tell him the story of Wade's importuning the guide girls. After checking with the staff, the supervisor had quickly replaced the offensive Wade.

Thus, from a very negative situation, Janice was now dramatically transferred into a positive situation. She couldn't say enough, of course, to thank us for "all we had done." Granted, we had taken steps to help her, but we had done no big ritual or spell—we had merely guided Janice to correct her own astral energy levels to compensate for the time she spent in the cave, shielded from the natural sources of life-giving astral energy. She simply was not receiving enough astral energy to stay healthy.

If your work requires that you spend much time underground, or if you feel that you are "down" more of the time than you would like to be, you will also benefit from following the regime we outlined for Janice.

RECHARGING YOUR BODY AT SUNRISE

Every Christian agrees that probably the most uplifting service in his calendar of religious festivals is the Easter Sunrise Service. Almost anyone you ask who has attended one of these services will tell you how inspiring it was. What did the priest or minister say? He can't tell you. What hymns were sung? He doesn't remember. What then inspired him so? Could it be that just by uplifting his hands to the sun he had let into his body a tremendous burst of astral energy? and that this astral energy then gave him enough of a high to carry on for several weeks afterward? We believe very firmly that this is precisely the case, and that ancient people knew this recharging procedure as a natural and accepted non-mystical part of life.

How can you put this ancient knowledge to work in *your* life? We suggest that you learn the following recharging ritual and that you do it occasionally, especially when you are feeling low.

Before dawn some morning, go to a quiet place out in the country where you will have an uninterrupted view of the eastern horizon. Wait until the very tip of the sun appears above that horizon at dawn, and stand facing it with your arms uplifted and outstretched as shown in Figure 4–1, "Star Position." If you are right-handed, have the palm of your right hand up and the palm of your left hand down. If you are left-handed, reverse them. Close your eyes and wait as the sun climbs clear of the horizon. Feel its life-giving rays enter your being. Say a simple affirmation like:

Welcome, Sun, Giver of Life.
Give me energy and calm my strife.

Try to keep your arms up during this simple ceremony. You may find that once in a while you must lower them for a moment of rest, but keep at it as well as you can for about fifteen minutes. Then return home and go back to bed for a couple of hours. You will find you sleep very soundly; this, too, seems to be an essential part of the ritual as the body absorbs into itself and distributes the energy you have just received. When you awaken, you will be literally "high" as if you had taken some "upper" drug—but this is a non-chemical high that lasts; and it has no after-effects. If you are feeling a little bit down at any time, just stand in the star Position of Figure 4–1 and recharge yourself.

This is a small, personal ritual of recharging. It is not the massive dose you would get from a formal sunrise service with hundreds of people in attendance. But even this personal recharging will really help you get over those low times that occur in everyone's life.

PERSONAL ASTRAL ENERGY CAN BE STORED

You learned in earlier chapters how to charge up psycho-stores. These psycho-stores were designed to accomplish very specific ends. Clean, empty psycho-stores take in energy even when people are unaware that they are charging them. This is why the psychic bug works so well. If you deliberately set out with the conscious intent of storing energy, they work so much the better. You can put all-purpose or "full-spectrum" energy into a psycho-store, which can then be of value in recharging yourself.

The best psycho-store for this type of energy is engraved glass. We ourselves have a Swedish glass vase; on it is engraved a female figure looking at the moon. This makes an excellent store for general energy. After a sunrise recharging service, or when you are feeling especially good and "up," hold your chosen psycho-store in your dominant hand and mentally give it some of your energy. It is nice to say some little affirmation as you do this, such as:

"Yea, verily, when my need is sore,
I'll draw strength from this psycho-store.

When you have charged the psycho-store for a few moments, it is wise to wrap it in a length of white silk cloth which you have dyed a saffron color; then place it in a steel box in a quiet place until you need it.

The very next time you are down or feeling blue, take your psycho-store out of its box and drop it in boiling water[1] and it will give its energy back to you.

EMBY AND HIS MASCOT

Emby G., a native of Ghana, dwells in Accra, the capital city. He is employed as a VIP bodyguard. This is a job which calls for the utmost in mental acuity, for he must watch for any hostile or terrorist act, and be prepared instantly to counter it. One day, in the course of his duties, he was shot at by a gunman who was attempting to assassinate the Chairman (as the President of Ghana is titled). By taking the would-be assassin's bullet in his own left arm, Emby probably saved the life of the Chairman. That badly mangled bullet became Emby's mascot. He

---

[1] Be sure ahead of time that the psycho-store can stand the thermal shock without breaking.

carried it with him wherever he went and eventually had it made into the centerpiece of a silver necklace. As time went on, Emby realized that he actually felt better and more alert when he was wearing his necklace than when he left it off. In a land of charms, potions, hexes, and amulets, he felt he had the ultimate lucky charm. He became almost obsessed with the idea that as long as he had this charm with him, he could do no wrong, that everything would go well for him.

Because of this growing reliance on his psycho-bank mascot, Emby started to gamble heavily and to neglect his sensible diet. Very soon he began to lose more money than he could afford. After one such gambling episode, in his frustration he threw the "lucky" charm into the bottom of a drawer and tried to put it out of his mind. He resolved to stop his gambling entirely for three months, but he did not go so far as to revise his bad eating habits; for he had learned to like the canned, imported "dead" foods available in the port city of Accra. Just as Janice the cave guide did, Emby now began to pay the price. Now that he had exhausted the power in his mascot and had switched to dead foods, he was not taking in enough astral energy to maintain his alertness on the job.

Samuel B, Emby's captain and a personal friend of ours, took him aside for a private word. "Emby, if you ever expect to get promoted, you've got to sharpen up. A couple of times recently. I've had to cover for you. Your mind just isn't on your work. You got a new girl or something?" Emby replied that, so far as he could think of, he had no worries. Being on good terms with his Captain, he confided to him the story of the bullet charm and how he had become frustrated with it. Knowledgeable himself in occult matters, Samuel told him that he had overused his charm; but if Emby promised to eat properly, he (Samuel) would recharge it for him.

Emby followed Samuel's advice implictly. With the proper foods from local farms and with his charm recharged, his health improved and his alertness returned. When the time for review of employee performance came around, Emby became a corporal in the security services.

GETTING A HAPPY BUDDHA

You may not be unfortunate—or fortunate—enough (depending on the way you look at it) to receive a bullet for your mascot the way Emby did. You may not want or need that kind of mascot, in fact; however, almost everyone can do with a little more happiness in his life.

Today, you can go out and get one of the most potent happy mascots in the world. We told you in the introduction of Mr. Seito and his happy Buddha, Ho Tei. Why don't you have a happy Buddha standing inside your entry door? Are you afraid someone will think you're weird? If you are self-conscious about your psycho-store, you can keep it in your bedroom; that way only your more intimate associates will know about it. But if you do keep it in the bedroom, don't let it become overcharged with lusting sex energy; the energy that you want to put into your happy Buddha is light-hearted happiness. Perhaps you think you will feel foolish patting his round tummy. That is exactly the kind of energy he is best at collecting! Light-hearted, foolish, laughing energy: that is what Ho Tei absorbs.

For just a few dollars you can change your life with a Ho Tei; so why don't you try it? It is very simple. Place your Ho Tei in some convenient place. When you are feeling good, rub his little tummy with your dominant hand. When you are feeling down, place your secondary hand on his tummy and will him to give you energy. He'll do it, and you will immediately feel better.

WALK IN BALANCE

This ancient Indian blessing is meaningful on all levels of life: physical, mental, and psychic. For your work with psychometry and with its extension, Meta-Psychometry, you must be in good psychic balance so that your emanations neither color your surroundings nor affect your results unduly. Checking yourself out for balance is naturally a delicate matter. If you know of a local psychic who is trustworthy, you can have that person give you a balance reading; but otherwise you should use the procedure outlined in the following paragraph.

LOOK TO YOUR PERSONAL RAINBOW

In earlier days, the saying was that one should "look to the rainbow" to test his balance. This is a brief way of saying that you can check out your psychic balance by seeing how many of the colors of the rainbow appear bright and clear to you. Any color which appears dull is considered to be a sign that you need more of that color in your life. Of course, you probably don't want to wait for the next thunderstorm and its subsequent rainbow to run an astral-balance check on yourself. Fortunately, thanks to the work of such men as Sir Isaac Newton, you need not wait for the next rainbow.

Go to your local scientific supply store, or write to the supplier listed in the Appendix, and purchase a prism. Look through this prism at a white light; tilt the prism in your hand; you will see the colors of the rainbow. Look very carefully at them and decide whether you see each one with equal intensity and brilliance, or whether some of them are dull or perhaps even completely missing from the spectrum. If one is dull, you have a slight problem in your astral balance. If any is missing entirely, you have a very serious problem in your astral balance and this problem should be taken care of immediately. The way to do this is to make yourself a psycho-store and carry it with you so you receive the color energy that will correct this deficiency.

If you are closely observant of people's actions over a period of time, you will notice that they tend to bring into their lives the color that they lack. The cowardly youth gains virile energy from his shiny red "Go-Devil" auto. You may have painted your bedroom a special color that you felt you had to have.

Once you are walking in balance, you will find you are comfortable only in light, pastel-colored rooms. Many highly developed and well-balanced psychics have to have their rooms painted white, for this is the only color with which they feel comfortable. If getting into balance means painting your bedroom in the color you instinctively desire, or getting that fancy piece of jewelry you feel you must have, or whatever—well and good! Your astral balance is worth almost any action you have to take to attain it. Go out and do it; however, later in this chapter, we will tell you of some rather easier ways to gain that specialized astral energy you personally need.

As you continue to work at your psychic balance over the next few months, regularly check yourself and your balance by looking into the prism. You will probably be surprised at how quickly you are able to begin to see all the colors of the rainbow. You have "looked to the rainbow" and have become a more balanced person.

STEVEN LOVES JADE

Steven L lives in Laguna Beach, California. He is a seascape painter who specializes in those pictures of rough seas breaking on a storm-washed coast. In the past if you went to his studio you would have found that it was crammed with pieces of jade and jadeite ranging in color from dark yellow through light green. Now all good artists are sensitive, and Steven had instinctively collected all that jade because it made his studio feel "comfortable" when he was working on his storm scenes. He had found that if the jade was not around, he just did not feel right, and consequently his painting was of an inferior quality. He was investing a great deal of his own psychic emotional energy into his painting of storm scenes, and that energy had to be replaced from somewhere if Steven was to maintain good psychic equilibrium. To this day I can hear his wife Luana say, "You didn't buy another piece of jade!!" and Steven sheepishly admitting, yes, that bulge in his sweater pocket was indeed another piece.

We showed Steven how he could recharge his pieces of jade with pyramid energy and how he could let others recharge themselves naturally by simply laying them out in direct sunlight. In this way, he could get by with just a few pieces in his studio rather than the jumble that he formerly had. I think we gained Luana's undying gratitude when we showed this simple psychic trick to Steven, for after that he kept only a few of his more treasured pieces and sold the rest at the local flea market.

CHOOSING YOUR PERSONAL PSYCHO-STORE

When your personal rainbow shows you that you are deficient in a specific color, you should look at Table 4–1 and select from it a psycho-store to carry with you. If you are low on green energy, for

Deficient Color (shown by prism)	Psycho-Store
Violet	Aquamarine
Lavender	Amethyst
Scarlet	Ruby
Red	Red Jade
Yellow	Opal
Amber	Amber or Pearl
Orange	Diamond
Chartreuse	Agate
Green	Emerald ⎫
Turquoise	Turquoise ⎬ or Green Jade
Blue	Sapphire ⎭
Indigo	Black Onyx

Table 4–1

Balancing Psycho-Stores

instance, looking at Table 4–1 you can see that you might get some rough jade in green, or some emeralds, to use as your psycho-store. No matter what energy is missing, you can find the appropriate psycho-store from Table 4–1. When you first purchase your psycho-store, you should psychometrize it as you learned to do in Chapter 1 to make sure that it is putting out the right "color" emanations. If it is not, you should cleanse it as you have been taught and then recharge it.

You bought the psycho-store because you found you were low in a specific type of energy. Now that the psycho-store is cleansed and ready for recharging, you should plan to do the actual recharging in a light-box, or with a pyramid arrangement, or with "natural" energy. Clearly, if you are low on a particular color of energy, you will only make matters worse by trying to use some of the already deficient energy within yourself to charge your replacement psycho-store.

CHARGING YOUR PSYCHO-STORE WITH PYRAMID ENERGY

In recent years, the occult world has been intrigued with using the energy that is available from the flow of cosmic force into the earth. Specifically, Czechoslovakian patents on pyramids have shown one of the ways of focusing this tremendous flow of astral energy that too often is wasted. Just as you can recharge your body by standing in the Star Position, so you can use the geometric shape of a pyramid to focus the astral energy and make it work for you. The quickest way of charging a psycho-store is to place it in a pyramid, as shown in Figure 4–2. You

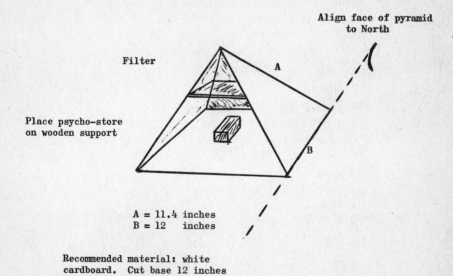

Align face of pyramid to North

Filter

A

Place psycho-store on wooden support

B

A = 11.4 inches
B = 12   inches

Recommended material: white cardboard. Cut base 12 inches square; cut three sides. Assemble with tape.

Figure 4-2

Pyramid Psycho-Store Charger

will select the filter "A" to match the color that is missing from your personal rainbow. Normally you will find that a psycho-store placed in a pyramid carefully oriented to the North, as shown, will very quickly recharge itself.

Steven puts a tremendous amount of psychic energy into his paintings; he draws this energy directly from his chunks of jade. Although these are powerful psycho-stores, they could not keep up with Steven's consumption of energy. We told him, therefore, to place a few of them in a pyramid so that they would become recharged with the astrally focused pyramid energy that would otherwise go to waste.

Pyramids are available for sale through the source mentioned in the Appendix; or you may construct your own, following the directions in Figure 4–2. Notice that one of the sides of the pyramid is left open so that you can readily change filters and put your psycho-store into the pyramid without disturbing the alignment. Also notice that the little support box is of such a height as to bring the center of the object that you intend to recharge one-third of the way up inside the pyramid. If you have a much larger object to charge, you may double or triple each of the dimensions given, remembering the Rule of One-Third: The center of the object must be one-third of the distance between the floor of the pyramid and its apex.

To do a proper recharging of any given object, first cleanse it of its present emanations. Then place your pyramid on a wooden table with its face perpendicular to true North, as shown. Place your psycho-store inside it, and leave it for a maximum of fifteen minutes.

Perhaps you don't own a filter of the appropriate color. Because the psycho-store has certain properties inherent in it, as implied by its shape, its material, and earlier uses to which it has been put, it can act as its own filter when it is allowed sufficient time to do so. If you do indeed lack the appropriate filter, leave the psycho-store in the pyramid overnight with no filter at all, and it will recharge itself with energy selected by its own inherent properties, though (again) it naturally takes longer to recharge itself in this wide-spectrum energy.

CHARGE YOUR PSYCHO-STORE WITH NATURAL ENERGY

Natural energy is energy that is obtainable from living or from recently killed flowers, plants and vegetables. We are not saying here that pyramid energy is not "natural"; we are just using the term "natural" to mean, in this context, that you are extracting energy from the growing things that nature supplies.

In recent years, Kirlian photography has demonstrated the fact that every living thing puts out astral emanations. This work in specialized photography serves to confirm what occultists and psychics have been telling us for centuries; and it confirms, as well, the work of such people as Dr. Burr who had shown many years ago that all living things had a measureable field around them.

Suppose you personally are short of green energy. To regain your balance, you can increase the amount of green living things in your diet, just as Janice did. Since living things are rapidly killed by stomach acids, this method of replenishment, though effective in the short term, is not as effective as a green psycho-store. Notice here we emphasize *living* green things in your diet. Many experiments have been conducted to determine how long the life-energy continues to flow out of a vegetable after it has been harvested, for instance. In general, provided you eat raw vegetables that were harvested not more than three days ago, you will gain psychic energy from them. If the vegetables are canned or were cooked at a high temperature, you will gain scant energy from them, because the processing makes the energy flow out of the vegetables just as it flows out of a heated psycho-store.

It is interesting to note that in green countries people tend to overcook and kill their green vegetables. This, again, is an instinctive adjustment. People in such countries do not need additional green energy, so they habitually cook it out of vegetables before they eat them. Conversely, in desert countries, even at the cool time of mid-winter there is great emphasis on crisp green salads in the diet, because in the desert there is a low level of green energy.

Charging your psycho-store with natural energy is simplicity itself. All you need to do is surround it with the appropriate just-killed plant or vegetable. Table 4–2 shows you the appropriate organic material to use. Notice once more we say "just-killed." If you were to place your psycho-store in among green lettuce out in the garden, in your quest for green energy, little or no advantage would accrue, because the plants themselves are absorbing all of the available green astral energy that is falling in the area. It is only when the plant is killed, and for three to four days after its harvesting, that it puts out the energy which it had absorbed during its life.

It is best to get a small steel box in which you can place your psycho-store and the organic material which will recharge it. If you wish, you can place the box in your refrigerator, for this will preserve the charging material. Remember once more that before you start this charging procedure, your psycho-store should be cleansed of formerly impressed emotion.

Psycho-Store	Charging Material
Aquamarine	Rhubarb, Lower Stem
Amethyst	Water-Lily Leaf
Ruby	Radish Leaves
Red Jade	Ivy Leaves
Opal	Lavender Blossoms
Amber or Pearl	Poppy Petals or Yellow Tulip Petals
Diamond	Sunflower Petals
Agate	Snowdrop, Whole Flowers
Emerald	Rose Leaves
Turquoise	Cactus Head
Sapphire	Asparagus Fern
Onyx	Thistle Root

Table 4–2

Organic Charging Materials for Psycho-Store

DECIDE WHAT YOU WANT

With the combination of your advanced psychometric ability and the Meta-Psychometric steps we have just outlined, you will very quickly have your life in balance. Now you are ready to proceed in obtaining the things you most desire. You learned in Chapter 1 how to psychometrize objects; you learned in Chapter 2 how to make sure your friends are really your friends; and you learned in Chapter 3 how to ward off evil. Now you have learned how to walk in balance: physically, mentally, and psychically, with the aid of Meta-Psychometry. You should next decide on what you really want first in life. Further, it is time to identify the root cause of any problem you plan to attack. You know by now that each solution will require a specific type of energy. If you go after all your goals at once, you will end up putting out only a combined color, perhaps a dirty gray, that will do no good at all.

Perhaps today you feel a vague unhappiness; you think a procedure for serenity would be suitable. This makes no sense, though, if your unhappiness stems from a lack of companionship or a lack of money or whatever. Decide first what it is you lack; then work on that. We constantly get letters from people saying such things as, "I am unhappy. I have no money. People don't understand me. I would like a new lover." When we ask in turn, "Which of these wants on your list is the most important one?" they get all uptight with us and write back telling us that we don't understand their problems. They want *all* the things on their list right *now*—and we are obviously very poor Witches if we can't immediately fulfill their complete list of requests with a swift wave of our broomstick. You may guess, that kind of letter is destroyed without further action, because we know full well that the most powerful sorcerer in the world can't fulfill all a person's wants instantly. The sorcerer, too, would end up mixing his energy outputs, rather than tuning them to specific results. Moreover, if the sorcerer could by some miracle make the wishes all come true, the next day the seeker would come up with an even longer want list to be instantly fulfilled.

Discipline and definition are two absolute requirements in successful Meta-Psychometric work. So decide first what are the major things making your life uncomfortable; then place them in a logical order or priority. If you want (1) money and (2) a new companion, it will be easier for you to get the money first and the new companion second. All things have logical priorities, so arrange your personal want-list and go to work.

ALICE PICKS HER GOAL

Alice J is an orphan. She was happily married to Stewart, her childhood sweetheart from the orphanage. Because their two backgrounds were so similar, they could understand one another; they loved each other very dearly and felt no need for outside friends. Stew took Alice to Los Angeles as a treat for her twenty-first birthday. On the way home from that pleasant evening, tragedy entered her life. Stew ran the car off the freeway, killing himself and severely injuring Alice. When she was finally released from hospital, Alice found that she had to sell almost everything she and Stew had owned to meet the medical bills.

Abruptly she became a typical Cinderella case: lonely, disheartened, and broke. She thought that her heart would break from loneliness; though she had loved Stew dearly, she felt that her first priority must be the finding of a companion. After several painful misadventures, she turned to the occult to help her in her quest. She visited several mediums and readers in the Los Angeles area. They all gave her advice on how to find a new loved one, and gave her charms to wear and affirmations to repeat. Typically, she would go in for a reading and ask, "Where do I find my soulmate?" The psychic would read the cards or the crystal ball, and would duly tell her how to find her soulmate. By now Alice was a drooping waif of a thing, poorly dressed and showing little to offer that might attract the opposite sex.

Eventually she went to a spiritualist church in Santa Ana; there she received a communication from Stew saying that he was disappointed she was searching so soon for a new companion; he thought she loved him sufficiently to let a decent time elapse for him (as he said) to get cool in his grave at least. This communication was a further blow to Alice of course.

In a private reading with Dorothy, the leader of the spiritualist church, Alice described her problem. Now besides being a very capable reader and medium, Dorothy was also a practical woman with both feet solidly on the ground. She could see that Alice was in no shape to attract the man she desired, that she had gotten her priorities mixed up. What Alice really needed most was some self-confidence and a bunch of money in her bank account. In psychometrizing Alice, Dorothy could read the "perfect-man" heavily sexual emanations of her psycho-stores and perceived how far off base they were. "No wonder Stew was upset," Dorothy told us later. "Here was his wife going around putting out emanations like a nymphomaniac when what she really needed was confidence and a square meal."

Dorothy told Alice to get rid of the psycho-stores that the previous readers had given her to attract a man, and, instead, to wear a psycho-store giving her confidence and attracting money. Within a matter of a few days, Alice's previous anxiety had vanished. She obtained a new job with a firm of female lawyers, a job she had earlier rejected because it would give her "too little contact with men." She showed so much promise in her job that the lawyers helped her go to night school; they were all proud when, six years later, she became a practicing attorney. She was moderately successful, and was soon bringing in a salary of over $20,000 a year.

Her work with her clients took her to many interesting places and served as the means of meeting many attractive and capable people. In the course of her work, she was introduced to a brilliant young defense attorney who fell in love with her—almost overnight it seemed —married her, and took her away on a world cruise honeymoon.

By rearranging her priorities, and with redirected Meta-Psychometric aid, Alice got everything in her life that she had previously desired; whereas, if she had persisted in trying to find a man first and worried about money later, she might have killed herself in the effort; for one must eat, after all, and eating takes money.

YOUR COMPLETE META-PSYCHOMETRIC
RECHARGING PROCEDURE

This chapter is designed primarily to help you get your astral or psychic batteries charged and into proper balance. This achieving of balance is the first super-critical step to being able later to make full use of your Meta-Psychometric ability to make things happen. Once you are physically healthy and mentally alert, the steps in this psychic procedure are extremely simple.

1. Look to your private rainbow, the prism, and find out whether or not you are currently in balance. If you are not in balance, decide what energy you need in your life to bring yourself into balance.

2. From Table 4–1, select the appropriate psycho-store for your needs.

3. Cleanse and charge this psycho-store, either in a pyramid or with the aid of natural energy sources.

4. Wear the psycho-store constantly, remembering to take it off and recharge it at regular intervals.

5. Every week or so, recheck your view of the rainbow. When you are sure you can see all the colors equally well, substitute a happy or high-energy psycho-store for your previous specialized one. In order to reinforce and sustain the effectiveness of this happiness psycho-store, you should occasionally recharge yourself in a sunrise ceremony and in Star Position recharging rituals.

Now that you have your energy in balance and are fully charged, you are ready to start taking steps to bring your dreams to fulfillment. Take a few moments to chart your course; then read on to learn of the Meta-Psychometric procedures that we will recommend you use toward the fulfilling of your dreams.

5

MAGNIFYING YOUR POWER WITH MAGNA-PSYCHOMETRY

WHATEVER YOU WANT CAN BE YOURS

You learned in Chapter 4 how you can use a mascot or psycho-store to give you energy, and you learned how you can put a little bit of psychometric energy each day into a mascot like a Ho Tei happy Buddha—energy which you can later withdraw and use to help you in your life. You can use these same procedures, which we call Magna-Psychometry, to increase your own control of the future. You may never become the Charles Atlas of the psychic world, but you can lift just as much weight as any Charles Atlas could by persistently lifting it one pound at a time rather than by attempting to do it all at once. No matter how serious the obstacles which confront you, you can succeed by trying successively more powerful procedures until your task is accomplished. Your psycho-store is your energy battery; just like the battery in your car, you will charge it up, a little at a time, with Magna-Psychometric techniques until you are ready to release the stored energy in a mighty surge of power that will overcome all obstacles.

Just as with your car battery, you must be sure that when you store psychic energy, it is all of the right voltage and polarity. This is why it makes sense to use the most elaborate procedure you are capable of and to tune yourself in precisely to the right color energy for your intent before each attempt to charge your psycho-store.

For some tasks, one battery may not be enough. Sometimes life's circumstances will mean you require as many as four or five psycho-stores that you can discharge simultaneously to give you the necessary blast of energy. Each psycho-store must naturally be charged on a separate occasion and then be put safely away until you are ready to use it with its companions in your Magna-Psychometric procedure.

HARRY GETS HIS WAY

Harry S was an independent trucker working in a New England mountain state. He was doing well until one of the "big boys," let's call the firm King Transport, moved into his territory. It seemed to Harry that within just a few weeks his comfortable life suddenly collapsed around his feet. A couple of his regular large customers told him they would no longer be shipping with him. This was a blow, but worse was to follow; for more and more of Harry's shippers left him—especially after a few mysterious fires broke out at plants which still persisted in hiring Harry and his independent buddies.

The main problem, however, was not violence or the threat of violence, but the fact that King Transport was apparently shipping goods for less than what it would cost the independents to buy even the fuel for the same job. Soon stories of repossession of tractors were common in every roadside cafe, and it became apparent that another one of the big firms (let us call them Queen Transport) was buying up the repossessed tractors and offering jobs to the out-of-work independents.

Though poorly educated, Harry was known among truckers for his self-reliance. He could see that this situation promised no good to his own future. He could not move to a non-organized area because he had a son in a special school for handicapped children, and his wife flatly refused to consider relocating the boy. Harry's tractor was paid for, so he decided he would get another job until this storm blew over; he knew that once the freight war was done, things would normalize again. But on what was to be his last run, Harry's load was hijacked, he was beaten up, and his tractor was burnt.

Little did the "big boys" know what a tiger they had roused. The special irony was that this tiger had always been a pussycat. But the violence done to Harry made him more angry than he had ever been before. He determined he would use the insurance money from his burned tractor to get even.

It seemed, though, that even getting his insurance money was going to take a long time. "Somehow," every time he tried to get the money, more questions came up about arson and about his business position. Harry also found that he couldn't seem to get a good job with anyone unless he became a member of the union; yet "somehow" he never could get that card they said he needed.

In many ways, though, Harry was still far better off than some of his buddies. His financial position was stable enough to enable him to spend time in figuring out what to do. The majority of the legal advice he received indicated that it would cost far more money than he could raise to fight this case; for it would probably have meant going all the way to the Supreme Court and getting the Federal Interstate Commerce Commission to do a full-blown price-fixing investigation. His early letters to Federal authorities had taught him that they could do little about a single company coming into an area and cutting prices; this was not price fixing, but rather harsh competitive practice. And since King was not operating interstate, it was really out of the hands of the Federal government.

About this time, with idle hours to spend, Harry heard of Uri Geller: how Uri was able, with power from his mind, to stop a ship's engines in mid-Atlantic by bending one of the pipes in the fuel system. Harry made up his mind that he would learn to do something similar.

It took him nearly three months to learn to bend small copper pipes; he found he could do it only by actually holding a piece of copper pipe in his hands at the time. His technique was to think "bend!" into his piece of pipe for about an hour; then when he physically bent this psycho-store and thought "bend!" other pipes in nearby locations bent from the released energy. At last he was able to pack enough energy into his hand-held psycho-store to bend about three nearby pipes in any given day. Then he started visiting various truck stops near his home. Each day he would bend the fuel lines of some of King Transport's trucks. (Whether he actually bent the fuel lines or not we don't know; but the trucks he was near almost always had trouble soon afterward.) This seemed to cause some annoyance and delay in King's scheduling. But more: everyone started to fear Harry's presence, for he jinxed trucks.

Remember that this was a mountainous region. Harry let it be known through various friends that the damaged fuel lines were only a start; that soon, brake lines, too, would begin to fail at critical places. The drivers now insisted that King Transport guard their trucks at night and use extra mechanics to check them out before going on the road. Curiously, one of the first trucks to report a damaged brake line was driven by one of the bullies who had beaten Harry up and burned his tractor. This individual had a brake failure on a notoriously steep grade and found himself in the hospital with multiple fractures. Soon, other trucks of the fleet began having brake problems; no matter how many guards or mechanical checkups were set up, still these problems persisted.

Now truckers are in some ways superstitious people. Many a time you will hear of a driver who simply won't drive if he feels that today is a "bad" day. Imagine how these people felt when faced with an entire geographic area under Harry's jinx. Soon, King Transport found it almost impossible to operate in Harry's state, and the independents were once again beginning to get full loads.

After Harry's very practical success with the trucks, he thought he would turn his attention to his insurance claim. He was pleasantly surprised when (after a week of concentrated effort) he received in the mail a check for full settlement.

This might have been written off as coincidence, but there was more to follow. Harry's six-month-old letter to the Federal authorities now paid off, too. For after they had achieved their semi-monopoly of the area, King and Queen Transport had both increased their tariffs simultaneously to new and high levels, and had, in fact, applied these rates across several states. Thus, the Federal government now had a case against the companies and told Harry in a letter that they would be pursuing the matter.

Harry the Tiger is once more Harry the Pussycat. He is well-known among his friends for his unorthodox ways of getting things done. Currently, he turns his talents to making himself a few dollars a month on the stock market and to helping his friends with their various problems. Harry accomplished his intent by making one little thing happen at a time. He was fortunate that he could develop a gift similar to that of Uri Geller; for if he had not had this gift, he probably would have had not only to attack one truck at a time, but also build up his psychic energy store one drop at a time in order to accomplish his aim. To this day we don't know whether Harry really damaged those trucks or whether it was all in the minds of the drivers; but the scheme worked. Best of all, Harry's Magna-Psychometric endeavors broke no laws.

IT'S JUST LIKE WATER IN A GLASS

A simile often employed in occult circles is the comparison of occult power to tinted water—a water which can flow over and into things, yet cannot be detected except by occult means. With the flow of this water-like power, a psycho-store then becomes the equivalent of a glass or bottle of water. Each day you can put into your store perhaps a few drops of water; or maybe, if you are not feeling good, you will take away enough of this psychic elixir for a small "drink."

The essential secret of Magna-Psychometry is to make sure that every time you add to your psycho-store you (1) add only water; and (2) you add the specific color of water that will not alter the color of the water that is already in your psycho-store. If you wish, by adding one drop at a time over a period of months, you can build up a huge reservoir of psychic energy; but unless you exercise strict caution, you may find that you are mixing different-hued water, thus diluting rather than accumulating the specific energy that you intend to store. In Magna-Psychometry, when you wish to store energy, you must be sure that you have sufficient mental keys to be able to store energy always of precisely the same type in your psycho-store.

Normally, people's view of a given symbol can change with time and with outside influences. This is especially true when a symbol becomes synonymous with something occurring in the mundane world. Currently, for example, to many young adults the seagull is a symbol of love and spiritual growth; whereas, in the past, most people who knew anything about seagulls regarded them as smelly carnivores. Thus, the image of the seagull has changed dramatically. If you had been putting seagull energy into a psycho-store in representation of love and spiritual growth—but then had abruptly been exposed to real flying seagulls as greedy, scavenging carnivores—your store would become a useless mixture overnight.

Changes of a more subtle nature can also occur in symbols. If you think a moment, you can probably name several such instances. In your reality, is a "pinto" a piebald pony or a cute little car? So if you are using the ram sign this week to help your mind store some Arian energy for a Magna-Psychometric effort, but during the week you read a book about sheep tending, perhaps you cannot be sure that your next attempt at storing power will result in energy of the same "color." You must use as many different psychic keys as you can, so that, even if one changes slightly in your mind, you are still sure that altogether they will give you consistent results. In most procedures, you should use a minimum of three keys, though five keys are much preferable.

FILL YOUR BANK AND DRAW IT OUT

When you are putting your colored energy into your psycho-store, obviously you must arrange matters so that you can also key yourself to withdraw that same energy. This can be compared to making deposits in a bank account or into a safety deposit box. You must have the correct key in your possession to allow you to draw these deposits back out again when you need to use them. Just as with your bank account, so it is with a psycho-store. The psychometric key that allows you to deposit energy is the same psychometric key that allows you to draw it out.

Do you remember in Chapter 1 how you chraged the desk calendar holder by using a colored candle and colored cloth, and, finally, by holding it against a specified part of your body? You were using three psychometric keys. This same technique can be adapted in endless ways to suit your personal need. Later in this chapter, we will show you how to construct your own individual, five-key Magna-Psychometric Table of Correspondences, which will then serve as your personalized set of keys for any ritual you attempt.

When you have constructed your Table of Correspondences, you can set up a work center. In this work center, you will arrange an altar on which your psycho-store can be placed, to be surrounded by the five items from your Table of Correspondences.

When you feel "up," go to your altar and get in tune with your psychometric keys, then address your psycho-store in words like these:

"Power, flow from me to thee.
Magnify my power, each magical Key.
As I will, so mote it be."

Then clap your hands sharply to signify the end of the charging ritual. If you have lit a candle as part of the charging procedure, clap your hands in such a way as to extinguish the candleflame. Then quickly leave the area.

In occult circles, some practitioners may use as many as 300 chargings for a single ritual; but we recommend no more than thirty.

Finally, you need some way of releasing the stored energy from your psycho-store as Harry released it from his psycho-store by bending the pipe in his hands. When the time comes to use the energy, at the height of the ritual drop your psycho-store into boiling water or throw it into a brazier of glowing charcoal. The thermal shock releases the stored energy to do your will.

EVELYN SUCCEEDED ON HER FIRST TRY

Evelyn H lives near Corpus Christi. A half-Navajo, she had been brought up on a reservation until she was 17. At that time, she had been "saved" by a Baptist missionary and had left the reservation and her Indian heritage. After living with her for three years and having two children with her, the Baptist missionary dumped her out of his home because his new congregation proved to be unsympathetic to his mixed "marriage."

Evelyn now remembered with longing her Indian ritual training and decided she was going to teach the congregation something they did not know—not for vengeance, of course, but to give them some instruction about life which she felt they now lacked. Unwisely, she let her feelings be known to her ex-lover, and he got the congregation together in several prayer meetings so they could call down the "lord's" protection on themselves. Witches and occultists in general have a rather low opinion of Christian ritual—but it does sometimes work. In this case, it successfully prevented Evelyn's hex from getting through, for the congregation's belief in their own ritual obviously pulled them together in psychic oneness of defense.

As is the law in psychic work, so it was in Evelyn's case. Since her hexing thoughtform had no effect on the congregation, it bounced back and affected Evelyn herself in a negative way. By the natural laws of the universe, the effect on Evelyn, a one-person target, was far more devastating than the thoughtform she had put out toward the whole church membership. Her life was destroyed; she became so terribly ill that the children's father put them into a foster home. She felt the only way left open to her was to return to the reservation and seek help from her medicine man.

Hitch-hiking and begging food, she made her way back to her own people. When she arrived at the reservation, she was ready to die. She told the medicine man her story; he counteracted her negative attitude by saturating her with love and understanding. He counselled her: If she really wanted to jolt the congregation, what she should do was not to hex them, but to love them; for none of the Christian rituals could stop love-emanations. After all, their own Book required they do nothing to stop the love of another person.

He also counselled her to use a prayer rug or Indian blanket to help her in her work. This rug she should weave herself, and she should do it while constantly thinking thoughts of love and consideration. She should weave into the rug a representation of each of the leaders of the church. These representations should be done in light yellow and green, and she should weave only when she was feeling in a loving mood, not at times when she felt upset or distressed.

Evelyn needed almost three months to complete that rug. When she was done, she took it to the medicine man and won his smiling approval. Then he had further instructions for her: First, she should return to Corpus Christi; then, once a month, at full moon, she should light a candle; by its light, she was to take apart her rug again, unraveling one or two representations of church members at each full moon—all the while holding thoughts of love and compassion and kindness in her heart.

She did exactly as he told her, though it took several months. The effect on the congregation was dramatic. Suddenly, leaders started liking one another better; bickering among themselves died down to a record low. They even passed a resolution to welcome Evelyn into the congregation, to waive their precious biased rules in the case of this one "half-breed." It was even suggested to the minister, Evelyn's former roommate, that he should have more love in his heart. But, since Evelyn could not find it in her heart to work a love spell on him he remained as biased as ever. When it was time for the minister's contract to be renegotiated, the congregation almost unanimously decided they could well do without him.

Meantime, Evelyn married one of the elders of the congregation; her magic had, indeed, worked well on this particular man. She may unconsciously have been half in love with him anyway, and she may have held even more loving thoughts for him than for some of the others when she wove her ritual rug. Happily, Evelyn was also able to recover her children from the foster home, so that the family was reunited.

The laws of the universe are indeed strange in their workings. At the time of this writing, Evelyn and her new husband had left the Baptist church and were starting their own church, which will teach a natural religion of love and harmony.

A SIMPLE TRIAL FOR YOU

Just as Evelyn changed the direction and the mood of the Baptist congregation, you, too, can use a similar technique to change the feelings of any group that you have to deal with. It does not matter whether you want to stop the Ladies' Aid from bickering with one another or you want to make your work fellows like you or their new supervisor better. Evelyn's technique can be modified by anyone; it provides a good test of the powers we have been talking about.

Instead of weaving a rug, you can collect photographs of the people whom you wish to affect. You can charge them yourself with whatever emotion you are trying to instill into the group. If this is a loving emotion, you know from Table 4–1 that amber energy is appropriate, and you can use any of the techniques we have described to charge the photos. If you perhaps decide on using pyramid energy, you must place an amber filter over each photo when you put it into the pyramid. Since the photograph itself will normally collect pyramid energy right across the spectrum, just putting the photo into the pyramid would only give the subject an increase in his level of energy; whereas placing the amber filter over the photo results in the subject being charged with exactly the right astral energy for your purposes.

Place each of your photographs in your charging arrangement for 24 hours. Then, some time late at night when you are sure they are all asleep or at least resting and quiet, you can do your final ritual to bring them together as a group. Because this is a Cancer-home-friendship-love kind of ritual rather than one for sexual attraction, it is appropriate to base your final group melding on a water ritual. Take the photos that you have charged and place them in a small copper or brass bowl containing slightly sugared hot water. Mix them together with your fingers until they are all formed into a single mass of papier mâché. While you do this, think of love and friendship and the warmth of the home hearth. You might wish to say a short rhyming spell several times, such as:

"Friendship now among these hearts,
Come to them as I blend their parts.
As I will, so mote it be."

When you have thoroughly melded all of the photos into one ball of material, squeeze the water from the ball; make sure that the water in the bowl retains no fragments of the former photographs. Place the squeezed ball of material under the amber filter in your pyramid and leave it there until it is completely dry. Filter the water through a plain linen cloth. Make sure that each of the persons who are to be a part of this new family gets some of this water to drink. You could, for instance, offer to get coffee for someone and add a little of your charged water before handing him the cup. There are dozens of ways to make sure everyone gets some.

When the paper ball is dry and you are sure everyone has drunk of your ritual water, it is time to send the ingredients into the ethers; because Venus, the Goddess of Love, is an air deity, and this offering to her signals the completion of your ritual. Boil away the water in its copper bowl until the bowl is dry. Carefully burn the papier mâché ball in a ritual charcoal fire. Within a few hours after you complete the ritual, you will notice major changes in the attitudes of the various people involved when they approach one another. There will be far more touching than previously, and a great deal less bickering.

This is a nice test ritual for you to try, because it is so easy to do; and because it brings so much more love into a group, it is really very rewarding.

REFINING YOUR TECHNIQUES

Just as a harpist learns her concert pieces and plays music ever more beautifully, so you should learn your rituals and make them work ever more effectively. The various tables given for psychometric work in this book are called by occultists "tables of correspondences." Each table is taken from a grand master table Yvonne compiled, originally based on ancient secret manuscripts called "grimoires."

These tables had been refined over many centuries of occult work, and Yvonne refined them further so they would work for us in twentieth-century terms. But they may not be right *for you,* because, as we have said, your background may have in it certain specific associations that will prevent your keying onto some of the necessary psychometric feelings in the manner in which the table is designed for you to do. Table 5–1 is our master Meta-Psychometric Table. Table 5–2 is a similar, but blank, table; into it you should enter the colors, odors, shapes, herbs, and other things that *you* associated instinctively with the left-hand columns of illnesses and needs.

We would recommend that you try to fill in for yourself first the column headed "color." When you have filled in this column, refer back to Table 5–1 for our color keys. See which of the color keys makes you feel most comfortable. The ones you filled in for yourself will be those which you can use the best in ritual work; for one of the closely

Intent	Planet	Sign	Element	Quality	Color	Stone
All unconventional enterprises Esoteric knowledge Disrupt friendship	Uranus	Aquarius	Air	Fixed	Violet	Aquamarine
Solve mysteries Develop mysticism	Neptune	Pices	Water	Common	Lavender	Amethyst
Courage Exploration Military success Athletic ventures	Mars	Aries	Fire	Cardinal	Scarlet	Ruby
Money Business and commerce	Earth	Taurus	Earth	Fixed	Red	Jade
Advanced technology Electronics Prediction Writing non-fiction	Lucifer	Gemini	Air	Common	Yellow	Opal
Safe journey Astral travel Writing fiction Gain by water	Moon	Cancer	Water	Cardinal	Amber	Pearl
Friendship Patronage Create harmony Renew youth	Sun	Leo	Fire	Fixed	Orange	Diamond
Exams Theater Influence people Merchandise	Mercury	Virgo	Earth	Common	Chartreuse	Agate
Acquire beauty Love, friendship Pleasure Joyous undertakings	Venus	Libra	Air	Cardinal	Emerald	Emerald
Inheritances Win legal conflict Gratify lust	Pluto	Scorpio	Water	Fixed	Turquoise	Turquoise
Career Luck and wealth General ambition	Jupiter	Sagittarius	Fire	Common	Blue	Sapphire
Knowledge of astral Business affairs Study for exams All home matters	Saturn	Capricorn	Earth	Cardinal	Indigo	Onyx

Table 5-1

Master Meta-Psychometric Table

Metal	Flower	Herb	Scent	Symbolic Creature	Body Part	Illness
Uranium	Buttercup	Winter savory Rhubarb	Lemon	Phoenix	Ankles	Ulcer Epilepsy Diarrhea
Neptunium	Water lily	Water betony Thrift	Water lily	Dolphin	Feet	Insomnia Irritation Tumors
Iron	Geranium	Anemone Radish	Tobacco	Ram	Head	Arthritis Blood pressure Depression Exhaustion
Nickel	Cowslip	Ground-Ivy Carpet bugle	Sandalwood	Bull	Neck	Polio Melancholy Tuberculosis
Aluminum	Orchid	Calamint Lavender	Cloves	Magpie	Hands Arms Lungs	Constipation Hepatitis Diabetes
Silver	Night-scented Stock	Poppy Moonwort	White sandalwood	Crab	Breast Stomach	Bronchitis Circulation Digestion
Gold	Sunflower	Rosemary Saffron	Saffron	Lion	Heart Spine Arms Wrists	Thyroid Mononucleosis Menstrual cramps
Mercury	Snowdrop	Caraway Bittersweet	Cinnamon	Virgin	Abdomen Hands Intestines	Cerebral palsy Mental retardation Colitis
Copper	Rose	Alkanet Black alder	Myrtle	Swan	Lower Back, Kidneys	Fever Blood disease Hypertension
Platinum	Cactus	Sweet basil Soapwort	Orange blossom	Scorpion	Pelvis, Genitals	Boils Burns Impotence Muscle tension
Tin	Narcissus	Balm Asparagus	Nutmeg	Centaur	Hips Thighs Liver	Nausea Shingles Goiter
Lead	Thistle	Barley Ivy	Civet	Goat	Knees Bones Skin	Glaucoma Palsy

Intent	Illness	Planet	Sign	Element	Quality	Color
All unconventional enterprises Esoteric knowledge Disrupt friendship	Ulcer Epilepsy Diarrhea					
Solve mysteries Develop mysticism	Insomnia Irritation Tumors					
Courage Exploration Military success Athletic ventures	Arthritis Blood Pressure Depression Exhaustion					
Money Business and commerce	Polio Melancholia Tuberculosis					
Advanced technology Electronics Prediction Writing non-fiction	Constipation Hepatitis Diabetes					
Safe journey Astral travel Writing fiction Gain by water	Bronchitis Circulation Digestion					
Friendship Patronage Create harmony Renew youth	Thyroid Mononucleosis Menstrual cramps					
Exams Theater Influence people Merchandise	Cerebral palsy Mental retardation Colitis					
Acquire beauty Love, friendship Pleasure Joyous undertakings	Fever Blood Disease Hypertension					
Inheritances Win legal conflict Gratify lust	Boils Burns Impotence Muscle tension					
Career Luck and wealth General ambition	Nausea Shingles Goiter					
Knowledge of astral Business affairs Study for exams All home matters	Glaucoma Palsy					

Table 5–2
Your Personal Table of Correspondences

Stone	Metal	Flower	Herb	Scent	Symbolic Creature	Body Part	Illness

held secrets of psychometry is that it works in your own personal reality or frame of reference.

Now, try a simple ritual using your color key and then do the same ritual using the historic color key. Compare the results of the two rituals. Again, the color that you filled in should both suit you best and it should also show the best results. Remember another fact: From day to day these keys to power may change for you. Suppose you are driving along the freeway and see a terrible accident involving a bright blue car. Then, for at least a few days afterward, bright blue will have heavily negative, destructive connotations in your mind, rather than the positive, lucky connections you would expect it to have. Remember, too, that if you have been using a blue key to make a psycho-store, you should wait several months after that accident before using a blue key again; for most assuredly it will give you mixed, rather than pure, energy in your store.

Now that you have learned the technique of filling in the Table of Correspondences, over the next few weeks you should work on the other columns of the Table by psyching yourself into the mood of each line in turn and by filling in the mood keys across the Table. You will find this technique is easier than the one you used for the colors, where you had to change moods some twelve times for a single column of correspondences.

AVERY CHARGES HIS PSYCHO-BANK

Avery B, a San Francisco businessman, had little interest in the occult and no knowledge at all of Magna-Psychometry. In his work, which was the selling of hamburger chain franchises, he had been relatively successful; but he found that of late he was losing customers to another chain, though he believed in his heart of hearts that his franchise was far superior to that offered by his competition. It was also true that franchise managers in other parts of the nation were still doing well, not experiencing the reduction in business that Avery's area was showing. Avery decided that what he needed were some sales aids; so he ordered the preparation of various little models of restaurant facilities to help increase his sales.

The man who fabricated these sales aids for Avery also made him a large gold-plated hamburger just for the fun of it. Avery spent many hours working with his sales aids; they were his audience when he rehearsed his sales talks; often he hoped over them that he would get better sales because of them. And of course he did! Both because he was able to tell a better story to prospective buyers with the aid of the promotional devices, and also because these promotional devices were loaded down with positive sales emotions.

Once when traveling to meet a prospect in Denver, Colorado, the airline lost Avery's bag containing all his sales aids. He was left with just his golden hamburger—but with the aid of this one object he was still able to sell the prospect.

That golden hamburger became Avery's mascot. Every time his sales record showed a lag, he would wish over it—you might say he prayed over it; and every time he did so, his sales picked up again. Without realizing it, Avery was using a standard Magna-Psychometry technique totally keyed to hamburger sales. The prospect, seeing the golden hamburger and feeling its stored emotions, knew that he himself would be successful selling hamburgers.

This was a very down-to-earth but straightforward use of a psycho-store, not mystically keyed to any color or ancient grimoire, but one which was keyed only to Avery's own reality—one which couldn't help being eminently successful.

SEVERAL ACCOUNTS ARE BETTER THAN ONE

In earlier chapters, we gave you all the historic methods for charging psycho-stores or psychic banks. In this chapter, we have shown you how to magnify your energy. So far, we have been talking about doing one thing at a time. We have emphasized very strongly that you should work on each psychic or mundane project with undivided intent. Now, in every project, there are two ways of affecting people. For instance, in a group-closeness ritual, you wanted to bring them together in friendship and at the same time perhaps you wanted to prevent that splinter group from going off and joining a rival group. In this case, you should instill into the members of the splinter group not only the loving feeling and the wish to be at one with their existing group, but also a dislike of the competition.

Though you are working on a single project, you are going to use two new different sorts of energy to, if you will, both pull and push the people involved—to push them away from the competition, and to pull them into your group. This concept can be called positive and negative energy, or hating and loving energy, or simply gay and sad energy. Notice that in each case the two energies are of opposite polarities and yet in ritual can be used to reinforce your purpose.

Let nothing go to waste. Sometimes you feel happy, sometimes you feel sad; both these types of energy can be stored—and *should* be—for later use. Use Ho Tei to bring happiness into your life, and use an image of a skull as a general-purpose store for sad energy. An overworked cliche in the mundane world says that love and anger are closely related emotions; as proof, love can turn quickly to anger. Again, this is the mundane world's recognition of the fact that these emotions of opposite polarity can be used in the same situation. When you want to gain a mate, you can use the loving emotion to pull that person toward you, and the emotion of anger to push the person away from your rivals.

This push-pull system is one of the best-kept occult secrets. It is this secret which will make your Magna-Psychometric work so effective.

SAD OR GAY, STORE THE ENERGY

Every time you return home from the outside world, whether you are just in a pretty passive mood or in a high state of emotion, you should put that energy in the appropriate store so you can use it later. This means that you should define what are the best psycho-stores for you in your own reality; at the very least, you should have one for each of the emotions listed in Table 5–1. Look at your personal table, 5–2, right now. Do you possess all the psycho-stores you have listed? Are they cleansed and ready to receive a charge? *Caution:* Make notes on sheets separate from the book; do not mark this book, as so doing will negate the psychometric powers.

Perhaps you come home extremely angry and frustrated at your boss. You are pouring out this negative energy, but it is going to waste! Pick up your chosen psycho-store, hold it for a few moments in your dominant hand, and say a few words over it, like:

> "Hot red anger, bide in here.
> Leave me free from hate and fear.
> Remain, vital Energy.
> As I will, so mote it be."

Not only will you be charging up a psycho-store for later use, but you will also be removing these destructive emotions from your own astral energy field, thus putting yourself more and more back into balance. You will find, particularly in cases of anger, that a good psycho-store really calms you and halts the production of harmful adrenalin in your body. This in itself is a very healthful thing for you to do.

Once you have charged the psycho-store in this manner, you must put it out of sight, preferably locked into a steel box. If you just leave it on the shelf, it will affect *you*. You will have unbalanced your environment, and you have already learned from earlier chapters how damaging this can be to you. For this reason, some people go to the extent of burying their psycho-stores in the garden; you may find (especially if you are a very emotional person) that you have to follow some similar procedure. We have found that by keeping twelve psycho-stores charged, an individual one for each of the emotions mentioned in Table 5–1, the twelve together put out wide-spectrum energy rather than unbalancing our environment. So if you keep each of your stores in its box, and the stores all together in one location, you will be all right.

Whether the emotion you feel is sad or cheerful, loving or angry, if you don't have an immediate use for it, store it for future use.

KAY USES SAD ENERGY TO SLOW THE KIDS DOWN

Kay R runs a pre-school class in mid-Missouri. She is dependent on this pre-school for her livelihood; yet she found that each successive year she seemed to have less and less ability to keep the children in order. Finally, she went to her doctor, who put her on a regimen of tranquilizers to help her handle the children. Though this calmed Kay, it certainly did not help the reputation of her pre-school; in fact, she eventually became so doped up that the kids ran wild.

During the summer months, following the worst winter Kay could remember, she managed to get away to a summer camp and occult convention in Virginia Beach. While at the convention, she talked of her problem to several of the women there. One of them told her of Magna-Psychometry and the trick of storing one's excess emotion in psycho-stores such as we have described. This woman also pointed out to Kay that taking tranquilizers was not going to help her school, because it was the kids who needed slowing down, not Kay herself. If anything, Kay needed speeding up to handle the high energy level of the children.

All of this made a great deal of sense to Kay, so when she got home she bought a dozen orange candles. This color, being ruled by Taurus, brings on depression and melancholia. Throughout the rest of the summer, every time she felt down, even if she only stubbed her toe in the garden and felt irked, she pushed these emotions into her orange candles. When school time came around again, she was prepared.

Those candles were fully charged—and Kay was as bright as a cricket. She had thrown her tranquillizers into the trash, for now she was sure she could handle the children. On the very first day, the kids started to act up as they had been accustomed to doing the previous year. Kay lit her first candle, thus dissipating into the air some of the melancholia that it contained. As it burned, the kids magically slowed down and became manageable. Kay found that as little as five minutes of candle-burning would accomplish her needs and that as the year progressed, she needed less and less of the sad energy to control the kids.

Soon the parents who had previously heard bad rumors of her school were bringing their children to her. They could see for themselves that children attending Kay's pre-school came home in an agreeable frame of mind. Kay's use of sad energy on the children in school lasted, staying with them into their home environment. There, of course, it served to balance the intense negative emotional energy they received from the violent shows they all watched on television.

You can greatly help your own children by balancing their energy. It is very difficult, if not impossible, for a mother to stop a child watching TV programs of heavy emotional intensity and violence. She cannot constantly be the warden of the TV set. If you try it, your children will come to dislike you. So instead of being a big negative ogre, why don't you follow Kay's example? Give your children an orange candle for a night light. When you feel sad, charge up this candle with sad energy. When you look in after your child is safely asleep, you can put out the candle, for it will have served its purpose. You will be amazed at how quickly and comfortably you can get a child to fall asleep with the aid of an emotion-charged candle of this sort.

USING YOUR ASTRAL BANK

In Kay's case, she used the standard table of correspondences to choose the color of her candles. But you should use *your* psychometric ability to decide on the color (and the other properties) of *your* psycho-store. Perhaps your child tends to be very uptight when you are trying to settle her down for the night. Sit back and figure out what emotion she is putting out, then select from your bank of psycho-stores the appropriate one that will either absorb this undesirable energy or balance it. If you have a full bank of psycho-stores, you should use both an absorber and a balancer, of course, to obtain the full Magna-Psychometric effect. You can place something near her that will help absorb the excess energy, and you can also place something nearby that will give her some balancing energy. These are the steps that turn your psychometric ability into Magna-Psychometry. You are magnifying the benefits that you yourself have felt to be desirable by employing your previously charged astral energy psycho-stores.

YOUR COMPLETE GUIDE TO UNLIMITED POWER

You may not have psychic muscles equivalent to the physical muscles of a Charles Atlas. But you can do all the things a Charles Atlas can by working persistently and continually, getting one small unit of astral energy into your psycho-store each day. Eventually, just as a slow rain fills a great reservoir, so you will fill your psycho-store. It is vital, of course, always to put the same color energy into any given psycho-store; for if you put different colored energy into the same psycho-store, it will be ineffective against specific obstacles.

You have two ways of deciding on your own astral keys: the first is to use the standard table of correspondences that has been worked out over centuries of trial and error; the other (and better) way is to make up your own table of correspondences and then, having understood this table, learn to key yourself to specific energies without having to refer to it. Remember, the only effective psychic keys are those that are meaningful in your own reality; and no one can tell you, for instance, what the meaning of a given word holds for you at any particular instant.

Now you have one type of psycho-store; let us say it is a positive one. You should also make its negative equivalent. The use of the push-pull technique in occult work has regularly been shown to produce results at least four times as effective as the simple one-way-only ritual. Pull the lover toward you, push the lover away from your rival, and you will succeed in utilizing all your energy, not just half of it. For sometimes you will be happy, sometimes you will be sad. By storing both of these available energies, you not only help to keep yourself in good balance, but you literally build a psycho-store bank of various energies that you can use in your work. You will find that when you put anger, for instance, into a psycho-store, it makes you feel infinitely better; because you feel better, those around you are made to feel better. Thus your life is automatically improved.

Again we emphasize that these techniques are simplicity itself. A few moments' work each day, and you can possess all the power you will ever need.

6

YOU CAN ALWAYS WIN WITH MAGNA-PSYCHOMETRY

YOU CAN BE AS LUCKY AS ANYONE

Having followed the instructions in the first five chapters of this book, you should now be living in a psychometrically serene environment. Moreover, with the various techniques set out, you probably have been able to improve your life considerably. Still, you may feel that you need that extra lucky break, the luck that a favorite talisman might be able to give you, that little extra boost that would make all the difference.

Magna-Psychometry can give you that extra edge. As with all psychometric procedures, you have to work at it a little and understand what you are doing in order to get the edge. Luck won't knock on your door; it has to be invited. The easiest thing to do, of course, is to use the psychometric procedures given in Chapter 4 to construct a sapphire-blue lucky psycho-store for yourself; then, when you are going to go into any enterprise where you need that extra edge, you should wear that psycho-store. This, however, is only part of the story.

All the lucky emanations in the world are not going to help you if you're sitting at home watching TV. You must get out and put yourself into the world and work at the enterprise in which you want to succeed. Initiate a Meta-Psychometric mate-attracting procedure, use your luck psycho-store, and go where the action is, if you are to succeed. You should not place your full reliance on just being "lucky." Use all your developed psychometric abilities to help yourself.

With the aid of this book, you can take on the world and win for yourself a comfortable place in it so you can then use your developed powers to help others. The world is your battlefield, and you must use every psychometric ability you can develop if you really intend to win your victory.

ELI AND THE POKER GAME

Eli V is a retired army major living near Springfield, Missouri. He had a comfortable pension, and the mobile home he lived in was paid for. Throughout his army career, Eli had regularly played winning poker; he attributed many of his winnings to his "mojo," a lucky mascot which he had acquired while stationed in Korea.

As any good poker player knows, the psyching out—or psychometrizing—of your opponents is a crucial part of the game. With your developed psychometric ability, you should be able to look beyond any poker faces and tell whether or not the players hold good hands. This is especially true when you play with strangers, for no prior knowledge of their personalities can warp or filter your readings. The double step of psychometrically reading your opponents and using a lucky psycho-store like Eli's mojo is a winning combination.

When he retired, Eli started playing poker in the trailer court every day with the same set of retired people. What he didn't realize was that his mojo would lose its lucky influence if it was used constantly. Moreover, because he was always playing with the same bunch of cronies, he found it more difficult to use his developed psychometric ability to read their hands and their poker faces.

At first, as he had expected, Eli did indeed win; but after a matter of weeks, he began to lose steadily. This was not so much a matter of financial loss to Eli as it was what Orientals would call a loss of face. He was thoroughly frustrated that every day he lost a few dollars. He became nervous and ill and, in many ways, a thoroughly disagreeable old man. He spent a small fortune on visiting his physician, who could do nothing for the pains and complaints which Eli showered upon him; in fact, the doctor's tranqulizers further depressed Eli's winning psychometric abilities.

The downward spiral was fully under way. When he lost money, Eli either took tranqulizers or drank heavily. The effect of the drinking and the pills was, of course, that his capabilities were further depressed; thus, as week followed week, he lost more and more money, and his health deteriorated in an alarming way.

In a moment of deep depression, Eli wrote to us and asked us to send him a lucky charm. This is something we do not do, because we feel that a lucky charm must be individually tailored to the needs of the person who will carry it; and, further, that the person using a charm must be able to understand how it should be used and charged.

Once having corresponded with us, however, Eli was extremely persistent. Nothing would satisfy him short of coming to visit us in person. On his visit to our farm, he talked with us for perhaps a day and a half; then he took the opportunity to go the local Legion Hall and play a little poker. He won, and returned to the farm as happy as a lad with a new jackknife. He became even more convinced that *we* were his new mojo. What he actually wanted to do was to draw out his life savings and take us with him to Las Vegas, or even to Monte Carlo, and break the bank. It took us almost a week to convince Eli that the reason he won at the Legion Hall was that (a) he was playing with strangers and (b) his original mojo had had a chance to recharge itself by being out of use for a couple of days while he had been talking and working with us at the farm.

We are still not sure just what we did or said, but whatever it was, it must have impressed Eli enough to follow our rules from then on. We're happy to say that even today he continues to play winning poker.

MAKING LUCK COME TO YOU

To bring luck unto yourself, as we have instructed, you should make a sapphire psycho-store, then charge it with the appropriate blue energy, either from yourself or in a pyramid arrangement. Remember that you can get out of any psycho-store only what you have put into it. Therefore, if you have been very unlucky in the past, it would be best for you to get two or three psycho-stores and wear one while you charge another. Step 1 is to charge a cleansed psycho-store in your pyramid, placing it under a blue filter. Step 2 is to wear this charged psycho-store as you go about your daily tasks, while another similar psycho-store is being charged by the great cosmic powers in your pyramid.

Just as with any charging procedure, use a suitable filter so you maximize the lucky Jupiter power instead of merely increasing the general energy level of your psycho-store. If to you blue does not "feel" like a lucky color, by all means charge your psycho-store with the color you selected when you made your individual Table of Correspondences in Chapter 5.

When you have great need, you should also use one of the (till now, highly secret) Magna-Psychometric procedures that will give your psycho-store an added psychic punch. Take a small iron box (for iron is naturally associated with military victory and aggressive adventure). Place into it a powerful Alnico[1] linear magnet. On the eve of the day when you expect that final decision in your favor, place both your psycho-stores on the south pole of the magnet. Place the magnet and the charms in the box and fill the remaining space in the box with tobacco taken from the finest cigar you can buy. This Magna-Psychometric system will draw to you that extra luck when you need it most.

Again we mention: Do not totally rely on luck. Many other people besides yourself have potent mojos and lucky charms. Using a Magna-Psychometric charging technique will ensure that your psycho-store is more potent than almost all others; still, it is best to combine your luck with a good, solid second-string Meta-Psychometric procedure that will ensure success.

You must always use your developed psychometric ability to its fullest extent. This gives you a multilateral advantage over the world: even if luck proves to be insufficient, you should never be at a loss, because one of your Magna-Psychometric advantages will always be available to you for instant use. Not only will your lucky charm fit every occasion, but one of your other techniques can be tailored to the specific need of the moment.

USE MAGNA-PSYCHOMETRY SPARINGLY

You may think that Magna-Psychometric techniques will work for you on a continuous basis, but this is true only when you have adequate charging potentials; for, just as Eli found, you can easily discharge your mojo or lucky charm, and then it will become a psychic vampire in your hands, sucking your good fortune from you to recharge itself. It is better, then, to reserve these procedures for those very serious situations where you really need to have the edge, than to scatter your energy by using Magna-Psychometry on every minor problem. This is not to say that in your early use of Magna-Psychometry you should not practice your talents and make sure that you can adequately psychometrize the situation and select the winning color combinations; in order to keep your skills in shape, you must practice them constantly.

We would especially warn you not to show off these talents to

---

[1]See Appendix.

friends and relatives: not only because this dissipates your energy, but also because it gives these people a warning of the things you can do; and the old chiche that "forewarned is forearmed" is very true in occult matters. Every neophyte occultist and many Christian ministers can advise people how to defend themselves against the invisible forces of psychometric power. In most cases, of course, these defensive techniques will require only that you exert a little more effort to accomplish your intent; but if the person had not been forewarned in the first place, you could more surely and quickly have achieved your aim.

SHARON GETS THERE FIRST

Sharon P was a draftswoman in Minneapolis. She was a charming, slightly overweight woman who quietly and constantly did excellent work. Her self-constituted rival in the office was Liz M, a slim, vivacious type who really couldn't be bothered with detail work, but made up for her lack of good solid productivity by her lively chatter.

Sharon was a practicing Witch and a very knowledgeable occultist, though she never mentioned these facts at work. She was amused and fascinated when Liz suddenly became aware of the occult and its possibilities. Of course, Liz, being a talkative type, told Sharon how she was making her life better with her lucky charms, and demonstrated for Sharon her ability to detect various colors psychometrically. Sharon gently warned her that this type of activity could cause problems; but in her typical chattery, scattery, scattery way, Liz ignored these warnings.

The situation came to an unspoken showdown when there was a possibility of a trip to Europe to draft plans for a new auditorium for Minneapolis. Feeling that they wanted to give an old-world Italian rococo effect to the proposed building, the developers had decided to send their engineer and a draftswoman to Europe to make on-site sketches. Vivacious Liz assumed that she had the assignment wrapped up; for not only was she more presentable than the other girls in the office, but she was also quite friendly with the engineer who was going. Liz decided that she should use her psychometric skills to clinch the job. As always, she told Sharon all about it; how she was recharging the vice-president's personal coffee cup every evening so that he would have a picture of glamorous Liz in Europe presented to him every time he drank coffee from the cup. Now, even though Sharon saw what a plum the European assignment would be, she never really thought she could get it; but knowing what Liz was doing, she felt (a) she should teach Liz a lesson and (b) maybe she could get to go to Europe after all.

In her quiet, thorough way, Sharon charged the coffee in the vice-president's office. Into it she put a very powerful thought of Liz' superficial workmanship and her shrill blatant sexuality. She impressed into the coffee a paraphrase of the Hertz slogan: "Behind the smile there's no brain." Every time the vice-president's secretary perked coffee in his office, these thoughts were released. All Liz's glamorous emanations in the coffee cup did were to reinforce Sharon's thoughtform of "nothing behind the smile" and easy sex. Very quickly it became apparent to Sharon that her technique was working, because Liz was told with increasing frequency to do her work more thoroughly.

When the engineer left for Europe to do his on-site sketches and plans, Sharon was with him. To her unutterable frustration, Liz was left home to mind the store. In the end, Liz decided that her occult dabblings had been the cause of her disappointment, and she discontinued her experiments. A sudden keen interest in macramé and houseplants now forms the basis for most of her breaktime chatter.

YOUR SILENT PERSUADERS

In earlier chapters, you leaned how to charge and use psychobanks to aid you in obtaining the things you wanted. These psychobanks were either discharged slowly to affect an environment gradually, or instantly so as to release a large pulse of energy that would make an abrupt change. Both Sharon and Liz used instant-energy-release systems in their Magna-Psychometric procedures; but because Liz had shot off her mouth, Sharon was able to add to her procedure a little negative twist. This extra fillip is the very essence of Magna-Psychometry because it shows how you can, though using very little energy, add to the work of others by hand-tailoring a little energy of just the right sort to get your way.

Suppose that your rival for a loved one's affection is putting out all sorts of good heavy sexual emanations. By adding a little Scorpio energy, you can make those emanations so intense that most people would boggle at even the thought of a date with that rival. Then, if you add some Venusian loving emanations to your own aura at the same time, the pushpull effect will accomplish your desire.

How then can you ensure that you add these extra emanations to the environment of the right person? Sharon and Liz used the vice-president's coffee cup and his little coffee percolator that sat on the table behind his desk. Their situation was as near to being ideal as possible, because very few people are going to have the gall to drink from the vice-president's personal cup, and probably only his secretary is going to fool around with his percolator. Thus, the energy that Sharon and Liz were directing was bound to hit the vice-president or his secretary. If you work in an office where employees have individual coffee cups, you can follow these same routines. Remember that whatever it is you elect to charge with Magna-Psychometric energy, that object must be broken or bent, or have its temperature dramatically changed to release the energy you have stored in it if the Magna-Psychometric procedure is to work.

Let your imagination expand, and think about this problem. Perhaps the person you intend to affect is a smoker. Well, then, you can charge up a single cigarette of the brand he likes, and arrange it in the pack so that he automatically gets that one when you offer it to him. Perhaps he loves log fires. Why not go to his wood pile and charge up one of the logs he will soon be burning? Or perhaps he chews gum. Offer him a stick whose foil you have charged. When he crumples the foil and discards it, the energy you have placed in it will be released.

Your opportunities for using these silent procedures are limited only by the scope of your imagination. The effects you can achieve are truly dramatic, and it is fun to think of all the different ways in which you can send your energy to do your bidding.

CONTROLLING YOUR DESTINY WITH MAGNA-PSYCHOMETRY

Everyone wonders from time to time whether his life is going to continue on its present track, or get better, or change for the worse. Scientists recently have discovered that they know all too little about a thing which they thought was fixed—a thing called "Time." It seems that the scientists are now discovering what occultists have known for centuries; that is, that Time is *not* fixed. It is beyond the scope of this book to discuss all the various planes of consciousness and all the various simultaneous-time theories; but we can say that prediction works because time is variable, and a capable psychic can bend time and somehow look around the bend of the river of time to see into future time continuums.

To prove how true this is, you may select a favorite object of yours that you expect to keep for a long time. Sit quietly with it in your secondary hand and psychometrize it while you imagine time running into the future. With your advanced abilities, you should find that it will give you very powerful emanations regarding the next few months, and then weaker and weaker emanations for the years into the future. By psychometrizing it this way, you can get a very good idea of the things that will happen to you in your own future.

This is exactly the same procedure that you used when you wanted to find out what happened to some object in the past; and it works just as well for the future time continuum. The emanations in the closer time frame are powerful, though the emanations in the longer time frame are quite weak.

Suppose you detect in your future some monetary loss. What you must now do with your Magna-Psychometric ability is find out how to change that loss to a gain; or at the very least, how to make sure that such a loss can be absorbed by your bank account. You know that, by introducing into your life certain color keys you can make many different things happen. If you introduce into the environment of your test object other psychometric emanations, you can detect the effect those emanations will have on your own future.

So the thing to do to learn how to have a serene future is to psychometrize the combination of this test object and various colored pieces of paper—paper of the color that you would expect to alter the future favorably for you. In the case of a monetary loss, you might first introduce orange and then green, and observe whether or not the orange Tauran colors correct the problem. If they do, you should introduce more orange into your life.

You can affect the future; your life is in your own hands. You have, as we say, personal volition. By checking out your future ahead of time and by correcting it, you can obviously improve your life.

KEEPING OTHERS OFF BALANCE

A favorite trick of executive interviewers with job applicants is to ask questions which seem to be way off base from the normal run of job-related topics. Typically, a secretarial applicant will be asked some mildly sexually oriented question; this question will rapidly be followed by one of the more conventional job-related questions. What the interviewer is doing is swinging the applicant into an off-balance position in one direction by asking her a perhaps embarrassing sexual question, then swinging the applicant hard over in the other direction to see how well she can handle that conversational balancing act.

This is the technique you should use in Magna-Psychometry. Swing the pendulum, and swing the person's life with it. Whether your aim is to help or to harm the target person, either way you can get better results by employing the swing technique. Imagine a heavy automobile stuck in snow. You could spend all day and all your strength trying to push it out in one direction, yet be totally unsuccessful. But rock it and swing it, and it will gradually rock further and further until it frees itself and is off and running.

To demonstrate this to yourself, you can make someone fall over by influencing the way he walks! Sit in the park some pleasant day and wait for someone who is aimlessly strolling. (Don't try this on someone who is hurrying purposefully to an appointment.) Watch the stroller carefully. You will observe that, as he walks, he sways a little to the right and to the left with each step. Every time the sway goes right, think at him, "Sway right further!" Every time the sway goes left, think, "Sway left more!" After you have practiced this a few times, you will find that you can make the person stumble. If he stumbles into the path of an oncoming car, you have hexed him; but if he stumbles onto the park grass and wakes himself up from his reverie, you have probably helped him. The push-pull technique has worked again.

You could sit outside all day thinking at someone, "Fall over," and it wouldn't happen; but the double-whammy push-pull of your Magna-Psychometric technique almost always works.

SID GETS HIS PROMOTION

Sid F was the assistant sales manager of a St. Louis electronics firm. The situation in the sales department of the company was rather confused: the previous sales manager had suffered a nervous breakdown and had not yet been replaced. Now three assistant sales managers were vying for the vacant spot, and company management had let it be known that not one of them would get the job unless they showed a more improved performance. This was no more than normal management policy, of course, designed to win more contracts. But after thinking it over for a time, Sid went to the president and laid it on the line:

"Look, Bob, I have three major sales opportunities over the next three months. If I can bring two of those in within my sales budget, do I get the job?"

Bob hemmed and hawed about that, saying that Alex had also been to see him with a similar offer. Bob felt that since Sid's sales prospects were expected to be a little more difficult than Alex's, it would be unfair to Sid to stipulate that he bring in two out of three to get the promotion. After some further talk, Sid persuaded Bob to make it a race between Alex and himself; and, further, that the company would not hire someone from outside until the results of the sales race were in.

Sid had two avenues of action open to him: he could work against Alex and ruin his sales prospects; or he could concentrate on his own sales and get them in. He felt that he should do something to lower

Alex's chances, but he felt that a destructive act would be negative to the future prospects of the firm. He determined that he would try only to get Alex's contracts delayed, while bringing in his own ahead of time. This would gain the most favorable attention for himself because the firm was in need of work and faced layoffs.

The first thing Sid did was to sit down privately with the three contract proposals that were assigned to him. By careful psychometric analysis, he found that he could win one of them with a relatively minor time-limited price reduction. Company management agreed to his proposed price reduction, because he could show the Manufacturing Department that if he got the contract in before his proposed time span expired, they could avoid those costly layoffs. When the proposal was rewritten, Sid took the first copy off the press and charged it with Arian military-success type energy, while at the same time recharging his sapphire ring with blue lucky power. Then he hopped a plane to Washington and sold the proposal to the Army. Within two weeks of Sid's pact with the firm's president, he could chalk up his first win.

Alex was not far behind. His first contractual win of the competition seemed assured. The key meeting was to take place the following day. The night before the meeting, Sid went to the company board room and impressed on the top sheet of every note pad feelings of delay. The next day, Alex was extremely disappointed with his customers' announcement that they had to postpone the contract for at least a couple of months.

Meantime, Sid had run into some difficulties with his second contract proposal. Every time he psychometrized it, he could get nothing from it but emanations of loss. He tried psychometrizing it with different prices; he tried psychometrizing it with new schedules; all the answers kept coming out negative. Finally, taking a deep breath, he went through the document, page by page, trying to feel what each page meant to the customer and what its effect would be in a future time frame. He finally narrowed it down to a problem with six or eight pages in the engineering section. He had the firm's Chief Engineer reread these pages and recheck the calculations on them. Sid was no slouch when it came to engineering; yet he could find nothing overtly wrong with the engineering proposal.

At last, over the objections of the Chief Engineer, Sid called in a top-flight engineering consultant. Those objections turned to praise when the consultant told the Engineering Department that there had been a recent breakthrough in computer logic circuitry which meant that their proposal would soon be totally obsolete; further, that by the time the proposal was reviewed by Navy personnel, the new technology would be widely known; and therefore their proposal, as it now stood, would have been rejected.

With the aid of the consultant, the proposal was rewritten on a crash basis. The rewritten version required a longer time period and a slightly higher price, but when Sid psychometrized it, he could feel pure "win" emanations. Leaving nothing to chance, he charged this proposal with positive Luciferian advanced-technology emanations. It won the competition, and Sid got his promotion.

CHARGING AND USING YOUR WINNING PSYCHO-BANK

There is an old saying, "If you're going to be nasty, be positively nasty." This is more true in the psychic world than in any other realm of activity.

Of course, Sid dealt a foul blow to Alex by charging with psychic energy the top sheets of the note pads that he knew would be used in the board room. Sid was scrupulous, though, to slant his charge in a strongly positive way; for although to Alex delay was a negative thing, still, the thoughts that Sid put into the pages were a positive emotion: "It will be better if you delay."

In order to win, when you charge your psycho-bank, you must always charge it with what you regard as positive, winning emotions. Table 6–1 shows you the three critical, winning emotions that you can

Winning Intent	Planet	Sign	Color	Psycho-Store
Legal	Pluto	Scorpio	Turquoise	Turquoise/Platinum
Money	Earth	Taurus	Red	Red Jade/Nickel
Contract	Mars	Aries	Scarlet	Ruby/Iron

Table 6–1
Basic Winning Psycho-stores

generally rely on to ensure the attainment of your goal. These three emotions cover the spectrum from winning a legal battle, through gaining more money, to winning a contract or a competition. If you have a specialized case like Sid's advanced-technology proposal, you should naturally refer to your complete Table of Correspondences for the best possible tuned-in color to gain your end.

The procedure is simple enough: charge whatever document is critical to the conflict with positive "I will win" emotions of the "color" selected from Table 6–1. If possible, enclose the charged document in a cover of the appropriate color, and take with you to any relevant conference the appropriate psycho-store of energy plus your own highly charged winning sapphire lucky psycho-store.

ZENA GETS FIRED

Zena S was a much-disliked executive secretary in a Chicago advertising agency. She came to our attention when another secretary in that same agency, which had been handling our own account, asked us whether we could use our specialized skills to sweeten Zena up, especially as she seemed to be passionately negative about the agency's handling ads for Witchcraft. Olive wrote that Zena was a strict fundamentalist Christian but, at the same time, she was a recent divorcee, who to all appearances was enjoying her new self-reliance and sexual freedom.

We told Olive we thought it was the conflict between Zena's fundamentalist beliefs and her liberated life-style that was probably making Zena so unpleasant. Zena was constantly being confronted with two diametrically opposed forces. She was the pendulum-bob swinging violently from one extreme to the other, and in this unstable situation she could hardly be expected to maintain a detached outlook or a sweet disposition in the office environment. Olive wrote back to say that this was all very well, but just because Zena had problems, Olive didn't see why she (and incidentally our account) had to suffer because of them.

After a rapid exchange of letters, we told Olive she had two choices: either she could push Zena a trifle further into her conflict situation and completely unbalance her, or she could try somehow to diminish the internal conflict—perhaps by teaching her that sexual adventures are not evil but, in fact, could be construed to be in accordance with her "holy writ." For non-adulterous sexual relations between consenting adults are nowhere forbidden in the Bible. Olive decided that Zena was completely unapproachable with respect to holy writ; thus she decided to see whether she could push Zena over the edge in the sexual direction by having her feel an obsessive lust for Ephraim, the extremely conventional, gray-haired corporation lawyer retained by the advertising agency.

Olive used the coffee-cup technique. Soon, the whole office was buzzing over the way Zena was salivating over Ephraim. The office rumor mill had a ball with the relationship, but in management it caused more amusement than annoyance. Since it seemed to have no undesirable effect on Zena's work level, "why bother?" seemed to be the general attitude.

Without discussing it with us, Olive now pulled a double-whammy on Zena. The boss's rather brilliant protege had worked up a whole new advertising campaign for a new brand of cigarettes, basing his work on a rather explicitly sexual illustration of a bikini-clad model. It was Olive's job to make up the proposal packages and distribute them to the agency's executives, to the customer, and to Zena, so each could study the proposal in depth before the final decision conference, at which the customer would decide whether to start the multi-million-dollar campaign. Olive charged both the manager's and the customer's proposals with Arian scarlet contract-winning energy; but she charged Zena's with all the Scorpio raunchy lust emanations she could; she even bound it in a turquoise folder.

During that vital decision meeting, as more and more of the company executives, and the customer, showed enthusiasm for the ad campaign, Zena became increasingly irritated. So unbalanced did she become that she literally exploded at the customer himself over (of all things) whether he regularly took sugar in his coffee. In advertising circles, this type of irrational blowup—at a customer—is an unforgivable sin. Zena dug her own grave even deeper by following up her outburst with a further diatribe against the whole advertising campaign and sex and desire in general. Her boss tried unsuccessfully to get her to leave the room, but she was much too unbalanced for any such rational behavior.

Olive's whammy had worked far more potently then even she had expected. Zena went through a classic nervous breakdown. Fortunately, she was young enough to be fairly resilient, and a brief stay in the hospital, combined with excellent psychiatric care, fully cured her. Today Zena is a well-balanced woman, free of her fundamentalist guilt and enjoying life. We are also glad to say that Olive learned a lesson from her psychic attack on Zena; to wit, it is best to stop short of overkill.

WE CAUTION YOU TO BE REALISTIC

In her push-pull procedures, Olive obviously went too far. Luckily, Zena recovered, and both women are now more balanced people for their experiences. We have not yet found an ultimate limit to the things you can do with the power of Meta-Psychometry, but in your procedures you should decide ahead of time whether or not you will like living with yourself when you get the results you are working for. It is always wise, in all magical procedures, to spend a few moments taking the results of your contemplated procedure to their logical conclusions and deciding (before it's too late) whether the game is, as they say, worth the candle.

In the same vein, remember that these procedures should be regarded as an aid to any given problem, rather than an answer in themselves. When you first start using these very real powers, neither your judgment nor your effectiveness will be as sure as they will become when you have gained more expertise.

What can you really aspire to? If you try from your present level of knowledge to grab directly for the moon, you may fail; furthermore, even if you succeed, you might not be prepared to enjoy it when you get it. Yes, stretch your imaginings. Reach out there and grab for realistic goals. But don't, especially at the beginning, overreach yourself. If you do, you will surely fail. Even the great power that is inherent in Magna-Psychometry can not build you a mighty rocket and take you to the moon; but it can take you down the road a long way toward all you can realistically desire.

YOUR COMPLETE MAGNA-PSYCHOMETRIC LIFE GUIDE

In Chapter 5 you learned how to magnify your psychometric powers; in this chapter, you have learned how to add the power of winning luck to your procedures. You have also learned how to read what the future holds for you; not only that, but also how this future can be changed for you by psychometrically adding different-colored emanations to your life. These steps, though they may seem complicated, are in fact simple when executed singly and in order. Reviewing them, you see that you must perform them in the following order:

1. Obtain and charge a winning psycho-store that you can use to smooth your winning path through life.

2. Find some favorite object that you expect will be in your future life. Carefully psychometrize it and find out from it what your future life holds. If you wish to make some change in your destiny, then re-psychometrize the selected object in combination with different colors so you can read the effect of these colored emanations on your future. During this reading, you may find that there is a particular point in your life where you must overcome some opposition. You should very carefully note this point and be prepared, when you come to it, to use your developed abilities either to win or to face it in readiness and knowledge.

3. Bring the necessary destiny-improving color into your life,

together with that indefinable extra pizazz you can get from a winning psycho-store.

4. Remember, when it comes to overcoming a specific opposing force, you should work both by pushing and by pulling. Don't expend all your energy pushing in one direction, because people learn very quickly how to resist a one-way force. You must decide how to push and to pull psychometrically to gain your end.

5. Select the appropriate psycho-stores at each step of the way, and charge them so you can Magna-Psychometrically influence the future to your advantage. Because you may not get all you desire on the same day that you work a procedure, it is wise to develop a logical life gameplan that will lead you step by step to your goal.

7

HEAL YOURSELF WITH MEDI-PSYCHOMETRY

AGE-OLD HEALING

When Great-Grandma set out to heal the flux, an essential step in her procedure was the hanging of a little sack of something around the neck of the patient. This practice traces back in time to earliest man; and it is still used by many native tribes and Amerindians today as a potent healing method. The connection between the articles in the healing pouch or Medicine Bag and the illness often seems to be quite remote. What, for instance, has a rabbit's foot or a wolf's fang to do with curing a flux?

Having come this far in your study of Meta-Psychometry, you know that such articles are energy accumulators into which Great-Grandma has poured energy that her patient needs for a cure. From these empirically proven traditional methods stems our claim that, in our practice of healing, especially of ourselves, we use a methodology tried and tested—and found to work—through many centuries of trial and error. This procedure we will call Medi-Psychometry.

In the same vein, nowadays, much to the amazement of orthodox physicians, thousands upon thousands of people have found relief from arthritis through the wearing of a copper bracelet. As you will see later in this chapter, certain metals have been associated for centuries with the curing of specific diseases. Copper is one that cures blood diseases; and since arthritis is caused by deposition of tiny crystals from the bloodstream into the joints, there apparently is some arcane connection between the copper bracelet and the curing of arthritis. We personally have found that the gold bracelet so beloved by German matrons is a far more effective arthritic aid than the copper, because it specifically helps the joints of the arms and wrists. We cannot believe it is by mere chance that women of Germany suffer so little from arthritis.

We know most surely that certain metals aid in the curing of certain diseases; yet we know, too, that the metal bracelets seem to lose no weight in the performance of their healing task. Thus, we believe that each metal sends out special unique energies which affect the human body in a specific way. Each is a natural energy store, constantly working night and day, yet never depleted.

Thererefore it is good to remember that when you use Meta-Psychometry to heal yourself, two different techniques are at your disposal: first, the use of the appropriate metal energy bank; and second, the use of the wolf's-fang type of energy store into which you consciously first put energy before it is released to help you.

YOUR MEDICINE BAG OF HEALING ENERGY STORES

You learned in earlier chapters how to charge energy stores both with your own energy and with cosmic or pyramidal energy. If you are sick, your available energy will be depleted; so when you make a medicine bag for yourself, you should not attempt to charge it with your own energy. You should, rather, use pyramidal energy. It is true, however, that just as metals give off specific natural energies, so certain herbs, flavors, colors, and odors also help, as they have properties that absorb and return the specific type of energy needed to cure a given disease. Table 7–1, for instance, shows the four items that should be in your medicine bag for the curing of a specific illness.

Say you are suffering today from common diarrhea: what Great-Grandma called the "flux." Looking then at Table 7–1, you can see in the left-hand column the illness "diarrhea," and your medicine bag should contain a lemon, some winter savory, either a pressed buttercup or a picture of a buttercup, and an aquamarine. These four items, when placed in a bag around your neck, will help you of themselves; but if you place them in a pyramid, as instructed in Chapter 4, for six hours each day, they will gain that all-important extra Meta-Psychometric punch.

Popular wisdom has it that a medicine bag should be made of leather and hung around the neck on a leather thong. It has been our experience that this will work adequately with uncharged objects; but when the objects are charged with astral energy, there must be a minimum of contact with animal-derived substances such as leather. These substances tend to absorb and drain off the astral energy that you

Illness	Scented Object	Herb	Flower	Stone
Ulcer, Epilepsy Diarrhea	Lemon	Winter Savory	Buttercup	Aquamarine
Insomnia, Tumor Irritation	Water Lily	Thrift	Water Lily	Amethyst
Arthritis, Hypertension Depression, Exhaustion	Tobacco	Anemone	Geranium	Ruby
Polio, Melancholy Tuberculosis	Sandalwood	Ground-Ivy	Cowslip	Jade
Constipation Hepatitis, Diabetes	Clove	Lavender	Orchid	Opal
Bronchitis,	White	Poppy	Night-scented	Pearl
Digestion Circulation	Sandalwood		Stock	
Mononucleosis Cramps, Thyroid	Saffron	Rosemary	Sunflower	Diamond
Cerebral Palsy Retardation	Cinnamon	Caraway	Snowdrop	Agate
Fever Blood Disease	Myrtle	Alkanet	Rose	Emerald
Impotence Muscle Tension	Orange Blossom	Sweet Basil	Cactus	Turquoise
Shingles Goiter	Nutmeg	Balm	Narcissus	Sapphire
Glaucoma Palsy	Civet	Barley	Thistle	Onyx

Table 7–1

Items for Your Psychometric Medicine Bag

had intended for your cure. Further if a problem is centered princi-
pally in the area of the stomach, it seems to us that we get better results
if the energy source is applied directly against the stomach.

We strongly recommend, then, that your medicine bag be made
of cotton, and that you wear it as close to the affected part as possible.
In hundreds of other experiments, we have also found that man-made
fibers tend to build up electrical charges, which sometimes seem to
change subtly the healing energy so its effectiveness is diminished.
This is why we urge that, in construction of medicine bags, you avoid
all man-made synthetic fibers.

In using these healing aids, remember that they work on the
body's *psychic energy field.* They do not work on the mundane body;
but they aid the psyche, which then instructs the body to heal itself. If
you are under a doctor's care for some specific disease, the doctor is
aiding the body to cure itself by giving it chemicals and drugs that it can
use on the mundane level. *So your Meta-Psychometric healing is an
adjunct to, but not a replacement for, your doctor's procedures.*

JUNE P AND HER OPAL

June P is a resident of Sydney, Australia. She wrote to us
because she had a severe case of diabetes that seemed to resist every
technique the doctors employed to alleviate it. We advised her first to
make her diet more acid and to replace all the sugar she took with
honey. These are the mundane steps—the steps to ensure that the
body has the right materials available for the mechanical aspects of its
healing. We told her, further, that to improve her psychic field pattern
of energy, she should make herself a medicine bag containing cloves,
lavender, a pressed orchid, and an opal.

After about a month, she reported to us that wearing the medicine bag seemed to make her symptoms worse, rather than better. Of course, we immediately told her to stop wearing the bag while
we attempted to figure out what was wrong. It seemed obvious to us
that either June's disease must be proceeding from her surroundings
and her life-style, or something in the medicine bag was exerting a
negative Medi-Psychometric influence.

We asked a local psychic in Australia to visit June and to see
whether or not June's house contained any heavy diabetic energy that
it might have picked up from previous occupants. Our psychic friend
reported that, so far as she could ascertain, June's house was clean and
that our friend, too, was at a loss to understand why that medicine bag
was not working properly. In psychometrizing the medicine bag, the

psychic had picked up a feeling of diabetic rather than anti-diabetic energy. We instructed June to send us her whole medicine bag without further delay. We were going to pin down the trouble or know why it happened. When the package arrived, we found that she had included it in a very beautiful black opal in a gold setting. As it turned out, this opal was putting out the negative energy.

Throughout this work, we have been talking about the importance of the right "color" energy to get good results. Nowhere is this color more important than in Medi-Psychometry. Later in this chapter, we will be talking of the importance of color in healing yourself.

The color to heal diabetes is a light yellow or white—the color of most opals. What we had not realized was that, in Australia, the very best opals are considered to be the black fire opals—an inappropriate gemstone for curing diabetes. Also, though gold may be used in the treatment of arthritis and such things as menstrual cramps, it is not at all appropriate for the control of diabetes.

We returned the medicine bag to June with instructions to substitute a white, unmounted opal for the black stone. By using this medicine bag, then, she was able to forgo the very painful daily insulin shots and depend on a far milder oral medication to keep her diabetes under control. Today, she is at least able to carry on all normal activities, and she is shortly to be married.

USING METAL JEWELRY TO HEAL YOURSELF

In the introduction to this chapter, we noted that one of the best-known Meta-Psychometric healing tricks is to use the natural energy from metals to heal yourself. I am sure you have seen many people wearing copper bracelets in an attempt to heal themselves of arthritis. We said earlier that gold would be better. "Stop!" I hear several ladies cry. "My ring finger is the most arthritic of my whole hand, yet I really believe that my wedding band is gold." This brings up probably one of the most important points in the use of metal amulets and bracelets for healing—they must never totally encircle any part of the body or have closed rings within their structure.

Centuries ago, the Mohammedans, a ruthlessly patriarchal and woman-demeaning people, found that women had more inborn power to influence natural events than did men; and in a time when men sought to maintain their dominance, they had to come up with a device through which they could limit the natural psychic power of women —that device was the wedding ring. When you wear a wedding band on your finger, your energy field is badly distorted. This distortion of your energy field causes disease. It was a sad day indeed for western womanhood when those 12th Century crusaders brought back the idea of the wedding ring to northern Europe; for with it they brought a diminution of women's innate powers and an increase in women's diseases. Specifically, they brought on the all too common problem of menstrual cramps.

Thus, when you use a metal bracelet or ring, make sure it is constructed in an open design or is of a clasp type similar to those you have probably seen made by the Amerindians. Any ring you wear should be a wrap-around or split type, rather than a "perfect circle." Neither bracelets nor rings should completely enclose any part of the body; they must have a gap to allow the natural energy flow of the body to pass by undistorted.

Similarly, if you are going to use a golden amulet, you should not plan to suspend it from a chain of links. For each minute link of the chain is, again, a closed ring—an absorber of astral and body energy. Whatever the gold astral energy is, it flows around the closed circuit of the link, unable to leave the chain to perform the healing you intended. It is far better to suspend any amulet by a natural-fiber ribbon as close as possible to the place where the healing energy is needed. The color of the ribbon will be discussed later in this chapter.

In considering jewels made of metal, it is also important to make the jewel in the most appropriate shape. You learned before that a good absorber and transmitter of energy has a rough texture; in addition to this rough texture, it is also advantageous to form the jewel into certain traditional arcane magical shapes. So far, we have found that the best way to do this is to have someone rough-cast the shapes listed in Table 7–2. Do not have the metalsmith polish your work, though, because the rough-cast works better than a polished surface.

YOUR HEALING TABLE OF METALS

In general, if you have a minor ailment, you do not need to go to the expense of having a jewel specially made. Just carry any small piece of the appropriate metal with you wherever you go. Table 7–2 shows that if you have a temporary problem with digestion, for instance, the best metal to use is silver. You may already own something like a silver spoon and, to achieve relief, you could carry this in the pocket of your skirt or trousers for a few days.

On the other hand, if you have a continuing problem such as menstrual cramps, it is well worth your while to go to the expense of making (or of having made) a golden lion amulet in accordance with Table 7–2. You should attach this amulet to your belt, or arrange it in a special sachet that you attach firmly inside your garments. The idea is that you must wear it constantly, every day, so that the very low level of Meta-Psychometric energy which it puts out will have the best possible long-lasting effects.

Illness	Body Part	Metal	Shape
Ulcer, Epilepsy Diarrhea	Ankles	Pewter	Phoenix
Insomnia, Tumor Irritation	Feet	Zinc	Dolphin
Arthritis, Blood Pressure Depression, Exhaustion	Head	Bronze	Ram
Polio, Melancholy Tuberculosis	Neck	Nickel	Bull
Constipation Hepatitis, Diabetes	Hands, Arms Lungs	Aluminum	Magpie
Bronchitis, Digestion Circulation	Breast Stomach	Silver	Crab
Mononucleosis Cramps, Thyroid	Heart, Spine Arms, Wrists	Gold	Lion
Cerebral Palsy Retardation	Hands, Abdomen Intestines	Mercury Amalgam	Virgin
Fever, Hypertension Blood Disease	Lower Back, Kidneys	Copper	Swan
Impotence Muscle Tension	Pelvis Genitalia	Platinum	Scorpion
Shingles Goiter	Hips, Thighs Liver	Tin	Centaur
Glaucoma Palsy	Knees, Bones Skin	Lead	Goat

Table 7–2

Natural Healing Metals and Shapes

CHERYL CHOOSES HER OWN AMULET

Cheryl B. lives in Mountain View, Missouri. She used to be a chronic insomniac. Cheryl was what we often refer to as a "fringe occultist." She had enough interest to read occasionally about psychic activity and paranormal research, but had never actually put such information into practice in her own life. She was not, for instance, sufficiently dedicated to get involved in such esoteric practices as psychic healing or psychometry.

Then she accompanied her husband on a business trip to Phoenix, Arizona. During his conferences, she spent some time at a psychic seminar that was being conducted in their motel. At that seminar, she met Kay Meadows* who makes a line of fine occult jewelry. Kay and Cheryl became good friends during the five-day seminar, and over coffee, Cheryl mentioned to Kay her problem with insomina. Kay told Cheryl that some people had reported good results in alleviating insomnia with the aid of a particular reproduction of one of the arcane Seals of Solomon, which Kay carried as part of her jewelry selection. She offered to let Cheryl try it overnight. Cheryl did, but found that it seemed to give her little or no help.

The following morning, the disappointed Cheryl returned the seal to Kay with her thanks. Because she felt she owed Kay something for the loan, Cheryl decided she would buy one of Kay's pieces of jewelry. Kay showed her how to hold her hand over the display of jewels to see which "felt good" and which felt neutral or negative to her. Much to Cheryl's amazement, some of these inanimate objects did, in fact, feel "warmer" than others. The warmest one of all was a simple rough-cast dolphin form; this she bought from Kay.

The very next morning, as they were leaving to return to Mountain View, Kay was also in the lobby checking out.

"How did you sleep last night, Cheryl?" Kay inquired.

"Fine—now that I come to think of it!"

"Well," smiled Kay, "I am not really surprised; for the dolphin amulet you chose is another well-known cure for insomnia. You are very typical of people on the fringe of the occult. If we tell such people ahead of time that this or that amulet will cure their problem, they seem to set up mental blocks so the amulet can't work. On the other hand, when I teach them to psychometrize the jewelry just as you did, Cheryl, the amulet does its healing work unhindered by the mental set of the buyer."

---

*See Appendix.

Cheryl thanked Kay for her help; today, she still swears by her dolphin jewel as a sure-fire means of curing insomnia. She had used her own little-suspected psychometric capability to select the jewel. Even though Kay had not called it psychometry when she had shown Cheryl how to pick the best-feeling of her thousands of jewels, psychometry was, in fact, what Cheryl was doing.

YOU CAN'T FOOL YOURSELF

Cheryl's experience with the original seal that Kay had selected for her is quite common in people's efforts at healing themselves. Many people suffer from a given disease because of what are called negative vibrations in their life. These vibrations may be proceeding from other people, or from the very house in which the sufferer lives: a disease in these cases being the result of the ability of the patient's unconscious mind to psychometrize and pick up these vibes and tell him that he must be sick.

Everyone, unconsciously, is a psychometrizer and picks up such vibrations, feelings, energy fields—whatever you wish to call them. You may not have a dramatic psychometric ability at the conscious level; but unguessed, unsuspected by you, you are constantly being affected by your surroundings and by other people.

Regrettably, your conscious mind has been trained since you were a small child to ignore these low-level feelings because, after all, anything you can't explain in concrete terms *must* be the work of the devil. "You must love your neighbor (that is, unless you are 'odd')." If you respond "But I don't like him," but cannot give a "real" or "objective" reason, you are suspected of being crazy.

This constant training and bombardment of your mind with anti-occult ideas has its own side-effects. If an occultist comes to you and says, "This jewel may help you," your mind immediately turns on its warning siren and cautions, "This is what I have been taught to avoid." Consequently, all too often, the mind deliberately prohibits the jewel from doing its healing work. Now, as you will see in Chapter 8, when you are dealing with other people and healing other people, you can prevaricate so they will believe that what you are giving them will heal them; and their minds, trusting you, will allow the healing procedure to have the desired effect.

However, when you are healing yourself, you cannot consciously select a jewel of a specified metal and shape and expect it to cure you, or even to relieve your symptoms, when your mind has been trained to reject totally the possibility of such a result. In order to avoid this resistance when you are selecting a jewel to help in your own disease, you should do as Cheryl did with Kay's display of jewels. You should use the psychometric ability that you developed in accordance with the training methods outlined in Chapter 1 to psychometrize the jewel and merely to identify the one that feels "good" to you; in this way, the conscious mind knows and accepts that this amulet feels "good" without reference to any possible healing ability it may have.

If, on the other hand, you are a practicing occultist and know how well these methodologies work, it is far better for you to use the arcane tables to select your amulet with care and accuracy; because the more effort and care you, as an experienced occultist, invest in its selection, the better it will work for you.

We have no way of telling you ahead of time which mind-set you have, whether favorable to the occult without any trained-in reservations, or negative anti-occult. You must make this diagnosis for yourself. You can, as Cheryl did, buy an amulet selected in accordance with Table 7–2 and its guidelines; and if that doesn't work, go to a dealer in occult objects and psychometrize the available amulets, letting your sensing hand tell you which one feels good to you. It is most probable that this jewel, the one you select through your own capabilities, will be accepted by your conscious mind and will be able to work successfully on your illness without interference from your conscious mind. But you cannot fool yourself. You must decide what your mind-set is before you can select a jewel with certitude for your individual needs.

YOUR HEALING TABLE OF COLORS

You have been trained from earliest youth to make certain emotional color associations. In the western world, black is associated with death and funerals; white is associated with love and purity. In contrast, if you had been brought up in China under the benign doctrines of Confucianism, you would connect white with funerals and black with beauty and strength. Table 1-1 shows the associations trained into the minds of most people brought up in the western world.

Psychiatric experiments have proven over and over again that these colors are intimately connected with your thought patterns, both conscious and subconscious. From this research, we know that, for instance, certain colors help people become less nervous and can be used to cure nervousness; and that other colors, conversely, make people more nervous and can therefore be used to cure conditions of lethargy and passiveness. Table 7–3 shows a comparison between color and disease. Again we should warn you that this table is applicable only to those who have been brought up in the matrix of western culture.

Now is the time to add color to your healing medicine bag and to your amulets. The first step is to dye your medicine bag the color which you can select from Table 7–3 for your particular needs. The second step is to use a correctly colored natural-fiber ribbon to suspend your amulet next to the diseased spot on or in your body.

BELL LABORATORIES AND THEIR THINKING-ROOMS

Many major industrial firms have what are called "think-tanks." Probably the best known of these are the Rand Corporation think-tank in California and the Bell Labs think-tank in New Jersey. These

Illness	Body Part	Color
Ulcer, Epilepsy Diarrhea	Ankles	Violet
Insomnia, Tumor Irritation	Feet	Lavender
Arthritis, Blood Pressure Depression, Exhaustion	Head	Scarlet
Polio, Melancholy Tuberculosis	Neck	Red
Constipation Hepatitis, Diabetes	Hands, Arms Lungs	Yellow
Bronchitis, Digestion Circulation	Breast Stomach	Amber
Mononucleosis Cramps, Thyroid	Heart, Spine Arms, Wrists	Orange
Cerebral Palsy Retardation	Hands, Abdomen Intestines	Chartruese
Fever, Hypertension Blood Disease	Lower Back Kidneys	Emerald
Impotence Muscle Tension	Pelvis Genitalia	Turquoise
Shingles Goiter	Hips, Thighs Liver	Blue
Glaucoma Palsy	Knees, Bones Skin	Indigo

Table 7–3
Color and Healing

think-tanks employ top-flight scientists whose job it is to think out solutions for today's problems. Such highly intelligent and intensely emotional scientists have found that sometimes their thoughts run ahead of them but at other times their mind seems to refuse to function.

As an aid to these highly paid specialists, most think-tanks (specifically that of Bell Laboratories) have colored rooms where the scientists can go to find the atmosphere they need. When the scientists have a specific problem, they pick the room that is most likely to help. The cool blue room will slow them down so that their thought processes can be more rational; but the harsh red room will speed them up and give them angry-type emotions to make them forcibly attack the problem at hand.

COLOR YOUR CEILING HEALTH

Just as large companies like Bell Labs invest millions of dollars in think-tank aids, so you can, on a smaller scale, dramatically improve your life, by coloring whole rooms in your home with emotion-keyed colors; or if you have a specific problem, you can merely paint the ceiling of your bedroom in the appropriate color taken from Table 7–3.

Let us say that you are asthmatic. In the general color scheme of your home, you should avoid the light bright colors and rely more heavily on subdued wood tones. In your bedroom, you should specifically color the ceiling dark orange and, if you can afford it, you should use dark orange throws and covers on the furniture and the bed. When you make these changes, you will be automatically exposed for several hours of each day to healing energy specifically tuned to your own individual needs. You will have emulated in your home the trick that the multi-million-dollar company uses to help itself; and all it cost you was a few dollars' worth of paint.

BLUE-EYED MARION DOES IT TO HERSELF

We first met Marion D. at a conference in Chicago where she had come to seek advice on her apparently incurable asthma. To put the matter bluntly, she was a physical wreck. Almost every second word she spoke required the use of an inhaler. She could hardly eat because of her continuous wheezing and retching. What could have been an attractive 25-year-old woman looked like a 50-year-old bag of bones. Her only remaining attractive feature was her beautiful, slate-blue eyes. Though they were heavy-lidded and dark-ringed, they were still an unusual and compelling color which Marion had always played up, as the beauty handbooks told her, by color-keying her wardrobe to her eyes, wearing only blue and gray and silver. When we met her, we were totally engulfed in blue energy.

Marion had been everywhere in her attempts to get her asthma cured. She had even undergone a painful operation designed to strengthen her throat muscles. We spent a lot of time counselling her, but we could identify nothing in her life-style or background that would explain her crippling infirmity. Finally, the answer dawned on us, and we told her to wear orange clothes. She, of course, immediately protested, "But they won't match my eyes. I always wear blue!"

What Marion had been doing since her school days was to surround herself with blue—which is the antithesis of the color she needed to help cure the minor asthmatic tendency she had inherited. Her constant exposure to blue-keyed energy had turned this minor inherited tendency into a genuine disability.

The next time we met Marion, we literally failed to recognize her, so much had she changed from a bag of bones to a curvaceous career woman. Rather than the bright oranges we had suggested she wear, she had compromised on tawny browns and rosy apricot tones, which were almost as effective—as well as very becoming—to her blond hair, which we had earlier perceived as just mousy. Hey eyes, no longer swollen, danced as she told us of improved health, job promotions, a new sports car, her new beige-tawny wardrobe, and an extremely active social life.

This is another example of the way people are subconsciously affected by Meta-Psychometry. Quite unwittingly, Marion had intensified her own disease. Look at your surroundings, with Marion's story in mind. Have you overemphasized one favorite color? And this color that you have overemphasized, has it now caused you to feel a little ill? Ask yourself, "Wouldn't I feel better if I exchanged this color so prominent in my life for another one?" If the answer to this question is "yes," don't delay! Get out and bring something fresh and positive into your personal world. You may, by doing so, save yourself from a debilitating disease in the future.

OTHER PEOPLE'S VIBRATIONS CAN BE DANGEROUS

I am sure you have met people whom you just don't like to be around. There is not necessarily a trait you can pin down; they just put out "feelings" which you would rather not associate with. Often what you are picking up is that they are sick and are putting out powerful vibes containing the energy of their sickness. These vibrations will make you sick, too, if you stay around them for any length of time without adequate protection.

In reflecting on this, you may think that all you need to do is to depart from the place where the detested person is and you will be all right; but that is not necessarily true. When a person puts out powerful vibes, he impresses those vibes or "astral energy potentials" into his surroundings; and, quite unsuspectingly, you can be affected Meta-Psychometrically by the impressed astral energy—even when the person has long been buried.

MAVIS GETS A BONUS

Mavis Q is employed as an executive secretary by a St. Louis aerospace firm. She had worked her way up through the ranks and was next in line for promotion. She was fully trained and extremely capable; yet, as soon as she took over Paula C's desk outside the office of the division vice president, she seemed to go to pieces.

Curiously, Paula, too had been fired because, abruptly, soon after her promotion, she had seemed to become a scatterbrained incompetent. Again, when Paula had been promoted into the job, she had seemed the logical choice, but the change in her convinced everyone that Paula had been promoted beyond her level of competence.

Fortunately, Mavis had been taking our meditation training* program. During one of her home practice sittings, she asked for guidance in becoming more effective in her job. She got a long, rambling answer from her Guide: it said, in summary, that the plant had been built directly over an ancient Indian burial mound, and that her desk was positioned directly over the burial site of an elderly chief who had good cause to detest everything brought to the St. Louis area by whites. The only positive idea she received was something she interpreted as "protect yourself."

When her meditation session was over, she called us; and we told her that since her work space was pretty well fixed, and since she had to work in it, she could either get a new job or follow the advice given in meditation and use some form of protection against the astral energies that were affecting her. She decided that, rather than give up the job which she found so rewarding, she would go the second route; so she asked us to develop some form of adequate protection for her against the lingering resentment of the Indian chief. We promised to do our

_____
*See Appendix.

best and said that if she would call the following evening, we would have something for her to use.

When she came to the house, we gave her four horseshoes and six or seven old bent nails. We told her to place the horseshoes, with their points downward, one against each wall of her office, and to conceal the nails under the carpeting near her chair. The very next day, she was happily on the phone to report a dramatic improvement in her working conditions and in her ability to concentrate. We warned Mavis that, each weekend, she should take home the horseshoes and the nails, and boil them for three minutes in salted water.

After she had been following this technique for a few weeks, she told us that her boss had begun to haunt her office, because, as he said, it felt so much better than his own. Mavis was the complete executive secretary and, of course, was fully in her boss's confidence. She finally felt secure enough with him to tell him, in a quiet moment, what she was doing with the horseshoes and the nails, and why. He decided he should try the same technique in his office, figuring he had nothing to lose; he found that it also improved his working conditions.

In a very unofficial meeting, the vice president asked the firm's supervisors whether any of them had negative feelings about their offices. Several of them admitted that they preferred to work away from their own desks and spent very little time in their offices. On the pretext of renovating the plant, new office areas were constructed away from the area of the desecrated graves. The firm's efficiency improved so conspicuously that the head office gave the division a substantial bonus. Mavis, of course, got quite a share of this money; her boss realized that without her and her "weird occult" ideas, his division would have continued to produce mediocre results.

PROTECT YOURSELF WITH
META-PSYCHOMETRIC TECHNIQUES

Through psychometric techniques combined with meditation, Mavis was able to remove what appeared to be a nervous disability. There are many lessons to be learned from Mavis' problem and its remedies; from both the cure which she used and that which her boss arranged for his supervisors.

Psychometry works on everyone, often to such an extent that it can be regarded as Meta-Psychometry. Impressed negative vibes or astral energy can make your life a misery unless you either protect yourself adequately against them or are able to move away from them. As you learned earlier in this chapter, some metals put out positive energy; however, this is not the way to fight powerful impressed astral energy. What is needed is something to absorb the negative energy, the horseshoes and the nails filled this requirement for Mavis.

The age-old protective device, the horseshoe, with its open end pointing in the direction from which the astral energy is coming, is one of the finest protective devices ever discovered. In Mavis' case, the ends were pointed downward at the Indian chief's grave site. If you feel you are being attacked with negative energy from afar, the ends of the horseshoes should be pointed horizontally toward the direction from which you think the attack is coming.

Bent nails are also an excellent protective device, because they seem to disturb and change astral energy fields. You will notice in the table of recommended metals that iron is not used. This is because it is such a good absorber of energy that it gives out very little energy to help in healing.

Since iron absorbs energy, it must periodically be cleansed. Almost any high-temperature treatment will suffice for this purpose, provided the temperature is kept above that of boiling water. If you are fortunate enough to have access to an open fireplace, throw your horseshoes into it occasionally; they will work so much the better after this seemingly harsh treatment.

Of course, you should be aware that, at the instant the iron absorber hits the high-temperature fire, there will be a sudden release of negative energy; however, since you are expecting it, you can easily guard against it by using a standard protective magic Circle. The Circle is constructed by simply drawing a circle of salt on the floor around yourself and saying the words, "I am surrounded by the pure white light of the God; nothing but good shall come to me," as you stand facing east within it. Stay within the Circle while the iron absorbers are being heated in the fire. Once the objects are hot, you can safely leave your protected area.

To summarize: For best Meta-Psychometric protection, you should use iron-absorbing objects such as horseshoes, or field-disturbing objects such as bent nails; and when you wish to purge the absorbed energy from these objects, you should protect yourself with a magic Circle.

YOUR COMPLETE META-PSYCHOMETRIC HEALING PROCEDURE

Does all this seem far too complex for you to be able to use when you are ill? It really isn't, you know; it is really very simple.

Step 1–Find out what is wrong with you. An ordinary office visit to your physician should accomplish this.

Step 2–Look up in Table 7–1, and obtain the objects you need to have in your medicine bag to aid in your recovery.

Step 3–Look up in Table 7–3 the color the medicine bag itself should be.

Step 4–If it is a long-term illness, look up in Table 7–2, and select a jewel of the correct metal type and shape that is best for you to wear. Either buy or have made an appropriate jewel, remembering to use a ribbon of the correct color to suspend it on your person.

Step 5–Look up in Table 7–3 the color that will aid your recovery, and bring more of that color into your life, either by purchasing a new outfit of clothing or by taking the longer-term step of painting your bedroom ceiling in the favorable color.

These are the simple, straightforward steps you can take to heal yourself Meta-Psychometrically; however, you should not stop here. You should use the psychometric ability you developed in Chapter 1 to find out whether or not you are being unduly influenced by negative astral energy. If you are being so influenced, you have two choices:

1. Move away from that influence (whether it be a person or a place).

2. Protect yourself against that person or place through the use of various iron astral energy absorbers.

In conclusion, let us again say that we have little idea today as to *why* these techniques are so successful, why certain places like Lourdes exude healing energy, and others (like perhaps the Bermuda Triangle) are so destructive. Further research is obviously needed, and more statistical analysis is urgently required. When you have successfully healed yourself, therefore, would you be kind enough to write to us and tell us of your success?

HEALING OTHERS WITH MEDI-PSYCHOMETRY

THE WHOLE WORLD SEEMS TO BE SICK

One of the most rewarding things you can do with your developed Meta-Psychometric ability is to help heal someone who is ill. The technique that you learned in Chapter 7 for healing yourself can now be extended to the healing of others. We are indeed fortunate in the western world to have medical aid that is readily available; but there are thousands, if not millions, of people who still need something more than the approach offered by orthodox medical practitioners. Thousands of these sufferers, of course, would be cured if they could face the fact that they should really see a psychiatrist; but thousands more have diseases that seem beyond the present capabilities of either the psychiatrist or of the physician.

Case after case of people being permanently disabled by arthritis comes to our attention. We all know that such illnesses as multiple sclerosis, cancer, cysticfibrosis, and emphysema are becoming more amenable each year to conventional treatment. But today patients with these and many other illnesses suffer their lot with little hope of a genuine cure.

It is far better for these people that you attempt to cure them than it is to leave them in this slough of despond. When you first start these efforts, you may be discouraged by what seems like a lack of success, but suddenly success will come; and even if as few as one in twenty of your early attempts are successful, you will find that this percentage is reward enough. We must caution you not to hold out hope to people after your best shots have gone astray, for this is patently unfair. In these cases, for some reason which we may learn only on the Other Side, the patient is doomed to endure. If you have followed our Medi-Psychometric techniques precisely, do not blame yourself for an apparent failure, for it is not your fault. When a person *can* be psychically cured, the techniques we will give you will do the job.

This Medi-Psychometric work is not a place to hide your light under a bushel, for success breeds confidence and confidence breeds more success. You should stand at center stage. You should welcome newspaper publicity of your success, for that very publicity will bring you more success with the unfortunate people who will come to you for help. Please note in this context that if you hold unorthodox religious beliefs as we do, it is wise not to get the beliefs publicized along with your healing work. The word "Witch," for instance, immediately starts a whole series of negative thoughtforms when it is said to a Christian; and this is not the climate you want to create if you are going to heal successfully.

In any successful healing, the first step is obviously to find out what is wrong with the patient. This is where your developed psychometric ability will be extended and used.

THE BUDDHIST DOCTOR AMAZES THE HOSPITAL

Yeshi Donden was the personal physician of the Dalai Lama; Dr. Donden is an unprepossessing, stocky Tibetan who wears a traditional saffron robe and sandals and shaves his head. His appearance alone was enough to make the establishment doctors suspicious when he was invited to an American hospital to examine a critically ill patient. As Dr. Selzer reported in *Harper's Magazine,* this suspicion turned to amazement when Dr. Donden made the report of his findings to a group of American physicians. He accurately diagnosed the fact that the patient had what we would call in western terms, "congenital heart disease with a septal defect." Dr. Donden's analysis, however, did not use these clinical expressions. What he said was:

"Between the chambers of the heart, long, long before she was born, a deep gate had been opened that should never be opened and through it the waters of her river of life cascade."

How had the Tibetan doctor arrived at his diagnosis? All he had done was hold the patient's hand for nearly half an hour and concentrate on the emanations he received from her; additionally, he had examined a urine sample. When we say "examined" her, we don't mean a big chemical analysis; nor did he poke or prod or ask any questions; he just held her hand and used his developed abilities to read her disease from the emanations he received. To an observer, he seemed simply to look at her, instead of subjecting her to the discomfort of all the batteries of tests that modern hospitals require.

Dr. Donden had stood by her bedside and comforted her; yet, he was able to give an accurate diagnosis of her critical condition—of a patient whom he saw for the first time that day and about whom he previously had known nothing. The patient had been told, of course, that she would be examined by a foreign doctor and that this doctor would be accompanied by a group of the hospital's own physicians; so when the group first approached her, she was rather nervous, for she had been subjected to many uncomfortable examinations before.

Dr. Donden spoke only Tibetan, so he could not communicate directly with the patient. He actually said nothing to her; yet, by simply standing there and holding her hand, he was able to relax her, to comfort her, and to give her some of his store of serenity. As he left, she quietly thanked him for the time he had spent with her. Yet outwardly he had done nothing but hold her hand.

It is this same serenity and comfort that you too should instill into a gravely ill person when you do your Medi-Psychometric diagnosis.

START DEVELOPING YOUR ABILITY TODAY

The first step in any development of your Medi-Psychometric ability is to review the procedure in Chapter 1 to make sure that your fingertip Meta-Psychometry detector is still at peak sensitivity. Then take twelve slips of paper and write on them the twelve illness groups listed in Table 8–1. Place these slips of paper in clean white envelopes and shuffle them as you would a deck of cards. Now, number the outside of the envelopes and make yourself a table, as shown in Figure 8–1. Work your first trial by entering the number of the envelope you feel is associated with the illness in the column opposite the illness, as shown in Figure 8–1. For the second trial, you should place a card over the column of figures that you completed earlier so that during Trial 2

Group 1	Group 2	Group 3
Thyroid	Mental Retardation	Fever
Mononucleosis	Cerebral Palsy	Blood Diseases
Menstrual Cramps	Colitis	Hypertension

Group 4	Group 5	Group 6
Boils, Burns	Nausea	Glaucoma
Impotence	Shingles	Shaking Palsy
Muscle Tension	Goiter	Pimples

Group 7	Group 8	Group 9
Ulcer	Insomnia	Arthritis
Epilepsy	Irritation	Blood Pressure
Diarrhea	Tumor	Depression, Exhaustion

Group 10	Group 11	Group 12
Polio	Constipation	Bronchitis
Melancholia	Hepatitis	Circulation
Tuberculosis	Diabetes	Digestion

Table 8–1

Illnesses by Group

Envelope Number	Trial[1]					Best Choice	Actual[2] Illness
	1	2	3	4	5		
1							
2							
3							
4							
5							
6							
7							
8							
9							
10							
11							
12							

Figure 8–1

Development Test Chart

---

[1] Enter the illness group you psychomertize.
[2] From actual slip in the envelope.

you cannot see the numbers of the envelopes you selected in Trial 1. After five trials, list in the "best choice" column the numbers that you most often came up with for each of the illnesses. Now open the envelopes and, in the "actual illness" column of the figure, list the correct numbers for each illness. The first time you try this experiment, you may get only four or five of the numbers correct; but after eight or nine trials (remembering each time to use new envelopes), you will find that you are able to detect the emanations and get nine or ten of the illnesses correct.

Statistically, even if you get only two correct in your first trial, you are still doing far better than random chance; and when you get up to nine or ten correct, you are doing as well as the most developed psychic can—and as well as many Medical Doctors can with all their diagnostic aids.

YOU, TOO, CAN MEDI-PSYCHOMETRIZE OTHERS

In the actual psychometrizing of a patient, the first step is to establish a serene climate. If you glance at Table 7–3, you will see that if the patient is tense, for instance, she[1] would put out what we have referred to as emerald emanations—and you as diagnostician might be led to believe that she had back or kidney problems. Similarly, if the patient is depressed, you might diagnose arthritis, for the depression emanation would mask the true problem. Therefore your first task is to establish an atmosphere of placid serenity and rapport with the patient. After this atmosphere is established, we recommend you hold the patient's hands or place your hand on her forehead, and concentrate on feeling the Medi-Psychometric emanations in the same way that you felt the emanations in your practice sessions in the foregoing paragraph. When you have felt these emanations and in your own mind have decided what is wrong with the patient, then you can ask what the physician had diagnosed, for now this information will no longer confuse your conscious mind or bias your Medi-Psychometric reading.

Now is the time for the appropriate Medi-Psychometric treatment to aid the doctor's work in the healing of the patient. In most cases, this will be the same medicine bag that you would have used for yourself, and it should be constructed by following the instructions in Chapter 7. Some patients will resist this approach because they will feel it represents a quack remedy. In these cases, you should subtly introduce the appropriate color changes by suggesting, for instance,

---

[1]Throughout this chapter, we refer to patients as "she," though we could equally well have used "he."

that the patient eat a red fruit three times a day or have a green salad with each meal. You should also conduct a ritual at home to send more energy to the patient, either directly or through the medium of a charged psycho-store that you place in the patient's room. You can perform this ritual either by yourself or, more desirably, with a small group of dedicated friends. When you work with a group, you are able to take the power they voluntarily donate and direct it toward your goal. This support from other persons very much enhances your probability of a successful healing.

HEALING IS BOTH PSYCHIC AND SOMATIC

Often in our lectures we have some fun with the audience by asking those people who have had a broken limb to volunteer to come up on the stage. When they do so, we give them a little life reading. We say such things as, "You had one strict parent; yes or no?" With older people, we tell them, "You have had more than one marriage and you went back to college after interrupting your education." The statistics are so much in our favor in these off-the-cuff analyses that we are wrong only perhaps once in a hundred cases.

This is no great psychic, occult, or psychometric analysis; it is an analysis that was statistically conducted years ago, showing the intimate connection between the psychic and the somatic parts of an illness.[2] Any person showing a certain cluster of traits is liable to certain illnesses. Even such mundane things as broken bones follow this universal law. If you have ever broken a bone, beware: you are likely to break another one. Even though you pay moderately close attention to your health and are indeed in quite good health, broken bones will continue to be a hazard throughout your life. You have unconsciously absorbed into your being characteristics that make you prone to broken bones; though if, as we said in Chapter 7, you dramatically change your life-style, you can avoid this problem.

As a healer, you must now extend this two-fold psychic and somatic approach to your work with other people; for illnesses are caused by both mundane, bodily, "somatic" breakdowns, and psychically by the absorption from their surroundings and the transmission to them of energy from other people.

Remember that all diseases are partially psychic and partially somatic. When you go into a patient's home, you should psychometrize it, just as you learned to psychometrize your surroundings in Chapter 3; you should also psychometrize the emanations from the patient's

---

[2]Flanders Dunbar, MD, Ph.D., *Emotions and Bodily Changes* (4th ed.; New York: Columbia University Press, 1954).

family and friends to see whether any of these are causing the disease. If you can locate the psychic source of the patient's disease and can cure this, then you are well on the way to curing at least half the problem.

FRANCES R MOVES TO HEALTH

Frances R, an attractive blond in her late twenties, lived with her mother. To anyone glancing at her life, she would seem to have no problems; she had a good job and was beginning to think seriously about finding a husband and forming a life that would combine some work, some play, and some affection. But she started to notice a pattern in her life that was preventing her from forming that wished-for liaison. The problem was this:

As soon as she became serious about any young man, she would begin having irregular menstrual cycles that caused an extremely heavy loss of blood. After a very thorough physical examination, her gynecologist convinced her that the problem was psychic; there was nothing wrong with her body except a mild anemia caused by her continuing loss of blood. He connected the fact that every time she got serious about a young man, she had menstrual irregularity; so he persuaded her to see a psychiatrist.

After six months of psychiatric care, the problem seemed to be cured. Of course, during this time, Frances had no suitor. Who wants to date a woman with psychosomatic illnesses, after all? At least this was her own unspoken belief. But after some three months of regular, comfortable periods, in her new-felt confidence Frances met her ideal mate, the one and only dream man for her. No sooner had she satisfied herself that he was an ideal partner than she was disturbed to find that her menstrual cycle was again acting up. She was afraid that if she went back to the psychiatrist and let her new friend know about it, he would drop her—but if she didn't tell him about it and he later found out, it would be disaster. So as a last hope she wrote to us, asking how she could get out of her dilemma.

Quite frankly we were puzzled, for it seemed to us that the physician and the psychiatrist had made an accurate diagnosis. When we asked for a photo, Frances sent one showing herself and her mother standing side by side. In Medi-Psychometrizing this photo, we found that the mother's emanation pattern was totally empty of emerald-green color. Her mother had been rather older than most women at the birth of her first child; she had begun the menopause when Frances was five; but even this did not account for the total deficiency in her love-pleasure-joy green emanations. We eventually determined that the mother was extremely concerned about her own future if Frances should marry and move away, and to prevent Frances' marrying, she had become an unconscious psychic vampire. She had literally sucked away Frances' green emanations and had unwittingly caused Frances her problems.

Our advice to Frances was to move away from her mother. As soon as she did so, her menstrual problems ceased, even though her relationship with her fiance had become (for Frances) daringly intimate. After a relatively short period of readjustment, Frances' mother took a job, found new friends through her church, and altogether became a more complete person.

Of course, we could have supplied Frances with extra green emanations, but we felt that this would not help the mother to start a new life; in fact, it would have been a treatment of the symptom, not the disease. So we chose instead to advise Frances to move before she became trapped irrevocably in her mother's dependence.

PSYCHIC ENERGY DEFICIENCIES CAUSE ILLNESS

A balanced person, serenely at rest, has a balanced output of emanations. When you Medi-Psychometrize your patient, you are feeling for excess or deficient emanations in some part of his spectrum. Thus you can consider psychic illnesses to be deficiency diseases, because the excess energy that you detect flowing from the patient causes in her a deficiency in energy of that color.

Let us say you baked a cake with a nicely balanced set of ingredients; the cake would have a pleasant flavor. If you now had some way of extracting all the sugar from the cake, the cake would not taste as good; it would not be balanced. A deficiency disease works in the same way. The patient is losing something which is not being replaced. On the mundane level, a patient can be deficient in, say, iodine, in which case she'll get goiter. Medi-Psychometry works in energy deficiencies which are just as important to good health as a well-balanced diet.

You have seen how surroundings and tension and things of this nature can cover up or disguise the patient's real problem—that problem which you must diagnose in order to help her. The medicine bag that you learned to construct for yourself in Chapter 7 cures by replacing your lost energy; again, the sugar in the cake. This is shown pictorially in Figure 8–2. The little stick figure in diagram 8–2a is losing energy which must be replaced by gaining energy from some source so that a new balance is achieved, as shown in diagram 8–2b. This is where you, the healer, come in. The source of this replacement energy will be yourself alone, or yourself in combination with friends, or it will be a medicine bag that you construct. When you personally

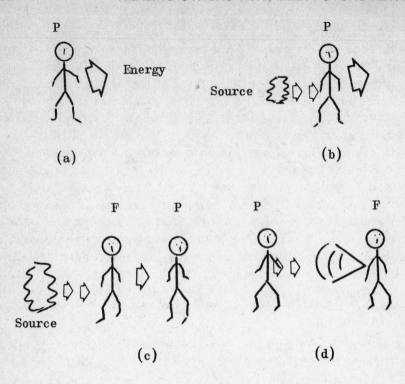

Figure 8-2
Energy Flows

supply the energy, you need to remember, of course, to replace it in your own field; otherwise, you will become as ill as the original patient, because you, in turn, will be creating your own psychic-deficiency disease (Figure 8–2c). Thus, when you have a patient who is emitting a large amount of green energy, for instance, you know that additional green has to be supplied to him to keep him in balance until the illness can be cured. If you are going to supply that energy, you too will have an energy deficiency which you must make up by adjusting upward the green emanations in your own medicine bag. In the case of Frances and her mother, we had what might be called a vacuum-cleaner situation in the mother, wherein she was sucking out Frances' energy (Figure 8–2d). Here, to cure Frances, you need either to supply Frances with more energy or to move the mother away so that she cannot draw on Frances so easily.

Every situation you come into will have its own little quirks and

peculiarities. You must be wide awake to detect interpersonal sub-
tleties, so that you can supply the right energies to the right people to
cure the psychic part of any disease.

LETTERS AND PHOTOS DON'T TELL THE WHOLE STORY

Once people begin to know that you are able to help them with
their medical problems, you will be asked to analyze hundreds of cases;
many people will want you to do this even by mail. Until you have
gained several years' experience, you should attempt to analyze only
patients whom you can actually visit. In Frances' case, we were, quite
frankly, lucky that the photo she sent showed her mother and that this
gave us a clue to the underlying problem. After years of practice, many
psychic healers can diagnose problems from photographs and letters
from the patient. You should be aware that oftentimes this is a
difficult procedure; after all, you have little or no idea of the patient's
state of mind at the time the photo was snapped or the letter was
written. In these cases, you should specifically discount any emanations you feel of such things as hypertension and depression, for
oftentimes the patient didn't want his photo taken or didn't want to
write the letter to a "swami," but is being pushed into it by some
concerned relative.

Remember also, as you learned in earlier chapters, that inanimate objects such as houses can act as both energy suppliers and
energy vacuums, and you should insist on visiting a patient in her own
home surroundings so you can analyze them just as you did in your own
personal surroundings, making suggestions on a total curative procedure rather than using a piecemeal approach. Obviously, with all of
these interactions to be studied, you should never make a hasty judgment; if at all possible, you should avoid any diagnosis until you can
make a personal analysis of all the factors.

GEORGE'S DAUGHTERS WERE NOT POSSESSED

George C, an accountant in a South American republic, was a
student of our School. He wrote to us one day very urgently because
his youngest daughter Rosa seemed to have an inexplicable, yet quite
serious, illness. She was unable to concentrate in school and wanted
nothing more than to stay at home and go for long walks in the
afternoons. He had taken her to three local doctors and had started her
on some sessions with a psychologist. All these worthy men were
unable to find anything significantly wrong with this strictly reared
teen-ager.

In response to his urgent letter, we asked George to send us a recent photograph of Rosa and a private letter written by her to us explaining her problem. A couple of weeks later we got a letter, not from Rosa but from George. We were obviously not very capable healers, he wrote: at the same time he had written us, he had also sought help from two other cosmic-wisdom or occult schools in the United States. One school had replied that Rosa was obviously hexed by George's jealous next-door neighbor; another had said that she had been hexed by her boyfriend, who had worked a love spell on her. In both cases, the advice was to confine Rosa to the house for the following week and to do various protective rituals for her around the house twice a day. George wrote in great jubilation that the recommended rituals had been performed, and Rosa seemed cured and was planning to return to school on the day of his writing.

A week later we received another letter from George. This one said his dear Rosa was as bad as ever—and his two elder girls, who had been visiting from nursing school in the capital, were also sick, apparently with the same disease, and refused to return to the capital. They, too had poor appetites; they too wanted to stay in the house except for afternoon walks; they too were very lethargic. It took all he could do just to get them to dress before lunch.

Again we wrote to George; again we told him we could do nothing for him until he sent up-to-date photos of the girls and had them write to us; again he refused to cooperate. By now he had received further instructions from his other psychic sources, telling him specifically who had placed the hex on his daughters. Further, the instructions continued, if he worked "the enclosed spell" at full moon, the girls would be cured. The next letter we got from George did in fact contain the photos we had been waiting for all this time, but still no letters from the girls. He ruefully admitted that the hex-on-the-hexer ritual had no perceptible effect on the girls' symptoms.

By now George was getting desperate. His three strictly reared daughters were treating him like dirt. All his plans for their going to medical school seemed to be destroyed. His carefully organized and strictly virtuous life was falling apart around his ears.

One glance at the photos of Rosa, Carlotta, and Dora was enough to disclose the whole story. It was—to summarize in one word—*pot*. Rosa's boyfriend was supplying all three with quite potent marijuana. The girls were sophisticated enough to abstain before being rushed off by frantic George to a doctor's appointment; but they had been so strictly reared that they would not disclose to a doctor or even to a psychologist what was going on, because (as we might have guessed) the marijuana had also been accompanied by a certain amount of sexual experimentation.

If George had not been so closed-minded, he might have spotted the truth himself; but he was so convinced by his other occult advisors that there was a hex, or perhaps a possession, operating here, that he could not perceive the more mundane explanation. Of course the girls didn't want to go back to the capital! Of course they didn't feel like resuming their classes at medical school! They were having a ball, and they certainly didn't want George to spoil their fun. Thus what could be considered to be perfectly normal behavior on the part of three healthy young women who had finally broken the bounds of their suppressive upbringing became a couple of months of terror and panic. Their worried father was willing to grasp at any straw, but until his back was to the wall, he would not take the necessary realistic steps that provided the psychic readers whom he contacted with sufficient information to do their work.

MEDI-PSYCHOMETRY CHANGES DIS-EASE TO EASE

Your whole aim with Medi-Psychometry should be to avoid subjecting your patients to the stresses that George and his daughters encountered. When a person is dis-eased, your first aim should be to bring as much ease into that person's life as possible. It is difficult to do this from a distance, especially in the early days of your career in healing. When you visit a patient in her home and family members are present, you should follow these rules scrupulously:

1. Just as the Tibetan doctor did, you should wear a saffron-colored garment with dull red or brown accessories. These colors inspire reposeful thoughts in the patient's mind. If you can't find saffron, a light yellow is permissible. Avoid all ornamentation, and dress "down" rather than "up." You are not going to the patient's home to make a big impression; you are going (hopefully) to blend with the background so that you can sit quietly and psychometrize the patient and her surroundings.

2. You will often find when you arrive that the patient is watching TV or listening to the radio. Now, unless she is listening to chamber music or watching educational TV, you have got to find a nice way to get her to turn everything off. One way we have found is to say something like, "I can't work around electrical appliances," thus assuming responsibility yourself for insisting on their removal. Then substitute for the light in the room a plain yellow candle. Part of the

therapy that you are going to recommend is a drastic cut in the time the patient spends watching TV and listening to the radio. Such programs as news broadcasts, soap operas, and hard rock are not designed to comfort or quiet a patient emotionally. They are designed to keep the listener's interest and to play on the emotions.

3. Be quiet and sedate. Do not put a time limit on the interview, and arrange with the family that there will be no interruptions during your stay. If the patient is highly tense, we would suggest you have her drink a warm glass of wine tonic. Such a wine tonic is made in the following manner:

2 cups boiling water
1 tbsp ground cinnamon
2 tbsp brown sugar
1 tsp ground nutmeg
¼ tsp ground ginger

Add all spices to boiling water and simmer very gently for five minutes.

Half-fill a large warmed cup with burgundy. Strain the simmering liquid into the burgundy until the cup is full. This recipe makes enough for two portions of tonic. You should drink one while the patient drinks the other, because it will relax you, too, thus enabling you to work more effectively.

4. When you have relaxed and quieted the patient, you can sit and soak up the atmosphere, holding the patient's hand if necessary, or her pulse, so as to get a closer rapport with her emotions. You will be looking for the same dis-ease emanations that you learned to read from your test envelopes earlier in this chapter.

5. Now you may ask the patient what the physician has said. If no doctor has seen the patient, we strongly recommend that you proceed no further until an RD (regular doctor) has been called in. If a physician has seen the patient, but his diagnosis strongly disagrees with your own—and you feel you are right and he is wrong—do not denigrate his diagnosis; instead, suggest that the family get a second opinion.

It is fashionable just now to criticize doctors. This is all very well when no specific patient is involved; but you certainly do very little good for the patient if you tell her you think she has a fool or a quack for a doctor.

6. With your psychometric analysis and the RD's diagnosis, you now can proceed to the supplementary healing work that you feel is most appropriate to give the patient psychic ease, while the RD works on the somatic problem and repairs the body of the patient.

SHAKE THE FEATHERS AND RATTLE THE GOURDS

The choice of the most appropriate method for attempting the cure of each patient concerns the psychic healer more than it does an RD, for you as a psychic healer are dealing in attitudes and feelings; you are dealing with some areas of the subconscious mind, and if you proceed in the wrong manner, the patient will set up mental blocks which you will not easily be able to overcome.

We are proud to claim as a personal friend a man who is probably the top exorcist in the United States; but Bill has a problem. His system of exorcism, which he has proved thousands of times to be effective, takes all of five minutes. His style of exorcism (not affiliated with any body of religious belief) involves no big exhortations or castings of holy water or screaming adolescents. Rather than donning the standard crucifix and magical priest-robe of the exorcist in popular mythos, Bill wears a western shirt and wash-and-wear slacks. A couple of times, people have left Bill who were totally cured, but still believed they were possessed, because Bill had not, as we say, "shaken the feathers and rattled the gourds" over them.

One day, two veterans of the Viet Nam conflict, veterans from whom Bill had successfully exorcised North Vietnamese spirits, came calling on the Witches. As Witches, we are naturally expected to put on a big show, and we did exactly that. The ritual we did was totally meaningless except in the minds of the two people to whom we did it. We burned some sulphur and exorcised away, shaking the censer with a will. Finally, at the height of the exorcism, we smashed a wine glass into the fire. Because the wine glass had a pinch of flash powder in it, this made for an extremely dramatic finale—one that fully convinced the two unfortunates that something important had really happened. They went away happy, and are still happy to this day, because of their conviction that they are rid of the malevolent spirits. We had not done anything except put on a show, but it had convinced their subconscious minds that they were cured.

This same show ("psychodrama" as it is now being called), which you can invent out of the whole cloth, will work perfectly with the person who believes himself to be possessed or hexed, whom your psychometry has shown to have no real problem other than a lack of confidence or a mental block. It is pure showmanship, but it works; and it is just as important in healing as the most careful and thorough procedure worked up by any RD. The results obtained through psychodrama are often dramatic.

Psychodrama does not replace long-term healing of physical illnesses. But occasionally, especially in cases of frigidity and impotence, it results in an immediate and total cure.

EDWIN REGAINS HIS POTENCY

Alicia is a very attractive 19-year-old Witch who clerks in a bookstore in Atlanta, Georgia. She called us in great concern one evening because, despite everything she could do, her latest conquest, Edwin, didn't seem to be able to turn on romantically at the right time. Edwin was worrying himself sick with the idea that he was really abnormal.

Alicia had followed all the standard Wicca practices to help Edwin, spending long hours with him, putting no pressure on him, and feeding him mild aphrodisiacs like sarsaparilla. During the month that she had been working with him, Alicia had become convinced that he was her soul mate and that she should do everything she could to make him "whole" again and be an appropriate all-round companion. It also came out in her phone call that Edwin had more than a million dollars in his own name; Alicia felt that some of this money could be used to help the occult movement and to start a healing foundation.

She had already convinced Edwin to go to a competent psychologist. She gathered from Edwin, after his visits to this man, that he did, in fact have a mental block caused by some unidentified traumatization in his youth. She asked us whether we could physically analyze his life in this incarnation so that the two of them could pin down the traumatization presently locked in Edwin's subconscious mind. Because this was a fairly definite case of a mental block, we suggested a very heavy ritual for him. This could be scheduled soon because we were going to be passing through the Atlanta area. But we didn't tell Alicia that this ritual would actually be something we dreamed up on the spot.

At midnight on the appointed day, Edwin was brought blind-folded and bound into the magic Circle. Great, ghastly shrieks startled his ears; incantations of unintelligible phrases boggled his mind. Sulphur was burned. Cymbals were crashed. Edwin was disrobed and lightly spanked. Some aromatic oil was rubbed on him. Altogether, we did as impressive a ritual as we could think up. As a finale, he drank wine from a glass which we then flung into the fire. As with the veterans of Viet Nam, we had put just a pinch of the right powder into the glass.

The following morning, Alicia assured us somewhat ruefully that Edwin was now more than fully potent.

YOU ARE THE PLUS FACTOR IN HEALING

Undoubtedly, Edwin's psychologist would eventually have rooted out the cause of his problem and cured him. We were able to do this rather more quickly by using the psychodrama of which Edwin was the central character. In the case of George C and his daughters, too, we were able to identify a very mundane problem and cure the girls on a purely practical level by cutting them off from their marijuana.

In any situation where healing seems needed, you must be constantly alert to look for the problems that the RD has not been made aware of, whether this RD is a psychologist or an MD. With his heavy load of patients, he is often unable to analyze fully all of the problems of any given patient; and today, of course, he does not often visit the home or feel its influence. The old-time small-town general practitioner knew everyone and visited his patients, thus becoming able to sense their problems more intimately. Today, it takes both a psychologist and a GP or specialist to give that same service; and even the two of them together do not make up the whole.

It is that *total* service that you are able to perform. Medi-Psychometrically you can analyze the patient and his surroundings, and you can fill in the gaps the RD's are unable to cover. You can be the plus factor in any healing.

MIRACLES DO HAPPEN

In this chapter, we have been discussing the standard everyday healings in which you can be of tremendous aid to the poor dis-eased people of this world. On a continuous basis, this is one of the most rewarding services you can possibly undertake. Occasionally, you will be called in on cases which have been given up as terminal by orthodox medical people. Once in a while, when you release your power for a healing in such cases, unexpected results will occur. In time past, these would have been categorized as miracles, and even today we are sometimes amazed at the almost magical results that can be achieved in healing efforts. So even in the most desperate of cases, you should at least try to heal. If the case seems to be quite hopeless, still, trying to cure costs you very little, perhaps a couple of hours of time from you and your friends of the healing Circle; and when total remissions occur in seemingly incurable cases, it makes you want to go on and achieve more and more.

BOB'S ARM STRAIGHTENED ITSELF

Bob C was a tire-maker working for the Firestone Company in Des Moines, Iowa. One day. he caught his wrist in the machine as the tire bead was being constructed. The heavy tire carcass wrapped around his wrist, snapping both bones and terribly lacerating the skin of his entire forearm. After several months of painful reconstruction effort, Bob was able to use his arm, but his hand motion was severely limited; and the best job he could get was that of a janitor. Besides being a tire-builder, Bob is also a gifted graphic artist, he is the editor and publisher of *Revival Magazine*, a leading publication on Craft and Wiccan matters.

When we were in Minneapolis teaching a group of people at the Gnosticon VI Psychic Festival how to do absent healing, we took the opportunity to work on Bob's injured arm. We will let you read Bob's own words as to the result of that absent healing, as he reported it in the Virgo 1976 CE issue of *Revival:*

> I've got some special 'Thank Yous' in order from my end, especially to Gavin and Yvonne Frost of the Church of Wicca. Yvonne and some 30 or so other folks at Gnosticon "worked" on my broken arm (I can't do a thing for myself), and the "bad" union of the radial is no longer crooked but absolutely straight. The muscles can function now without pain sensations, and I've increased the use and it's getting its old strength back again. Where it was limited before, I have almost recovered the full use; just give me a couple more weeks. By the way, the hair on that arm is even a little longer now. Thank you, everyone, may the Old Ones shower you with blessings. May your years be increased immensely . . .

These things will happen for you, too. For us, they seem to happen to this degree in about one in ten cases in which the RD's had given up hope of further improvement for the patient. You can do it, too.

YOUR STANDARD MEDI-PSYCHOMETRIC HEALING RITUAL

The class of thirty people who got together to learn about psychic healing had no idea beforehand that we were actually going to attempt a healing in the class meeting. They were from all walks of life. We had flower children as well as retired "blue-rinse" ladies, and even a hard-hat construction worker. Yet, after a half hour of instruction, these people were able to cause a miracle to happen. You and your friends can do exactly the same thing. It is childishly simple and, incidentally, children can do it too.

Sit around in a circle, either on wooden chairs or on the floor. So far as possible, have male alternating with female in the seating arrangement to balance the power. Arrange it so you can all comfortably hold hands. Now you, the Medi-Psychometrist, should explain to the group what you feel is the situation that you are going to attempt to cure. Explain color association and other tuning aids which you feel are appropriate to this healing. If possible, you should have in the center of the circle a piece of colored cloth of the color specified in Table 7–3 and a piece of the healing metal specified in Table 7–2. A candle of the appropriate color can also be used as a good focusing point for the group. You should get the group emotionally aligned with some singing of a light-hearted nature into which everyone can join in.

The actual procedure will take less than one minute. Have the members of the group hold hands for a moment and then, releasing their grip, position their hands with fingers parallel to one another and palms not quite touching. Each person's right-hand palm should be facing upward and each person's left-hand palm should be facing downward, not quite touching the palm of the person next to him. Before you do anything, see whether you can have the group feel the actual flow of power around the circle; most people will feel that their right palm is warm and their left palm is cool. Have them break the circle by clapping their hands, and the flow should cease.

Now re-establish the circle's flow of power, remembering to keep the fingers accurately aligned and the palms not quite touching. Begin now any repetitive chant you wish to use; we often recommend the "ee-aye-ee-aye-oh" from the chorus of "Old MacDonald's Farm." Gradually lead your friends to a louder and louder chant. At the peak of the chant, break the circle by clapping your hands together and shrieking at the top of your voice, "Heal X!", naming the patient.

It is usual then for the group to relax for a few moments before attempting another healing. We recommend that no more than three healings be tried in any given session. In our framework of religious belief, we ask the group to meditate before closing the session; but meditation is outside the scope of this book.

YOUR COMPLETE MEDI-PSYCHOMETRY HEALING GUIDE

We recommend that you take the following steps when you are approached be anyone who seeks healing:

1. Visit the patient in her own home surroundings; put her as much at ease as possible. Psychometrize the patient, her family, her friends, and the surroundings. Decide on the probable cause of her dis-ease.

2. Compare your diagnosis with the diagnosis of the RD. Decide in your own mind whether you or the doctor is closer to the truth. If the RD's diagnosis and your own are in wild disagreement but you feel strongly that yours is correct, recommend that the family get another opinion from a second RD.

3. Start your supplementary healing procedure. The first decision you must make is whether or not the patient will fully accept unorthodox procedures or whether, in fact, the patient needs unorthodox procedures to shake something loose in her subconscious. If the patient needs the impressive psychodrama ritual, do not hesitate to do one. If she will accept unorthodox procedures, make her a medicine bag as instructed in Chapter 7 and have her wear it. Also, adjust the color balance emanations in her room and make sure that none of the family or friends are psychic vampires. If they are psychic vampires, supply them also with medicine bags, or separate them by a great distance from the patient. Having the patient or the vampire move to a distant city is often best.

4. If your Medi-Psychometrizing of the patient leads you to believe that she will resist unorthodox practices, you should conduct the appropriate ritual in absentia. Choose a time when you know she will be at rest, so that her guard will be down and you can get through to her subconscious more easily.

We hope you will not read this chapter and lay it away as not being immediately rewarding to you. Both of us can positively assure you that when you get into helping people, people will help you; and your life will take on a far fuller meaning.

USE META-PSYCHOMETRY TO GAIN YOUR IDEAL MATE

SEX ISN'T EVERYTHING

In the western world, it seems that sexual compatibility is the top-ranked priority in the selection of a life companion.

Tragically, many young people put sexual compatibility and attraction at the very top of their priority list when it comes to signing that long-term contract called "marriage." Few if any of them really consider mundane compatibilities, and only one in a million considers the most important compatibility of all—psychic compatibility. If you are psychically compatible with another person, you have what in occult circles is called the "twin-soul" phenomenon: no matter what problems and stumbling blocks the world puts in the way of your mundane life together, your strong psychic compatibility will always bring you through the turmoil to eventual harmony.

No matter how sexually desirable that stranger seems at first glance, you should look to psychic compatibility before deciding that he or she is your ideal. If your present mating circumstance is not ideal,

Meta-Psychometry can help you; for through Meta-Psychometry you can:

1. Find your ideal twin soul.
2. Make love without becoming pair-bonded[1]
3. Break up unfruitful relationships without pain.

IT MAY NOT BE YOUR FAULT

Incompatible people can find all too many pretexts for getting married despite their unsuitability for each other. Some of the more popular excuses for marriage are:

- Loneliness
- Getting away from parents
- Two can live cheaper than one
- Stop the neighbors' talking
- Want sexual satisfaction
- File an orthodox income-tax return

No two people who are psychically incompatible should ever marry; if they are married, they should separate as soon as they can, for they will never be compatible. Very occasionally, they can be made compatible in a short-term sense with the aid of Meta-Psychometry, but even this is just a stop-gap measure.

When two people first meet, they are usually attracted to one another either by similar interests or by their differences. They either reinforce each other, or they complement one another. These situations are shown diagramatically in Figure 9–1. Figures 9–1a and 9–1b show the Law of Attraction of Sameness at work. These psychic fields meld and reinforce one another. Naturally the interests, being so similar, reinforce one another. Alternately, opposite (Figures 9–1c and 9–1d) fields meld and form a circle of completion; for between them they are interested in everything. This results in an interesting marriage, though not always a serene one.

In occult circles, the relationships just described are called "trines," and it is the Meta-Psychometric use of these trines that will help you identify your ideal mate. But Figures 9–1e and 9–1f show a situation where people are forced together by outside factors or by some of the reasons listed earlier in this section, though they are incompatible and will always remain so. Their fields do not meld; they

---

[1]"Pair-bonded" is the anthropological term for the phenomenon in which after copulation two animals are emotionally monogamous until the offspring are reared. In humans pair-bonding is often mistaken for love.

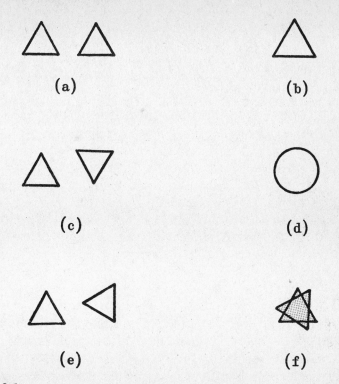

Figure 9-1
Examples of Psychic Compatibility

clash. It is not their fault that they clash, for no one has "sinned;" just like fire and water, though, they simply don't mix.

HEATHER QUICKLY OUTGROWS HER LOVER

Heather L was a quiet, pleasant senior at Texas A & M. In her final year, she was becoming more and more frustrated with herself because she kept seeing and hearing all the good things about sex from her sorority sisters: how great it was, how it made the whole world shine. Heather was born in mid-September and had the naturally reduced sex drive traditionally associated with those dates. Still, she felt that she was missing out on one of life's great experiences. She had tried in her sophomore year to dress sexily and to be attractive to men, but she had found that her grades had suffered during that time, so she had given up what she felt was a distraction.

Finally, almost in desperation, Heather contacted us through one of the covens on campus. We psychometrized her photograph to find that, although she was apparently attractive, she had rechanneled her sex drive into scholastic achievement and had so far repressed her sexual emanations, that they could not be detected from her photo. We turned this psychometric analysis into a Meta-Psychometric procedure by telling Heather to wear more clothing of turquoise and red; in other words, to increase artificially her emanations of desire and of adventure. The effect was, as we could have predicted, that she was soon able to choose a lover from among the several men who suddenly began to take notice of her in her new colors.

In those final months of college, Heather settled down quite happily to a live-in relationship with Greg, a virile athlete. When they left college, of course, Heather and Greg were firmly pair-bonded together; however, within a couple of months Heather was writing us again, this time to ask how she could most gracefully get out of this relationship that she now found so empty.

Her friends thought she had acquired an enviable catch in Greg. Her parents, who had earlier been worried about her being left on the shelf, were now pushing her toward an early marriage so her relatives wouldn't cluck about her living "in sin" with Greg. Heather confided in us that Greg was a great guy, and sexually all she could possibly need; but his interests were so far removed from her own that she felt a marriage would be a disaster. Of even more significance, her letter included the sentence, "He seems incapable of understanding my spiritual needs."

We asked Heather to send us a recent photo of herself and a separate one of Greg. When we placed these two photos together and psychometrized the resulting pattern, we could see the incompatibilities immediately. Instead of the colors meshing into an overall harmonious pattern, there were brilliant lines of color incompatibilities flowing between the photos. We told Heather that there was nothing she could do to make this relationship a long-term success, and that she should again change her selection of clothing colors so that Greg would be turned off.

Heather followed our advice and wound the affair down. She had found out that although sex was fulfilling and pleasant, it was not the be-all and end-all of a relationship—especially for her, who by her very nature had a somewhat reduced need for sexual fulfillment.

This is the system we told Heather to use to turn Greg off: She should bring yellow into his life, and she herself should wear muted shades of violet, purple, and gray. Since Greg was born in early June, this meant that he became even more frivolous while Heather appeared extremely square, dowdy, gray, and uninteresting to him.

Heather could have made an even better initial selection from the available men that she did if she had been willing to go by the psycho-mating chart shown in Figure 9–1. As it was, the relationship ended in quite a painless way. It seems almost impossible in the western world to bring the realization to people that spiritual compatibility is more important than sexual compatibility.

IDENTIFYING YOUR TWIN SOUL

One of the most delicate tasks in any psychometric analysis that you can undertake is that of psychometrizing yourself or someone with whom you are deeply involved emotionally. Thus, for at least your early attempts at psycho-mating, we recommend you use the rather coarse gradations given in the Psycho-mating Wheel shown in Figure 9–2. When you are closer to signing a life contract, we suggest you take

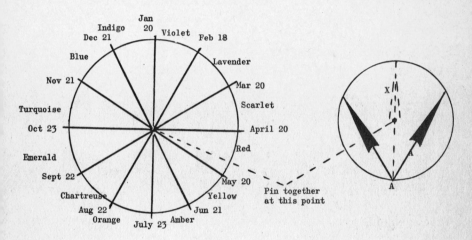

Figure 9-2

Psycho-mating Wheel

a photo of yourself and one of your tentative mate, place them face to face, and psychometrize the resulting energy pattern for colors of incompatibility. If you do detect a bright flare of a particular color, look up that color in your Table of Correspondences and decide whether you can both live with the discordance.

This Wheel is based on the ancient grimoires and on the fact that, in a time which no man can remember, certain elements were assigned to each group of birth dates and colors, as shown in Table 9–1. Each person can thus be associated with a specific element. People of the

Birth Date*	Element	Color	Sign
Jan 20–Feb 18	Air	Violet	Aquarius
Feb 19–Mar 20	Water	Lavender	Pisces
Mar 21–Apr 19	Fire	Scarlet	Aries
Apr 20–May 20	Earth	Red	Taurus
May 21–Jun 20	Air	Yellow	Gemini
Jun 21–Jul 22	Water	Amber	Cancer
Jul 23–Aug 22	Fire	Orange	Leo
Aug 23–Sep 22	Earth	Chartreuse	Virgo
Sept 23–Oct 23	Air	Emerald	Libra
Oct 24–Nov 21	Water	Turquoise	Scorpio
Nov 22–Dec 21	Fire	Dark Blue	Sagittarius
Dec 22–Jan 19	Earth	Indigo	Capricorn

Compatible Opposites	Incompatible Opposites
Fire and Air	Air and Earth
Water and Earth	Fire and Water

Table 9–1

Birthdate, Element, Color, and Sign

---

*Northern hemisphere. If you were born south of the Equator, add six months.

same elements are compatible, as are people of compatible-opposites; but people of incompatible-opposites will be unable to build a happy life together.

The easiest way to use this information is to construct the Psycho-mating Wheel shown in Figure 9–2. Just copy the two figures onto thin cardboard and pin them together at the center so the small wheel can rotate on the larger. Place Point A opposite your birthdate area. You will see that the indicator gives you two birthdate areas of highest compatibility. Within these two areas you will find your psycho-mate. The indicator line with the X on it is the balance psycho-mate line; occasionally a psycho-mate will be of this area. No matter how attracted you are to someone of another area on the indicator, you should be very wary of making a long-term commitment to anyone who is not in the areas indicated. Such mismatching cannot succeed, for it ignores the basic psychic laws of the universe.

We are often asked whether people of the same birthdate area can make a go of it. In psychic mating terms this is called the "siamese-twin syndrome." Yes, you can get along, because your tastes will be so identical that you will both be happy doing the same thing.

There is one other relationship that has been known for centuries to be successful; that is the relationship between the Wheel area shown as scarlet and that shown as turquoise. In some ways this is an occult mystery, the reason why this pairing is so often successful. Put these two into a jar and shake them up together, and often sparks will fly; but somehow the combination seems to have something unique about it (as yet unexplained by known laws).

READING BEYOND THE FIRST YEAR

The photo-psychometric technique that we use to analyze the relationships between people is an extension of the basic Psycho-mating Wheel technique. It can easily be extended to examine, not only the present relationship between the partners, but also the future potentialities of any given couple. We said earlier that to psychome-trize situations in which you have a large emotional investment is tricky; this is why you should get a capable psychic with whom you have no emotional ties to do this work for you. He may charge you $50 or so to give you a life analysis; but it is money well spent.

The procedure is not complicated. Take separate photographs of the two people involved, place them side by side, and psychometrize the combined emanations of the two fields. If they are harmonious today, let your mind travel forward in time while continuing to psychometrize the fields to see what effect future time will have on the harmony of the relationship. If the relationship gradually tends to go out of balance in one direction, a Meta-Psychometric procedure can be employed by adding specific colors in the future of the couple to bring it back into balance. If sudden dramatic color incompatibilities are seen to be developing, then there is very little that can be done to keep these people together, and consideration should be given to an early non-punitive separation.

People tend to make excuses to stay together when their psychic and physical incompatibilities are obvious. If these relationships stretch on, they cause damage to the partners and to any children in the immediate area of the incompatible couple. For incompatibility results in the release of tremendous bursts of negative emotional energy, and these bursts are absorbed by anyone in the neighborhood of the mismatched pair. Separations of this sort should not be looked upon as a tragedy; they are a logical and desirable development step toward personal fulfillment and the finding of your ultimate twin soul.

We should warn you here that just because a couple seems on the mundane level to be mismatched, this does not necessarily mean that they are not underneath it all twin souls. She likes Mozart; he likes rock and roll. This can be interpreted either as an opportunity for each to grow by learning the other's tastes, or as an excuse for violent quarrels and disharmony. If the partners are psychically matched and melded, their differing mundane tastes will be valued as giving the possibility of mutual growth rather than of mutual destruction.

COLOR YOURSELF SEXY

Whether you have decided that the lady you met last night is suitable as a playmate or for a serious, longer-term relationship, still unless you are experienced you probably need some help in attracting her sufficiently to establish that relationship. (We are speaking here of "her," but we are not so chauvinistic as to think that we couldn't equally well be writing about "him"; for the ladies are just as interested in pleasant relationships as are the men.) Before you enter a relationship, you should try to decide whether it is one that you hope will last, or whether it is going to be a brief interlude in your life. In either case, you may wish to influence the lady or gentleman in your favor.

This is where Meta-Psychometry can be of infinite value to you; for it allows you not only to color your own emanations sexy, but also to add to your own emanations those things which will balance the emanations of your prospect. When you balance another person's pattern of emanations, that person will feel comfortable with you and will seek your presence; for with a balanced pattern, he is what we call "homeostatic," or at rest. He is not being pushed or pulled in any direction, and he can relax. Of course physical relaxation follows immediately after psychic relaxation. Once a person is psychically relaxed, he lets down his physical barriers. This procedure, therefore, is again a push-pull system. You are going to make yourself more attractive to the prospect, and you are going to make the prospect feel more comfortable with you than with anyone else.

DOUG AND THE VOCALIST

Doug E is an aerospace executive whose career had been one of rapid advancement until, as so many junior executives do, he had gotten involved with one of the secretaries in the firm and had disastrously split up his home life. As a result of this upheaval, he had applied for and received a post in Taiwan. When he reached Taiwan, he quickly set up a housekeeping arrangement with a local girl and her mother; thus supplying himself with both a housekeeper and a mistress. He had been in Taiwan for more than two years when, on a visit to a local club, he met an English vocalist with whom, as he said afterward, he felt such an immediate empathy or psychic compatibility that he just had to push for a closer relationship. He immediately checked on his Psycho-mating Wheel and found that she was eminently compatible with him.

In his time in Taiwan, Doug had been studying with our School. He confided to us that in his opinion this girl, Eileen, was his twin soul. He asked our advice on how to attract such a popular vocalist to him, for she was so surrounded by admirers who Doug thought were bound to be more interesting than a stodgy, divorced aerospace executive. He felt that without psychic help, he was destined to fail in his campaign.

The first thing we told Doug was to send Eileen roses. We suggested that he send her one yellow rose each day, and at the same time get a photo of her and send it to us so we could tell him what balancing emanations would make Eileen feel warm and comfortable with him. When we received the photo, we could see that Eileen had trained herself to be sexually a very unresponsive person, and that she would feel very little interest in someone who, for all she knew, would be just another one-night stand. What she needed was security and strength. Because of her attitude, we told Doug to stop worrying about the macho types buzzing around Eileen. She was sure to reject them. What he should do was constantly reinforce his orange executive strength emanations when he was with Eileen. Since Doug's basic physical needs were being looked after by his live-in mistress, he could squire Eileen on dates without ever trying to overwhelm her sexually.

In order to reinforce Eileen's aversion to overly aggressive males, we also suggested that Doug give her a bracelet of platinum and turquoise, which he had carefully cleansed of all emanations, and that he find various excuses to re-cleanse this bracelet whenever he could. The bracelet was designed to work as a psychic vampire or magnet which would pull physical feelings of desire out of Eileen and make her even more bored with the constant overtures of lusting males.

We are happy to relay the information that Doug and Eileen have now been happily married for several years. Once the panting mob was removed from her environment, Eileen became a more than adequate partner for Doug. They now live in southern California, where Doug's executive prospects were never better.

GETTING TO HOME PLATE

You can follow exactly the same steps that Doug did. Let us review them in order.

Step 1—Look at Table 9–2. You will see the appropriate Meta-Psychometric keys for coloring yourself sexy. Notice that they are in the light greenish range. You can see also, by referring to the more complete Table of Correspondences, why the macho speed fiend in his red Rocketmobile is usually not so successful in sexual matters as he hopes to be. The red color is intimately associated with athletics and with military domination; nowadays, with our easing sexual mores, domination and sexual subservience are not the basis for even the briefest of encounters. So you must concentrate on an artificial increase in your emanations of green. Copper and turquoise jewelry is an ideal source, for such jewelry combines both the joyful copper emanations and the more desirous turquoise.

Type of Affair	Color	Metal	Flower
Love of Goddess*	Amber	Silver	Night-scented Stock
Light-hearted	Emerald	Copper	Rose
Lusty, deep	Turquoise	Platinum	Orange Blossom

Table 9–2
Colors That Give Sexual Emanations

---

*By "love of goddess" we mean that placing of the object of your affection on a pedestal: the non-physical type of love.

Step 2—You should obtain a photograph of your prospect and carefully read its emanations. In heavily emotional matters, it is better to work with a photo than with the actual person, because the emotions roused by the presence of your prospect will often confuse your reading. A good procedure would be to scan the photo through a prism to see which colors are stronger and which are weaker. When you have read the colors, you should wear a psycho-store designed to give the prospect something that will balance her emanations. This balancing psycho-store could naturally be a piece of jewelry for a lady; or for a gentleman, perhaps an article of apparel, especially if he is so uptight that jewelry is unacceptable.

Step 3—Most importantly, you should place your prospect's photo and your own together to see whether the combined emanation is in balance. If it is not, again you should arrange to carry some subtle psycho-store with you on your dates so as to bring the combined couple-emanations into balance. It is also better to approach a prospect first with amber emanations of goddess-worship, and then to introduce more of the lusty Scorpio feelings on later dates.

Remember to send your prospect. at first night-scented stocks or light yellow roses, and to change to orange blossoms when the relationship has matured. In this way, your prospect will progress comfortably from the light touching love affair into the heavier, more intimate relationship. Convention has it that only ladies like to receive flowers; but, Madame, if you have a hot prospect and you send him an orange rose, he will be your slave.

Step 4—As the relationship progresses, the most significant step occurs when rings are exchanged, for rings reduce the emanations of the person wearing them. Two people, both wearing rings, will more easily get along with one another because rings prevent the sparkling high-level emanations that are so necessary at the beginning of a relationship. Removal of this fiery interchange assures the relationship of longevity, even if that longevity runs the risk of becoming a little dull. Once there has been a physical blending, we recommend that, at the very least, you split[2] your rings so that they are no longer psychic barriers to a fair interchange; or a rather better procedure is to remove the rings, bind them together with copper wire, and throw them into deep running water.

COUPLING[3] IS THE ULTIMATE PSYCHIC LINK

It seems, as we have mentioned, that Mother Nature tries to trick human beings with the formation of pair-bonds; but apart from the pair-bonding, we find that, after coupling, major changes take place in the psychic emanations of the partners. This is not just a reduction in the emanations of unfulfilled desire; it is a subtle blending of each partner's aura so the emanation of the couple becomes quite distinctive. Often, you will see an elderly couple who have been together for many years; they not only think alike, but also seem to look

---

[2] By "splitting" a ring, we mean cutting it so that it no longer forms a complete closed circle.

[3] "Coupling" is a convenient euphemism for "complete sexual relations"; we feel that "coupling" more accurately conveys the idea of full physical and emotional blending.

alike. This impression occurs because you not only see their physical features, but you also sense their blended emanations psychometrically. At second glance, the couple may appear to be physically dissimilar, for now your conscious mind is in control; but the impressions from that first glance will stay with you so that you always think of those two persons as a couple.

From a psychometric point of view, honeymoon photographs are often dramatically different from the wedding photos; and with your advanced psychometric ability you can tell at a glance whether a couple have or have not melded during their honeymoon. If the photos have about them a brilliance and a bright, sparkly nature, you know for sure that each member of this couple is still within his or her own hard shell of individualism. You may see color areas where the two have partially melded, but some unfortunate people have been so rigidly trained that they are unable to get outside their identity, even in the ultimate joyful experience of affectionate sexual relationships.

Most people who are relaxed meld immediately when they couple. This is a very pleasurable situation, of course, when both partners want to make theirs a long-term relationship; but it can be disastrously painful when either or both of the partners are interested only in a brief affair. Fortunately, experiments have shown that psychic melding occurs most powerfully in the half-hour to one-hour period after coupling, rather than at first physical union or at orgasm. It seems as though during the initial sexual act each partner is more occupied with his or her own gratification than with giving pleasure to the other; but in the period following gratification, or on subsequent occasions, they meld more readily into a couple.

The rule, therefore, for affairs that you do not want to lengthen is for one of the partners to leave the arena immediately after orgasm, so that psychic melding and pair-bonding are minimized. In this way the partners can go their separate ways without the emotional storms that so often accompany the breaking of firmly established pair-bonds.

Just as closed rings reduce the psychic energy outflow of a person and prevent quarrels and high-energy interchanges, so too they prevent psychic energy inflow and proper melding. So, as an additional precaution against psychic melding, you can wear heavy metal rings (silver, gold, or lead) on your fingers.

CASEY NEVER KNEW HE HAD BEEN DUMPED

Casey G was a mechanic in a service station on the North Carolina coast. He was well known in the local community as a ladies' man, and the station prospered from the trade of many women who, though married, liked to be chatted up to by Casey and to feel that perhaps they could stray if they wished. Of course, Casey delighted in aggressive conquests of the local damsels. He took pride in never getting emotionally involved with any of them, and in boasting of the number of conquests through which he had come emotionally unscathed.

Megan, a local Witch, decided that Casey had had his way for much too long and that he should be taught a sharp lesson in humility. It was easy for her to get Casey interested, because he had never been able to seduce this previously stand-offish, svelte girl. He was quickly disabused of the idea that this was going to be one of his one-night stands, for Megan told him very candidly that unless he would spend a week at the ocean with her, she was not going to succumb to his blandishments. She was so slender, so flexible, so altogether desirable, that Casey finally agreed to spend his Christmas vacation with Megan at a beach motel. We should say that Megan herself was an artful lover; so she was able to keep Casey confined to their room for most of that week. What Casey did not realize was that immediately after each orgasm, Megan was dumping her emotional energy into a collection of psycho-stores that she had brought with her; and, further, that the rings she wore on all her fingers were, for her, a means of preventing emotional or psychic involvement with Casey.

Well, after a week of this treatment the boastful Casey was totally smitten. He was more thoroughly imprinted and bonded than Megan had hoped. Imagine his surprise when, on the day after they returned home, Megan drove into the station with her old beau, and strongly hinted that Casey now bored her.

Casey was flabbergasted. During succeeding weeks, Megan kept Casey drooling after her. Every time his interest was about to flag, she would dump on him the energy from one of the psycho-stores she had charged in the motel room, and all the emotion of those moments would be forced back onto Casey. As he relived them, the torture of knowing that Megan was now beyond reach became more and more unbearable.

Megan kept up this punishment for an unbelievable six months. In that time, Casey became a shadow of his former swaggering self. Megan had worked the traditional Witch's obsessive procedure. With her psychic knowledge and skilled technique, Megan had made the breakup of this affair a terrible experience for Casey. She had not cast a spell on Casey purely from spite, of course; she simply felt that this walking example of male domination should be taught a lesson.

From this experience, you can see that if you do not intend to be serious about an affair, you should take steps to prevent your psychic involvement with your partner, as these steps will save both you and the partner many painful emotional moments.

MAKE THEM WANT TO LEAVE

If you know that the relationship you are entering into will not be as desirable as a long-term affair, you can take precautions; but often you don't discover that a relationship is destined to an early death until you are so far into it that both of you are pair-bonded and psychically melded. Often the female, being more realistic in matters of the heart, realizes this problem before the male does, and, with perhaps some mothering and tender-hearted instincts, she hates to break off the liaison because she knows her act will cause pain.

You must learn, therefore, how to set up the necessary psychic barriers so that a relationship can quietly fade away, rather than be abruptly and emotionally broken up. Again, you should use the push-pull technique by pushing that partner out of your life but at the same time arranging for him to be pulled into other replacement activities. The first part of the push will be accomplished by a sharp diminishing of sexual activity and by a total cessation of shared sex as soon as possible. This is because, no matter what psychic defenses you employ, coupling still tends to reinforce the psychic bonding.

It is almost impossible to terminate a sexual relationship "cold turkey" in comfort, because your glands, having become accustomed to the various hormone and chemical changes that occur with orgasm, will tend to require that you continue to get fulfillment. Thus, if you cut your partner off cold turkey, the partner will experience many negative—even painful—physical sensations. What you should do is to make sure that, after sexual relations, the two of you immediately separate; or if you have to stay together, you should protect yourself, as Megan did, by placing closed rings on your fingers. An ankle bracelet on your right ankle will also help in closing you down emotionally. This ankle bracelet is a well-known symbol in Europe of the "ladies of the night." The lady of the night wears it for the same reason that you should wear it: It ensures that she will not get emotionally involved.

In order to push your partner away further, you must examine his color balance; then, by adding the appropriate color to your own emanations, you can make him feel uncomfortable with you. If you do not feel fully competent to psychometrize your partner's field, you can in any case wear the suppressed violets and yellows so you are at your most disruptive. This is the "push" side of your Meta-Psychometric procedure.

To work the "pull" side, you will invite many attractive friends to your dwelling so your companion will be pulled toward these more friendly alternatives. When a friendship develops, you can then push that friendship into a more intimate affair by giving your ex-partner jewelry that will make the blossoming friendship better balanced psychically. To do this, you follow the same procedure as before: Take a photo of your ex-partner and a photo of his new friend, place them together, use your developed psychometric ability to find out what that partnership lacks, and select a piece of jewelry that will balance the partnership.

YOUR COMPLETE META-PSYCHOMETRIC GUIDE TO MATING

Again, we have given you many keys to achieving a worthwhile and rewarding coupled life. To review these steps:

1. Decide what you want and what you are going to do before you start your search. You can best do this by having someone psychometrize your own photo and telling you what you need to balance your life. Alternatively, you can make up the Psycho-mating Wheel and give yourself at least some guidance to those mates who will partially fulfill your destiny, rather than selecting someone who will turn out to be a total mismatch.

2. If you can, decide ahead of time, in any given affair, whether or not you want this to be a long-term relationship or just a brief encounter. If you feel that it is to be a short-term relationship, you should take adequate steps to avoid the psychic melding and pair-bonding that occur with coupling; on the other hand, for a long-term affair, you should use your Meta-Psychometric ability to make sure that your emanations fully meld with those of your partner. In order to foretell the outcome of a relationship it is often useful to place the photos of both partners together and sit quietly psychometrizing them while you allow the wheel of time to run forward. In this way, you can sense whether any relationship you enter will develop positively and be long-lasting—or the reverse.

3. When you have decided that you really want to get serious with a particular person, you should psychometrize that person or his picture, and arrange your emanations so that they will balance his. Once this psychic balancing is achieved between you, the prospect will lower his mundane defenses and you can begin to Meta-Psychometrically influence him with the more physical Scorpio emanations that will eventually push the prospect into a relationship of deepening intimacy.

4. Probably the most important thing you can learn from this chapter is how to break off a relationship without emotionally injuring either yourself or your partner. First, you should understand that a cold-turkey cutoff of sexual activity results in very negative withdrawal symptoms; thus you should taper off this activity rather than taking the cold-turkey approach. Secondly, you can use your Meta-Psychometric skills to push the partner away from you and arrange for the partner to be pulled toward someone else. In this way, often the partner hardly realizes that he has been dumped.

Readers may feel that this chapter encourages them to use magical techniques for trapping and caging a partner. Perhaps in some ways, this is true; but notice that, in most cases, if you are to succeed, you have to think about the other person and his needs. In this very action, you are beginning to understand that if you are able to fulfill the psychic and mundane needs of another human being, that person will respond to you.

Rather than use the old-fashioned trapping rituals, we recommend here that you use your Meta-Psychometric ability in a non-selfish way to fulfill the needs of another human being. Rather than use the old-fashioned aggressive sexual-conquest approach, wherein the male gets only a physical conquest and the female only feels she has been used, we recommend that you take great joy in your sexual encounters, and that you attempt to bring friendship, as well as sexual completion, into your life. Thus the techniques in this chapter are not a means of getting your partner into your debt, but a means of exploring a life, activity that can bring release, companionship, and fulfillment without obligation.

10

USE MAGA-PSYCHOMETRY TO DOMINATE OTHERS

SOME PEOPLE NEED TO BE DIRECTED

Just as a teacher directs a child's learning, so the ancient Magus directed a whole tribe's psychic and mundane welfare. Thus when we talk about controlling and directing others, we use the visualization of the wise leader, and we call this psychic control of others Maga-Psychometry.

Maga-Psychometry uses the same system that we have been discussing throughout this work. First, psychometrize the situation and establish the psychic need; second, fulfill that need, whether it be in your own life or in the life of another. Many times throughout this book we have given you examples in which psychic means were employed to effect dramatic changes in the outcome of events. Some may protest that this constitutes an infringement of the freedom of another human being; but we firmly believe that when someone is violating the rights of another person, every means you have within your power should be used to halt that violation, even if this police action requires that you violate someone's rights. Moreover, we feel strongly that when god-given talents are being wasted you should help people by pushing them into a slightly different life-style.

Many young people, especially those coming from an orthodox family background, find themselves adrift and unable to make decisions when they get out into the world. You can help these people by giving their life a little guidance. At other times, you will find people who are compulsive alcoholics, gamblers, TV watchers, or whatever; often these people don't realize that they have fallen into the trap of wasting their lives, and can with relative ease be made happier and more productive.

A very small jolt can achieve a large result; millions of words are written annually about such topics as self-determination and psychic attacks. It is easy to argue that a person should be allowed either to destroy himself or to harm others without in turn being punished or redirected. But this laissez-faire attitude does not work, for the challenges of modern society are such that everyone must become a useful working member if the system is to survive.

In your work, try to imagine yourself as the Magus, and always try to redirect people psychically for their own good rather than for just your own ego fulfillment.

LUMMY AND HIS MOTORCYCLE

The other day, one of our more elderly practitioners told us this story because he was worried about possible infringement of another person's freedoms. In this case, he was concerned about infringing the freedom of his nephew.

Uncle Kay, as we shall call this gentleman, lived on a small farm in the estuarine country of Virginia. Many years earlier, he had taken in his orphaned nephew Lummy when the lad's parents had been killed in a highway accident. Lummy was raised with a great deal of freedom; provided he did his farm chores, the rest of his life (as is often the case with farm children) was his own. Uncle Kay was probably a more lenient guardian than Lummy's parents would ever have been, and at an early age Lummy got used to having his own way. This didn't particularly worry Uncle Kay, for he knew that no matter how children are raised, by and large they work out all right.

Uncle Kay's hobby was painting the marsh birds that came to breed in the river estuary near the farm. Everything went fairly smoothly until, as an eighteenth birthday present, Uncle Kay gave Lummy a small motorcycle. For the first few months after the cycle came to the farm, all was well. Then almost overnight, it seemed to Kay that Lummy had changed. He traded the small cycle for a much larger machine, which he promptly had fitted with straight-through mufflers. Soon he was to be seen constantly roaring up and down the dirt roads near the farm, which of course scared all the animals and birds in the vicinity. Uncle Kay was in a quandary: he didn't want the animals scared or his favorite birds driven away; nor did he want Lummy to feel crowded in and go drag racing on some highway, for the memory of Lummy's parents' traffic accident was still alive in his mind. Kay had never disciplined the boy, and he didn't quite know how to start in Lummy's eighteenth year.

Eventually, Uncle Kay decided to use his developed psychometric talent to see what was goading Lummy into racing his cycle around the neighborhood, and to see whether he could redirect Lummy's life psychically so as to fix the problem. Uncle Kay found that Lummy was feeling the normal sex drive of a young male but, having been raised alone, Lummy was rather shy when it came to dating girls; thus he was taking out his feelings of masculine virility on the motorcycle, without regard to the rights of the animals.

Uncle Kay did two things. First he shut down the farm and took Lummy on a trip to the Orient, where he arranged for the boy to receive proper training in sexual techniques from an accommodating lady. Second, on their return, Kay used what we call a "two-stage, triggered psycho-bank" which he made from a specially-charged medallion from Japan. He told Lummy this was a parting gift from his mentor which of course insured that Lummy would wear it at all times.

The trick of the triggered psycho-bank is one of the secrets of Maga-Psychometry. It worked this way: every time Lummy over-revved his motorcycle, he got an immediate headache. Thus, slowly but surely, he ceased to find pleasure in his cycle and re-channeled this energy more appropriately into getting better acquainted with the many girlfriends that he now met with such self-assurance. For not only had he overcome his shyness of girls, but the girls soon whispered around that he was an accomplished and thoughtful lover.

Uncle Kay's question to us was whether he had overstepped the mark in manipulating Lummy in this way. We told him we felt that he had done nothing but good for the boy. We still feel he was right in his actions, for he was thinking mainly of Lummy's welfare—even if a secondary consideration was the peace and harmony of the animals in the river estuary.

PROTECTING OTHERS FROM THEMSELVES
WITH MAGA-PSYCHOMETRY

Why should you interfere in the life of someone else? There are many reasons, as we have said. When you decide a life warrants your interference, the first thing is to proceed just as you would if it were a medical case. You must get to know the person and psychometrize him; then you must psychometrize the circumstances and all the people surrounding that person.

Let us say that the person whom you intend to help is a compulsive gambler: he lies, steals, cheats, all for money with which to play the ponies. When you investigate such a case, you will probably find that he has a total lack of Arian energy, and he makes up for this by gaining emotional energy from the crowds at the track. Conversely, he may have an overabundant supply of Arian energy, and he may find that he can dump it into the crowd when he loses. This second type of compulsive gambler can also be called the born loser; for it is only through losing that he can psychically rebalance himself.

To cure a case of this sort, you obviously must restore his balance of Arian emanations: either bring Arian energy into his life, or suck some Arian energy out by introducing an Arian psycho-store or a balancing Scorpio psycho-store. These possibilities also show you how to push and pull your subject out of gambling by introducing sexual adventure into his life. This will normally pull him away from the racetrack; and if you lower the need for excitement by draining the excess excitement out of him, then you are accomplishing the other half of the Maga-Psychometric procedure. You are indeed the wise Magus, thoughtfully helping someone in need. Every case brought to your attention should be carefully and thoroughly psychometrized, and corrective Maga-Psychometric steps should be taken. Remember that the mundane manifestation of the problem, whether excessive drinking, compulsive gambling, or whatever, can usually be traced to a psychic source.

The husband who is constantly at odds with his wife may be simply a victim of a psychic mismatch. You can aid this situation by getting them both to wear rings and bracelets, and you can use some absorbing or balancing psycho-stores to alleviate the worst of the mismatch. But, in the long run, it is far better for you to advise a psychically discordant couple simply to separate; for the band-aid procedures that you are doing can never totally overcome the psychic problem in such cases.

YOUR PSYCHIC TIME-BOMB

Often in your work with people who have a compulsive pattern of repetitive behavior, you need to psychically punish them when their indulgence becomes excessive. Naturally, one after-dinner drink or a couple of TV programs are not a problem. Only when the person goes on a drinking spree or constantly watches TV all night do you need to step in and change the life-pattern. This is where the triggered psycho-store, your psychic time-bomb, can help. Preparing these devices is admittedly tricky; and if you arrange for a mundane equivalent (like the wife moving a psycho-store into the TV room when she thinks he has had enough), your task will be easier and more sure of ultimate success.

Sometimes, however, your psychic time-bomb will be the only measure sufficiently drastic to do the job. Start by charging a psycho-store in the normal way. We normally charge with emanations of headache or of tiredness and melancholia. As you will see from your Table of Correspondences, the head is governed by Aries and melancholia by Taurus. You should charge these psycho-stores with personal energy rather than in a pyramid or other charging arrangement; because you want to be sure to get the exact "color" of energy for your intent. Now you must instruct the psycho-store in its task.

The easiest way to do this is to take a parchment-type paper and write very simple instructions on it, preferably with a nib pen, using a drop of your own blood as ink. Some people report that using the subject's saliva as ink provides a better psychic link, but we have found that using your own blood is effective. Using your own blood, of course, definitely indicates the level of your concern and involvement with your subject. Place the paper and the psycho-store in a metal box, and burn the paper. Now all you have to do is recharge the psycho-store and place it in the subject's environment. The psycho-store will follow the burned instructions. After perhaps two hours of TV or after a loss of $20 at the track, or after whatever you tell it, the psycho-store will automatically dump out its energy and cause the subject to feel tired, or to get a headache or whatever negative sensation you have impressed on the psycho-store.

(We should caution you not to be overly complex in your instructions to the psycho-store. Something very simple is all that's necessary.)

Sometimes your work will bring amusing results. In St. Charles, Missouri, we had a case of a teen-ager who persistently tossed empty soda cans into our yard. We charged up the iron fence around the yard as a psychic mirror. This worked so well that whenever the teen-ager tried to throw his can into the yard, it bounced back and hit him. Whether the fence was affecting his aim, or the charge was strong enough to affect a thrown can, we don't know; nevertheless, the "mirror spell" was effective and intriguing in its results.

THE CUSTOMER IS ALWAYS RIGHT

In recent years, this old saw of the retail business has been honored more in the breach than in its observance. Everyone you meet can tell some story of poor workmanship, sloppy service or maintenance, and what we call the "it's him, not me" syndrome, where the customer gets the run-around between the various people who are supposedly responsible for his satisfaction. How many times have you heard a salesperson say, "No, we don't service it; that's a separate department," or "It's management policy," or "I'd like to help you but I can't."

In these cases, you cannot win by simply pushing against the established policy of a company. What you have to do is make them want to help you. When you have created in them a desire to help, a gentle push or a threat with a big stick will overbalance them, and you will get your way.

GRANNIE MAKES THE MECHANIC BACK DOWN

In moving to a new home town, one of the most difficult tasks can be the locating of a reliable auto-maintenance man. Grannie Stovall retired to Florida when she was widowed. All her life, Grannie had been poking into and servicing her own cars. In her early days on the farm, she had done nearly all the servicing of the farm vehicles, because Wendell had little mechanical aptitude, being better suited in temperament to working with livestock. When Grannie arrived in Pensacola in her 1936 Buick Straight Eight, one of her first thoughts was to locate a reliable service station. Her new neighbor told her that JP's was the best in town. Grannie trotted her Buick down for its regular oil change; while it was there, she was coaxed by the service manager into a front-wheel alignment as well.

Billy, the mechanic who actually did the alignment, told Grannie that she needed several hundred dollars worth of new parts. Since the Buick had been giving no trouble and showing no symptoms of wheel-alignment problems, Grannie told him to forget it. When she got the old car back on the road, though, she found that it did in fact seem to have some front-end vibration. When she got home, she changed into overalls and crawled underneath to see whether she could tell what was wrong. She could see immediately, by the shiny threads showing on various adjustments, that Billy had slightly misadjusted the wheel alignment so she would be convinced that the Buick needed attention and would buy the parts he had recommended. Of course, this all made Grannie furious; she was quite a feisty old lady anyway. She decided on a campaign of education.

Carefully, Grannie charged two or three standard wrenches with irritation and clumsy energy; then she took her car back to J P's. She told the service manager that she wanted the same Billy who had looked at it before to realign it, and, since she had been having trouble with it, she wanted to watch him do the work. Once she was in the pit with Billy, her mechanical know-how convinced him that he had no chance of successfully putting one over on her; so he did his work properly. But while Billy was busy readjusting the alignment, Grannie substituted the charged wrenches for his own; then, having made sure it was correctly aligned this time, she quietly drove away.

Now Grannie's charging of the wrenches had been of the triggered psycho-store type. Her instructions were to cause Billy irritation and clumsiness only when he was deliberately attempting to mis-align front ends. It didn't take him long to find out that every time he tried a mis-alignment, he would injure himself or break a tool or in some way become extremely frustrated. Very soon, he had learned his lesson and was doing proper alignments in every case. Grannie is still well-satisfied with the service she gets at J P's.

A LESSON FROM GRANNIE

In her procedure, Grannie Stovall did very little work that was different from the normal psychometric charging procedures. She started out by being convinced that J P's was a reliable firm and that she was only dealing with the proverbial bad apple in the barrel. She felt that it was worth her while to bring Billy back into line, both for her own benefit and for the safety of future customers. She suspected that if a complaint to the manager got Billy fired, he would just get a job as an alignment mechanic somewhere else and carry on with his unethical practices.

Being a good mechanic herself, Grannie was in an ideal position to charge negatively the triggered psycho-stores that she used. She could perfectly visualize the use and the mis-use of the wrenches, and could finely tune the energy she put into the wrenches to create the result she felt was best. You too can do as Grannie did, but you must understand both the problem and the motivation of the person whom you want to redirect. You must carefully charge your psycho-stores with finely tuned energy, as you have been taught.

STORE YOUR CONFIDENCE AND USE IT

In any situation where you wish to dominate someone, you must exude confidence and knowledge. Attitude is everything. If you tiptoe to the desk of a hotel and say, "Would you mind very much changing my room?" in a cringing voice, in most cases the room clerk will attempt to talk you out of the idea. But if you go in and demand with absolute assurance that they forthwith give you a different room because the one you have is unsatisfactory and, if they don't give you a better room, you will call the Chairman of the Board of the hotel group, you will find that (if he has any other rooms available) the room clerk will offer very little resistance.

People tell us that if you go into a bank in old clothes or in hippy gear, the bank will tend to treat you poorly; but from our personal experience, we can say that this is not so. Everything depends on your attitude in the bank. There is a well-known saying, especially in Swiss banking circles: "Only the very rich can afford not to dress up." Bankers are well aware that wealthy people often dress casually or even sloppily; but when a very rich person goes into a bank, his attitude itself indicates that here is someone who expects (and consequently will get) the very best of the bank's attention.

Confidence and a feeling of security go hand in hand. If you can make the person that you want to bend to your will feel insecure, his confidence will drain away into the vacuum of his insecurity. If you push against the confidence of a claims clerk secure behind her barrier in the department store, you will have difficulty in overcoming her trained-in confidence. Being in her accustomed surroundings, looking down on you from her own stool behind her own counter, she has all the security in the world. To win your claim, get her to come out from behind her counter and view the disputed merchandise, preferably in the back of your car in the parking lot. Because you have taken her security blanket away from her and gotten her out into the wide open parking lot, she has lost that feeling of confidence and self-assurance. Now, by exerting your confidence or by dumping a previously charged "confidence" psycho-store, you can get your way.

ALWAYS A BRIDESMAID

Catherine L was the senior assistant of Dr. Jerry R, one of the leading microbiologists of a midwestern research hospital. In colloquial terms, Catherine was "on the shelf." She had dedicated her life to the study of children's diseases and to helping Dr. Jerry in his research. Underneath, of course, she was totally in love with the good doctor. She knew that one day he would take his place beside Pasteur and Schweitzer. On his part, he was a shy, retiring, mother's boy type of dedicated researcher. Though Catherine and Dr. Jerry got along well together, his social life consisted entirely of caring for his aged mother, whose battle cry was "We're not going to let any of those filthy bacteria get in here!"

When Jerry's mother eventually died, both Catherine and Jerry were approaching middle age; Catherine realized that now was her last chance to capture the brilliant but self-effacing researcher. She decided she would charge some psycho-stores with sexual and loving energy, and see whether she could arouse Dr. Jerry. She did notice a definite warming of his attitude toward her, and he became less restrained in the lab. She felt that an intimate dinner would tip the balance in her favor, and he could be tempted into at least an affair. On the evening of their dinner, she wore her most Venusian green frock and filled her apartment with several Scorpio-type emitters. She was dismayed after dinner when the doctor launched a diatribe against kissing and all the diseases that it might transmit.

Late that night, Catherine called us and tearfully told us of the failure of her plan. After thinking about it for awhile, we felt the doctor just lacked confidence with women. Obviously, his harangue about kissing indicated that he was being affected by the psycho-stores but was trying to keep his impulses under control. We told Catherine that what the doctor needed to be finally pushed into an affair, was a burst of confidence given to him at the critical moment in her campaign.

Again, Catherine invited Dr. Jerry to dinner; again, she heavily loaded psycho-stores with her excess sexual energy. In addition to loading all the psycho-stores, she also charged a ruby ring which she wore with all the Arian confidence she could muster. When they were sitting on the couch together and the doctor was having that last brandy before his departure, she rapped the ring on the edge of the coffee table, then took it off and dropped it into the flame of the brandy heater. Abruptly Dr. Jerry overcame his aversion to physical contact and promptly seduced his willing lab assistant.

They are now married and still having a ball. Not only that, but the doctor has gained sufficient confidence to publish more of his work and to obtain better funding for his hospital. That little push, that little domination exercise that Catherine went through, has not only improved her life, but is going to result in a lessening of children's diseases world-wide.

YOU CAN GET YOUR OWN WAY WITH MAGA-PSYCHOMETRY

No matter what the situation is or how black it looks, you can make it better with Maga-Psychometry. You may not always be able to direct people to do precisely the things you want; but it is also true that you may not have all the facts of any given situation at your command. Thus, if you should fail in a given attempt, you should go back as the Magus would and re-examine the basic premises upon which you based your actions. In almost all cases of failure, you will find that there is a reason for your failure. After your re-examination of basic premises, you can re-adjust your procedure to bring it more into tune with the needs of the situation. All you have to do is:

Psychometrize—Evaluate—Correct

If you prefer, you may think of these Maga-Psychometric steps as:

Psychometrize—Charge your store—Release the energy

We should give you one warning here: In your procedures, you should not use what we call "caging" rituals. With your advanced knowledge and developed techniques, you could, if you wish, trap almost anyone with a ritual cage; however, this is not the way the Magus would do it. *Help* the other person; modify his behavior patterns; yes, imprison him and rob him of his freedom, no.

"I WAS A TEEN-AGE LOSER"

Every day, we get letters giving us all the excuses why the writers cannot follow our procedures. A very common excuse is contained in those letters that start off, "I am a loser. I always have been a loser, and nothing I can do for myself will ever help me." This attitude, often brought about by constant parental repetition of such ideas as, "You are stupid, you can't win," is a real mental block. The only cure that we have found for these people is to help them actually win one or two conflicts, or to do a ritual psycho-drama for them, wherein their mind is convinced that their bad luck has been removed.

KELLY CHANGES COURSE

Kelly B was a young adult living in Tucson, Arizona. He was the son of an Army major general. Unluckily for Kelly, he was of a rather slight build; and all his father's insistence on proper nutrition and body-building exercises seemed unable to fill Kelly out. As with many young adults today, he also had an aversion to his father's profession. These two factors seemed to grate on the general. He was forever telling his son, "You will never be good for anything. You'll always be a loser." Of course this losing attitude built up in Kelly's mind to such an extent that he came to accept it and live with it unquestioningly; for by expecting nothing, he was never disappointed.

The only lucky break Kelly seemed to have had in his life was his falling in love with Eunice, a pleasant if rather overbearing young lady. They made a good pair because Kelly was happy to let Eunice wear the pants in the family. They planned to marry in the spring and settle down to a stereotyped suburban life.

For the long honeymoon they planned, Kelly bought a new car. It turned out to be an embodiment of everything summarized in the word "lemon." Even as Kelly was driving it away from the dealer's lot, the brakes failed and Kelly bent a fender on a utility pole. After many such surprises with the car, Eunice was fighting mad, but Kelly was his normal "I can't win" self. Nothing Eunice could do would make Kelly even write to the Lemon Motor Company in Detroit or to one of the consumer-protection groups to complain about his Lemon.

The final showdown came when the car heater poured rust-stained hot water onto Eunice's new pantsuit and coordinated boots. In her rage, she told Kelly that unless he did something about the Lemon, she was leaving. When she cooled off, she knew she didn't want to leave Kelly; she really liked him. She decided the only answer was going to be a psycho-drama to break his mental block. She made up with him and endured the Lemon a few more weeks while she arranged with us to do the ritual necessary to make Kelly feel he could be a winner. At the next full moon, we played out the psycho-drama, shaking the feathers and rattling the gourds with a will.

It produced a dramatic change in Kelly. Though he did not become a raging bull, he did at least find enough nerve to start writing letters to the head of the Lemon Manufacturing Company. He also advertised in the local newspaper, seeking other dissatisfied drivers of

Lemons, and he wrote to Ralph Nader's consumer advocate group. From the Lemon Company he received a standard form letter; the Nader group offered little more encouragement; however, Kelly's ads paid off. He collected more than fifty signatures on a petition to have the local Lemon dealer's license to operate in Arizona revoked. Taking this petition to the prosecuting attorney for Tucson, he got a strong letter written to Lemon Manufacturing. At the same time, Kelly wrote a personal letter to the president of Lemon, asking whether such dealers were typical of the corporation and whether the president realized what a bad image this dealer was giving Lemon cars.

Lemon Manufacturing concluded this Kelly was going to be a source of endless problems unless they could satisfy him. They arranged to exchange his Lemon for a new car and had the dealer make amends to the other dissatisfied people who were signatories of Kelly's petition.

This win made a conspicuous change in Kelly's character. As the saying goes, he never looked back. The changes wrought by the psycho-drama were reinforced by a victory over one of the major corporations of the nation. Kelly is now almost a by-word for his self-assurance. When he stands in the center of his living-room declaiming, Eunice quietly smiles.

YOU, TOO, CAN BEAT THE ESTABLISHMENT

Normally, the most common problem you personally will have in dominance is when you wish to influence a giant corporation. By practicing getting your own way at the complaints level, you can develop your ability to such an extent that minor problems can be easily solved by your dominance of the situation. But when it comes to the huge corporation, how are you going to exert your influence? Remember first of all that the more rigid they are, the more susceptible they are to your influence; for a rigid structure indicates lack of tolerance and lack of ability to bend with changing circumstances. You may have to exert a lot of influence, but when your work comes to fruition, you will find they will completely overbalance in your favor and do everything they can to satisfy you and restore their toppled structure to its original rigidity. They never seem to learn that a little flexibility would save them tremendous amounts of grief. This is why, once the edict comes from the top that this customer is to be properly treated, major corporations go overboard in their efforts to please you.

When you have a complaint, you will usually find yourself dealing with someone low on the totem pole in the corporation, someone who is powerless to do much for you; or you may work with the office of the president, who can do everything for you. There is little point in working at any other level because between these two levels you have the whole corporation in your grasp. Pushing at the bottom and pulling at the top will surely get you the results you desire.

Suppose you have pushed on the subordinate until he can be pushed no further, both at the mundane level of "Fix it!" and on the psychic control level; and still the subordinate is unable to move. Your next step will be to find out from a local stock broker the name and address of the firm's President. You should write this person a "how would you like it?" letter—a letter stating in simple, straightforward terms what has happened to you and asking him how he would like it if something similar came to his life. This is a double-whammy letter because before you mail it you are going to charge it psychometrically with loving, friendly emotions. The President will sense that you are a warm, friendly person, not the troublemaker that he has been hearing about from the subordinate. You can imagine what effect these contrasting emotions will have on the head of the corporation.

Two brief examples of this ploy will show you how to handle the corporate-dominance situation:

When we lived on our Ozark farm, we had a problem with our TV set which we had purchased from a major mail order house. The farm wiring had not been adequately protected against lightning, and during an electrical storm sections of the set burned out. After some three months, though we had pushed hard on the local service representative, Sears had still been unable to get parts out to our rural district for repair of the set. Living that far out in the Ozarks, three months of isolation can be a long time, too. So we wrote to Sears' home office in Chicago, telling them of our problem. We suggested that if the president wanted to achieve his multi-million-dollar sales goal for the year, this was no way to treat customers. In passing, we mentioned that we thought this was a pretty sneaky way of letting our expensive warranty run itself out. We saturated that letter with all the loving thoughts we could. Within a week, we received a most conciliatory letter from the president, and not only was our TV restored to perfect working order, but we were also given an extension on our warranty.

2. A similar incident occurred when Gavin purchased a coat for Yvonne from one of southern California's nicer department store chains. They promised faithfully to have her name embroidered on the inside pocket before delivering it on a specified Friday evening. Well, as things go sometimes, they were unable to fulfill their promise—but

we were leaving for Europe at noon on Saturday. It was time for drastic action. We would take the coat, we told them, whether it was mono-grammed or not. The poor little salesman really had a problem now. It was the store's practice to send coats out to a custom monogrammer for such work; and the chain of command was such that the salesman seemed unable to locate and return the coat in time for our departure. This time, we called the president of the store, person-to-person, and again used the "how would you like it?" approach, but blended it with as much understanding as we could get into the telephone conversa-tion. "I am going to the Paris Air Show and my wife won't have a coat to wear and it is your fault," was the gist of the conversation.

The coat was delivered to the airport desk for our pickup before our departure the next day.

In both of these cases, we followed up with a very nice note to the president, thanking him for his attention and saying that we were sorry to have caused so much trouble with the subordinate. In both cases, again, we got very pleasant return letters thanking *us* for our considera-tion in bringing this matter to the attention of the president.

It is easy. You can do it, too. Think about the balance and about the push-pull; think about whether you have a real case; and then go to work.

YOUR COMPLETE MAGA-PSYCHOMETRIC
GUIDE TO DOMINANCE

If you still feel that dominance is an evil thing after reading this chapter, you should not attempt it. But if you can put yourself into the position of the Magus, who has the responsibility for the future of the tribe and the smooth running of the group, then you can safely and properly use dominance procedures to help both yourself and others to a better life. You should follow these steps in your work:

1. Completely psychometrize the situation. Decide why the per-son involved is behaving the way he is. Is it some lack in his life? Or is it something that you are doing that is causing the problem? It is most important that you try to divorce your Maga-Psychometric work from the immediate mundane problem and look for the psychic causes.

2. Having established the root cause of the problem, you are in a position to correct it. You should work in a dualistic way. If it is a case where the person is, for example, an obsessive viewer of the TV late late show, you can work on the pleasure-pain principle: Charge up a triggered psycho-store that will cause pain every time the subject

views too much TV, and reward the subject, either psychically or mundanely, by fulfilling the other needs that he must have.

3. In dealing with large corporations, first establish your dominance over the subordinate with whom you have been working. You may have to use some psycho-stored confidence energy in this effort, but the first step is to establish your superiority over the person you are dealing with. Remember, as long as he is in the security blanket of his own office surroundings, he is one up on you, so whenever possible take him out of that environment before you confront him with the problem. If the subordinate is really helpless to assist you, or he cannot help you in a timely manner, you should start to pull the upper management of the group toward you by writing love-impregnated letters to them explaining your problem.

Maga-Psychometry can make a new life for you. Even if you feel you are a born loser today, when you have won a few conflicts with Maga-Psychometry, your life will suddenly become far better and more meaningful. The techniques described in previous chapters are easily applied, but you cannot win if you don't bother even to enter the race.

11

TAPPING THE UNIVERSAL GOLD MINE WITH MIDA-PSYCHOMETRY

LINKING YOURSELF TO THE MONEY THOUGHTFORM

The Law of Attraction is as valid today as it was when Hermes Trismegistus (the "Thrice-Master"), the ancient father of much sorcery, magic, and occult arts, first inscribed it on the fabled Emerald Tablet. Currently, we might phrase that Law as, "Birds of a feather flock together," for this expresses the same idea. The arcane secret of Mida-Psychometry is that money attracts money. In the chapter on love and mating, we illustrated that sexuality attracts sexuality. As you will see in the story of Olive, silver attracts silver. The Law of Attraction is a basic law of the universe, as is the law of the Attraction of Opposites, a law exemplified in the attraction between male and female.

In this and the succeeding chapter, we are going to show you step by step how, with only a dollar or two in your pocket, you can link yourself to the money thoughtform and with that universal gold mine available to all who understand it.

HEALTH AND WEALTH CAN BE YOURS

You learned earlier that to make something happen, you have to put out the correct emanations so that other people, and inanimate objects as well, can psychometrically discern that you are (in this case) wealthy. We might call this "putting out the right occult image." You also know from Chapter 7 that an outflow of energy can be equated to sickness and that if you fail to replace this lost energy, you will in fact become sick. You are probably aware that hypertension is almost universal among business executives, who have to rely heavily on "downer" drugs to keep in balance. Refer now to Table 11–1, where you will see the illnesses that correspond to the various money thoughtforms; you will see that hypertension is a probable hazard to those who deal in the green Venus thoughtform.

Eli Blake, president of a multi-million-dollar food conglomerate, recently committed suicide; you can immediately see why, when you consult Table 11–1. Eli overemphasized the earth or Tauran money thoughtform, which implies the risk of melancholia.

All you have to do is draw energy from a source such as a Money Bag to replace the energy you are putting out in your rituals, and you can stay healthy. One of the simplest ways to set about gathering riches is to construct your own Money Bag or Lodestone. This construction is in many ways identical to the construction of a medicine bag. Just as the medicine bag replaces the energy you lose because of your illness, so a money bag replaces the energy you use in putting out money emanations.

As you will also see, there is a very special occult balancing system which you can use to achieve good health and undreamed-of riches.

MIDA-PSYCHOMETRY, FABLED GOLD MAKER

We call the balanced techniques of making money and staying healthy "Mida-Psychometry," after the legendary King Midas whose very touch turned objects to gold. The myth of King Midas tells both halves of the story: that even a golden touch can have its drawbacks. In King Midas' case, he could not eat anything, nor could he touch his beloved daughter; for literally everything he touched turned to gold.

You too can become a modern King Midas, but without running the risk of anything as destructive as a literal golden touch. We will show you how you can turn your home into a golden treasure chamber, in a safe manner, through keeping in balance. But be warned: If you go overboard in gathering money to yourself, you must be prepared to live with the consequences of your decision.

MONEY MAKES MONEY

In the world of international finance, the name of Bernie Cornfeld is mentioned with awe and wonder. Though he started his career as just an ordinary guy working as a stockbroker in New York, Bernie seemed almost overnight to become a multi-millionaire, with chateaux in Switzerland and even his own jetliner. The story of his rise and his ultimate failure is still a textbook case in international finance. When you read of Bernie, you find that almost every article quotes his basic premise. That premise is: "If you wanna make money, deal in money."

From the psychometric point of view, this is excellent advice; for when you deal in money, you are handling it constantly and you are thinking of it day and night. As a consequence, by the Law of Attraction, you will inevitably attract money to yourself. This is because everyone around you will unconsciously pick up psychometrically that aura of money and wealth you radiate. Handling money is a basic method of acquiring wealth. The Law of Attraction is extremely powerful when applied to financial affairs: Money attracts money. If you have money, you can get a loan; if you have no money and you really need that loan, you can't get it. This experience is so well-known it needs no amplification; everybody knows it.

Happy Howie, the manager of the local finance company, will be glad to lend you money—if you have a selection of stocks and bonds in your portfolio. But Happy Howie turns into the most obstinate miser imaginable when you try to borrow from him without having strong links to the money thoughtform. As a successful manager, Howie has learned to Mida-Psychometrize his customers. He has the gift of sensing which applicant is good for the loan; that gift is nothing more or less than Howie's psychometrizing of the applicant and picking up the fact that the customer has money or is putting forth strong money emanations.

The rule of dealing with money to make money is also good advice in another practical way. If you, let us say, become a mortgage broker and you sell a $200,000 mortgage to some local businessman, you as the broker will make upwards of $4,000 for a few hours work. On the other hand, if you are out selling material things like encyclopedias or vacuum cleaners, you will have to spend weeks if not months selling to realize a clear profit of $4,000.

If you are unable to deal directly in money—that is, in cash—its nearest equivalents such as securities, diamonds, and gold coins can also link you to the Money Thoughtform. This means that there are thousands of jobs you can get which offer opportunities for you to deal with large sums of money each day.

Why aren't you working with money? Why don't you handle money every day? We hear you protest, "But I'm a clerk in a stock-room." If you really and truly want to be rich, you will become a cashier in a bank, or an assistant in a coin store, or one of the myriad other jobs that put you into close-linked association with the Money Thoughtform.

OLIVE AND THE SILVER DOLLARS

Many women of our acquaintance have a little piggy bank put away somewhere, whether it actually takes the form of a bank, a sugar bowl, a sock in the mattress, or a tin can nailed to the cupboard floor. Olive, a secretary in Los Angeles, is no exception to this pattern. She diligently collected every silver dollar and half-dollar that came her way. (This is a curious thing, too. It seems, somehow, as if President John Kennedy's sexual attractiveness started this trend, for almost any woman you ask will tell you that she saves Kennedy half-dollars.) Olive managed to save something over $100 every year in silver dollars; as time went on, in fact, she became a Silver Lady. She thought silver. She wore silver. She treasured silver. She had what amounted to a love affair with it. Olive radiated silver emanations. She was unwittingly using Mida-Psychometry to draw silver to her. Thus, people were constantly giving her unexpected silver gifts of coins and collectibles. Olive would go out of her way to attend silver shows and silver coin events.

As time went on and the Government changed the content of the silver dollars it minted, including more and more nickel in the metal, her association with the coins made her think more and more in terms of stainless steel and nickel; and in her comfortable home today you will find all stainless steel flatware and serving accessories. But this change occurred after Olive had made her fortune in silver coins.

Having no family, Olive was also interested in the occult; she decided to see whether the ancient Law of Attraction would work for her. Every evening, she fondled her silver coins, and she always held a silver coin in her hand when she talked of her hobby. Soon all her friends and work associates knew that Olive was interested in silver currency; so when they received any such coins in their change, they would give them to her. Returning from pleasure trips to Las Vegas, her boss would regularly bring her a dozen or so silver dollars.

Her intimate knowledge and love of silver had become the basis for freindships with all the coin dealers in her area, and she regularly bought from her friends coins that her study had taught her were worth many times their face value. Of course, her love of silver was so strong that she could not bear to part with many of these coins. In fact, she would occasionally go hungry so as to buy a particularly rare or valuable coin.

Eventually, though, she had so many that her banker advised her to convert her collection into securities. She thought about this for some time, but could not bring herself to do it. Instead, she decided she would open a coin store, specializing, of course, in silver coins. The store was an instant success, and seeing all the coins people brought in to sell, Olive was rapidly able to enlarge her personal collection. Today her collection is valued in the tens of thousands of dollars, and her business in the middle five-figure bracket.

Over a period of ten years, with the aid of Mida-Psychometry, this woman turned a pleasurable hobby into what can only be described as a big business. How many readers of this paragraph have coins saved, even if it is only one or two? If you wish to multiply those coins, handle them daily just as Olive did, and love them; and you too could rapidly become a big business person.

YOUR GUIDE TO MONEY THOUGHTFORMS

The first real step in making money is to look in Table 11–1 and see the correspondences between money and its thoughtforms. Start with Line 1, the basic money thoughtform. You will see that its astrological symbol is Taurus the Bull; that its color is red-gold; that it is associated with the earth. Notice also that it is linked with melancholia.

The second most important money thoughtform is that associated with Venus and the green color of a dollar bill. In astrological terminology, this is because Venus rules Taurus. Notice that the Venus money thoughtform is associated with pleasure—and with hypertension. This is both an outgoing and an incoming thoughtform associated very strongly with green dollars. In working with it, you must be sure to exercise care to make certain that the dollars' flow is, not away from you but toward you. In employing it, you become the giver of pleasure for which you will be paid. (Human nature is such, of course, that one who gives pleasure also receives it. But your work within the frame of

reference of the Venus correspondences means that, besides the al-
truistic rewards of giving pleasure, you will be remunerated.)

The final money thoughtform which you will consider here is the
silver form governed by the moon. This is the thoughtform that Olive
used in her business. Notice it is also associated with the diseases of
digestion and bronchitis; even today, Olive has a chronic complaint of
constipation. Because the moon is so important in the composite
money thoughtform, you must always be sure that any time you work
for money in a ritual, you do it at the time when the moon is between
new and full; for only in this phase of the moon will your money grow. If
you do a money-attracting ritual (especially a Venus-tuned one) in the
waning phase of the moon, your money will wane or decrease.

The most powerful money thoughtform you can work with is that
associated with Taurus the Bull and with red-gold. We have found in
our ritual work that South African gold is of a redder color than
American gold, and that the most successful rituals are accomplished
with the aid of South African gold coins. They have about them a raw,
earthy, bullish emotion that can lock your mind into the money
thoughtform faster than any handling of the more ethereal paper
equivalent. The only drawback with this Taurus thoughtform is that it
tends to work more slowly and with less pleasure than the Venus
thoughtform.

VINNIE AND HER MONEY RING

Vinnie was a pleasant but no longer young woman who operated
her own occult book store in Tucson, Arizona. Now book stores are
among those pursuits that are very pleasant to own and operate, but
they result in no large income for the proprietor. Consequently,
Vinnie was perenially wanting financially. But, conversely, she was
happy in her life.

One day there came into her store an elderly lady, obviously
well-off. Vinnie and Gladys (for that was the lady's name) became good
friends; presently, Gladys made Vinnie a gift of her money ring. This
was a red-gold ring that had been charged by a Navajo Indian to attract
money. Vinnie started wearing the ring; very soon she found that
people were coming to her for readings of the tarot cards and were
buying books in ever-increasing quantities. We do not know whether
the Indian's charge on the ring was effective for Vinnie or not, since the
ring had been passed from one wearer to another; but from our past
experiences we do know that a red-gold ring will in fact attract money.

As it turned out, the Mida-Psychometric properties of the ring did attract a great deal of money to Vinnie; but, regrettably, her increased prosperity brought with it the associated melancholia. Of course she was working very hard and she didn't have time to do all the reading for pleasure that her previous slow trade had permitted her. Her work, sadly, also separated her from her former friends; and good old Vinnie, wishing to relax some of her business tensions, began taking a little drink now and then in private, to help her through the day.

Vinnie was materially rich now, but in her personal life she had sacrificed much in the gaining of that wealth. Great wealth is too often associated with ill health and loneliness. If you want great wealth, it is your own decision whether to risk ill health in the gaining of unimaginable riches.

MAKING A MIDA-LODESTONE

Your first step on the road to reasonable wealth should be to construct your money lodestone, or Money Bag—the thing that will attract as much money to you as you could possibly use. For example, if you want the maximum possible long-term wealth, you will use the Tauran attraction system from Line 1 of Table 11–1. Make a bag of pure linen cloth about four inches in diameter and six inches deep. A simple way of constructing the bag is to sew it over a glass tumbler. After removing it from the tumbler, run a drawstring of linen thread around the opening of the bag. Dye the bag with a dark orange dye. Because it will be in contact with your skin, make sure that the excess dye is washed out by rinsing the bag thoroughly and allowing it to dry. Then in dark brown indelible ink on one side of the bag draw the symbol of the Bull; on the other side draw the symbol of the earth as shown in Figure 11–1. Place into the bag a piece of red gold (preferably a

Planet/ Sign	Element	Jewel	Metal	Scent	Herb	Health Hazard
1 Taurus	Earth	Yellow Jade	Red Gold	Sandal-wood	Ground-Ivy	Melancholia
2 Venus	Air	Emerald	Copper	Myrtle	Rose	Hypertension
3 Moon	Water	Pearl	Silver	Sandal-wood	Night-scented Stock	Digestion

Table 11–1

Thoughtforms Associated with Riches

Krugerrand from South Africa), a piece of yellow jade, a piece of sandalwood, and a dry leaf of ground-ivy.

Starting at the new moon, at midnight every night light an orange candle and place the bag on the table before the candle. Stand facing south, with the candle and the bag between you and the South Pole; chant four times:

"Money, money, come to me.
As I will, so mote it be."

Each repetition of the chant should be louder than the one before. At the end of the fourth chant, clap out the candle and leave the arrangement till the succeeding night. After eight succeeding nights of this charging ritual, take the bag with you and wear it for the next seven days and nights.

The next step, a most important one, is in the interest of safety. From the time the moon is full until it is new again, the bag should be locked away in a steel box and you should try not to think of it; for this is the time when the influence is diminishing, and obviously you do not wish to use a system that causes diminution of your riches. Each fifteen-day period from new moon to full moon, wear the bag around your neck (for Taurus is associated with the neck). If at any time you feel excessive melancholia or a wish to commit suicide, lock the bag away in its steel box and do not wear it again until the melancholia wears off. An alternative procedure is to use the balance system described later in this chapter to keep yourself in harmony.

You will find that the bag will attract to itself and to you untold riches. You will find that while you wear the bag, you will become a modern Midas, for the emanations from the bag will attract money to you. It is a money lodestone whose potentialities we have proved time and time again.

INSTANT MONEY (YOUR FIRST $100)

There may come a time when you need money instantly, but you will not have the leisure to wait and work for the great riches that will be yours through the lodestone. This is the time when you should move away from the slow, sure magic of the earth (Taurus) to the lighter, faster magic that is associated with Venus and the air. This is the magic of the green dollar bill, the magic that can be made to work quickly. As you know only too well, green dollars flow into and out of your hands far more rapidly than heavier metals such as gold. Referring to Line 2 in Table 11–1, you see all of the Mida-Psychometry tuning aids to be employed when you want to get your mind and body linked

Taurus   Earth

Front of Bag   Back of Bag

Figure 11–1

to the Venus green-dollar thoughtform rather than to the Tauran red-gold thoughtform.

Notice from the Table that Venus is an air sign; this means that anything you do should be done joyously, quickly, and lightly. This approach is most desirable and effective when you need a couple of hundred dollars to meet an urgent bill or to buy the necessary psychometric aids for the Tauran money lodestone that will draw to you long-term riches.

SIX FRIENDS GET $30,000

Having read in one of our books[1] the story of Hank the astrologer and his friends in Arizona, six young people of Des Moines, Iowa, met to attempt a similar ritual. Their leader was Clevis, a filling-station attendant in his daytime life. These young people knew very little about psychometric magical procedures; but they adapted the ritual as explained in our book, and at midnight on a springtime new moon, they joined hands around a Venus green candle and chanted their hearts out, for they were all genuinely impoverished. Even though, in this group there were four girls and only two boys, the ritual still worked. Within a month, all had received unexpected sums of money. Clevis the leader received over $20,000 from the settlement of his grandfather's estate, a matter which had been in the courts for some three years. Partly because the money was so unexpected and he had made no concrete plans, Clevis fulfilled the other aspect of the Venus thoughtform to perfection; within a year, he had spent the majority of his new riches.

The next highest amount received was by one of the girls of the group, Garnet. In her infancy, Garnet's parents had bought her a

---

[1] Gavin and Yvonne Frost, *The Magic Power of Witchcraft* (West Nyack, N.Y.: Parker Publishing Company, Inc., 1976).

lakeside lot in the Missouri Ozarks. Imagine her astonishment when she received an offer of nearly $10,000 for property whose ownership she had almost forgotten. Garnet very wisely reinvested her money, and today she lives in a modest home with her three children, enjoying the wonderful freedom that a substantial bank account in her own name imparts to a married woman.

The minimum amount received after the Venus ritual was a $50 bonus to one of the boys who worked as a box-boy at a local market. The boy's manager handed him the bonus for no specific reason except that he "thought he could use it."

These examples show once again how, by making even a little effort to get in tune with the money thoughtform, you can receive that insta-money that will help you overcome temporary difficulties or will become the magical seed money for a Tauran ritual.

YOUR OWN MONEY RITUAL

If you must work alone, a candle-magic ritual will be the most effective for your purposes. This ritual essentially tunes you in to the Venus money thoughtform. You can learn how to do it from our previous book; however, in order to tap this universal gold mine, we recommend you work with a small group of friends. The following ritual is designed specifically to attune you and your friends for a few magic moments to the Venus green-dollar thoughtform and to establish a good, firm link between you and it. Experiments in our own groups have shown that an ideal number for this ritual is five: three women and two men. We have found that if the group is larger than five, some of the people will tend to let their minds wander and spoil the pure essence of the emotional emanation. In groups of less than five, there seems to be insufficient power to get out there and attract vast amounts of money.

The group should choose one of the younger women to act the role of Venus. She should have long, straight, fair hair which has not been cut for at least a month prior to the working of the ritual. It would be preferable if this young woman were a virgin and also nude. If the lady is bashful in the presence of her friends, she should arrange to wear a light green mini-bikini during the ritual. We should emphasize now that this is a light, airy Venus ritual and though loving emotions should be raised during the course of the work, they should be kept on a very high plane. Animal lust is more suitable for Tauran bullish rituals. Here, for instance, any body contact should be of the light, hardly-touching variety rather than a vigorous embrace.

On the chosen night, the group should meet outdoors, preferably on a green lawn; if this is not possible, indoors in a building that
has the minimum of metal in it. If they are working in a building, green
should be the predominant color in the room. All the participants
should either disrobe or dress minimally in loose, light-green attire.
They will need a wooden bench of some sort for Venus to lie on, some
myrtle incense, four green candles, four new $1 bills, if possible an
emerald, a small vase of roses, and five clasp bracelets made in such a
way that they can be worn without forming a closed circle or ring about
the wrist.

When everyone is assembled, Venus should arrange herself comfortably on the bench with her head to the North, lying on her left side
so that she is looking to the East; for the East is traditionally the place of
greenness and rebirth. She should wear the emerald bound to her
forehead. Now, each participant should light a candle and approach
Venus in boy-girl pairs from the East, with the boy on the North and
the girl at his left to the South. Their copper bracelets should be worn
on the left wrist. Their bodies should be totally unbound, without
knots, without hairpins or fancy hairdos, without watches or jewelry,
and without cosmetics or any chemical substances present. The only
thing they should wear is their copper bracelets.

As the boy-girl couples draw near to Venus, they should bow low
and place the candles on the ground before her. Throughout this ritual,
Venus should not speak, nor should she be touched by the hands of the
participants. Now the group forms a circle around her at arms' length
from one another. Instead of joining hands, they should join the circle
together by holding the four dollar bills between the thumb and
forefinger of each adjacent pair of workers. Now a spokesman should
briefly state their purpose in meeting, something like:

"Venus, beautiful goddess of the air,
We are in need. We ask you, be fair."

The words are not as important as the sincerity of the participants. If
one of the group is not really lacking money as he has claimed, he will
probably give himself away by giggling. The leader has two choices
then: either to continue in full knowledge that the ritual has lost its
chance for effectiveness, or to try another time with different participants.

Now Venus rises from her couch and walks in a queenly manner
three times clockwise around the circle. She may lightly touch, and
even perhaps gently kiss the cheek of each participant. Her purpose is
to raise a strong love emotion in the participants. This force, called

"kundalini force" by occultists, will now be sent out to attract to itself the green dollars. Venus should now stand in a statuesque posture on her bench, and the group should chant the age-old sound, "Ee-ai-ee-ai-oh!"

If this seems strange or puzzling to you, listen for a moment to a recording of the folk tune called "Old MacDonald's Farm." The chorus chant of this ancient song is the one you are trying to use. Its building of intensity and its cumulative effect, rising to a peak of power, is traditionally the exact method used in the working of all success spells. If you are a very Christian-oriented group of workers, you might listen to the concluding bars of the Hallelujah Chorus from Handel's "Messiah." Then you can substitute in your Venus ritual the old pronunciation of hallelujah: "El-le-lu." You will find that this, too, is an effective magical chant.

Now in the candle-lit green room, or on the moonlit green lawn, the participants should imagine that green money energy is flowing clockwise around their circle, passing from the left hand of one worker through the green dollar bill into the right hand of the next worker, and so on around. They should concentrate all their attention on the woman representing Venus, and they should continue their chant, ever louder and faster. When they have attained the greatest volume and speed of chanting that they are capable of, all four should simultaneously scream out the word, "Money!" and Venus should jump immediately from her altar smothering the candles immediately after her leap. The ritual is complete.

The group should instantly hide or bury the dollar bills, then leave the circle area immediately. In their ordinary clothing again, they should adjourn for a snack, firmly turning their thoughts to unrelated topics.

This is an extremely powerful ritual, totally modern in its format. It does not use strange terminology, and it does not use any weird ingredients. It is a Mida-Psychometric tuning ritual. The whole purpose is to tune the people in to one another and to tune the group in to the Venus green-dollar thoughtform. After tuning, their emotions are raised with love and chanting; this emotional power is what is used to attract money to the members of the group.

We encourage you to do your own psychometrizing of rituals of this style and to develop your own personalized format. Change the ritual so that it feels comfortable to you; for if it does not feel comfortable to any member of the group, in all probability that member will unwittingly ruin the ritual for the others. Generally speaking, this is the reason why many people who work with ancient grimoires and "magical legendary spells" fail in their efforts. They are chanting what to them is meaningless mumbo-jumbo, even if it is "traditional," and they are naturally self-conscious and embarrassed. If sky-clad (nude) rituals embarrass you, work in robes. If all group rituals embarrass you, you should do a private magic. When you are doing Mida-Psychometry procedures, as with any other magical procedure, you should still use your intelligence. You are aiming at raising the most possible emotional energy tuned psychometrically to the right thoughtform; and anything that gets in the way of either the tuning or the raising of the emotional energy will foredoom the ritual to failure.

THE ADVANTAGES AND THE DRAWBACKS OF MONEY

We have said before that any time you tune in to a given thoughtform, you leave yourself receptive not only to the money associated with that thoughtform but also to the health hazard associated with it. This basic magical attraction procedure is based on the idea that like things attract one another. If, for instance, you are doing a Taurus lodestone procedure and you are constantly being associated with Medi-Psychometric melancholia thoughts, eventually these melancholic thoughts may create in you a mood of depression. The rule here seems to be that if you are melancholy, perhaps from the loss of a loved one, you can overcome your mood by doing a single Taurus procedure; but if you continue to do these procedures, things will come full circle and instead of curing your melancholia, the rituals will reinforce it.

There is another set of universal truths that also apply to magical procedures. This package of ideas is far less often used than the set called the Law of Attraction. They are the ones that show us that opposites such as male and female also attract, and that nature, as the saying goes, abhors a vacuum. If you have time to spare on the job, your work will expand to fill it. This illustrates again the same rule.

There are, therefore, two ways of curing melancholia. You can use either the Law of Attraction or the law of the Attraction of Opposites. For instance, you might follow some very light-hearted pursuit (Law of Attraction); or you could use the Medi-Psychometric procedure of reinforcing your melancholia thoughtform (Attraction of Oppposites).

In money procedures, Taurus and Venus, fortunately, are complements to each other. Whereas Taurus produces melancholia, Venus produces hypertension. Whereas Taurus is earthy and heavy, Venus is airy and light. Perhaps you have been doing the recommended Taurus lodestone procedure for some length of time and you begin to feel a

mood of depression coming on. It would be natural to change over to a
Venus happier procedure to overcome and rebalance your forces. It is
either very fortunate or it is the provision of an overseeing benevolent
Providence that in occult matters of Mida-Psychometry Taurus and
Venus balance each other so well.

LIFE TURNS SOUR FOR HERBERT THE MILLIONAIRE

Herbert is a financier of some renown. "Herbert" is, quite
frankly, our pseudonym, employed to protect his identity. He wrote to
us feeling that somebody must have hexed him, because he had been
riding a wave so high that everything he touched had truly been
turning to gold; then, seemingly overnight, he lost his money, his
friends, his position, and his health. He was so strapped by the time he
wrote to us that he could hardly manage to pay his medical bills; yet.
less than a year earlier, this same man had been the chairman of the
board of a major electronics firm in Texas.

What had happened? Had someone indeed hexed him? The
answer was, quite simply, No. What had happened was that Herbert
had been—all unaware—so locked on to theVenus thoughtform that
he had developed all of the Venus symptoms. He seemed to have an
almost insatiable sexual drive; he had hypertension so badly that he
was perpetually taking tranquilizers; and he was continually getting
colds. All this in a previously healthy and well-balanced man in his
fifties. He was worried about having a heart attack, and of course he
was constantly thinking about money. No longer was he a well-
balanced individual.

Looking at Table 11–1, you will immediately see that Herbert had
overdone the concentration on one very narrow aspect of life. Because
of his pursuit of secretaries to fulfill his Venus-originated desires, his
wife had divorced him. We should say here that he really didn't want to
make love to these Venus images as much as simply to enjoy them
esthetically. He was not lust-oriented so much as he was driven by a
desire to idealize a Venus image. This, of course, was something his
rather earthy wife could not understand. Why should a man in his
fifties want to surround himself with young attractive girls if he did not
want to make love to them? She was thus completely unable to understand his behavior.

Herbert also spent money on pleasure almost as fast as he earned
it. The inevitable crash came when he had what in current terms is
euphemistically called a "psychotic incident"—what used to be called a
"nervous breakdown." During his stay in the clinic, his "friends" voted
him out of most of his high-paying positions; from being a millionaire

Herbert rapidly went downhill, still spending his money, still being unable to give up the pleasure of the Venus thoughtform.

We had to tell him as gently as possible that no one had hexed him; no one had done him dirty; he had done it to himself by living such an unbalanced life. We supplied Herbert with directions for making a balancing psycho-store that were similar to those we gave you in Chapter 4. Gradually, we were able to remove his excess Venusian energy and get him to walk in balance again.

Today, Herbert has remarried his previous wife and is quietly farming in Colorado. He is not poor, nor is he very rich. But from his total-life point of view he has far more happiness than he did when he was a multi-millionaire.

THE MILLION-DOLLAR SECRET
OF COMBINING RICHES WITH GOOD HEALTH

When you made the Taurus money bag, we said you should wear it for fifteen days and then lock it away in a metal box for fifteen days. This procedure allows you to reinforce your red-gold emotional output during half the month and for the other half to have a lower-than-normal, red-gold content in your emotions. The procedure therefore works on the basis of "like attracts like" for the period from new moon to full moon (the period of increase), and "opposites attract" or "natural fills the vacuum" for the period of time from full moon to the next new moon. During this waning-moon period, your lower-than-normal, red-gold emotion will suck in money. It turns out that the suction process is just as efficient as the attraction process, and it helps you avoid the possible melancholia by lowering the red-gold emotions that produce it.

In addition to this method, there is a more effective way of balancing your life; that is, alternate between Tauran and Venusian emotions. Obviously, you must put out these emotions in monthly cycles; harmony with the moon's phases is of greatest importance. We recommend that in a two-month period you should begin at the new moon of the first month and work on Venus-emanating magic. This will give you the immediate seed money you need to work the more expensive Tauran magic of the following month. Figure 11–2 shows a typical schedule of how to work a two-month period, both to balance your life and to gain the maximum riches. By following this schedule, you will be able to avoid the health hazards that are associated with each individual sign. You should, however, be warned that doing this will increase the level of your sexual desire, and that (especially during the Taurus period) those sexual desires will be of a very animalistic, bullish nature.

In summary: Mida-Psychometry is the art of tuning yourself in to the money thoughtform that can make you infinitely wealthy. It is a simple and effective procedure. There are of course, as with all things, some catches in the procedure; but by following our simple guidelines, you can avoid the majority of these potential drawbacks and still reap all the benefits that will lead to a golden future.

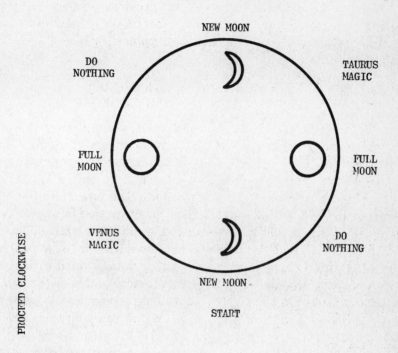

Figure 11-2

The Two-Month "Safe" Money Schedule

12

MILLION-DOLLAR MIDA-PSYCHOMETRY ACTION STEPS

RICHES FROM THE EARTH

You learned in Chapter 2 how various psychometrically induced emanations lock you into the reception of money and wealth. There is yet another principle that you must always use in achieving any ultimate desire; that is: The Gods help those who help themselves. Obviously, all the money spells in the world and all the reinforcement of your money emanations and all the linking to the money thoughtform that you could possibly do would benefit you very little if you were sitting on a lonely desert island without communication and interface with the real world. Nor will riches come to you if you sit idly with your hands in your lap. Therefore, in addition to taking your Mida-Psychometric steps to money, you must also help the universal forces to help you by putting yourself in the way of money.

We have strongly recommended that for an immediate gain, you work handling money. This actual working with money is designed to reinforce your Venusian emanations so that the Mida-Psychometric magic will bring green dollars to you. However, having read Chapter 11, you are also aware that the more long-lasting wealth is gained from the earth, and that you should in any case work with both Tauran and Venusian emanations to achieve a balance.

The psychometric link between the red-gold earth thoughtform and the green air thoughtform is clearly demonstrated by the fact that green things grow from the earth. Magically, we extend this thoughtform to say that if you deal in earthy jobs, the green will grow for you, whether it be green dollars or green crops. So in considering ways of putting yourself into the flow of money, you should first think in terms of working daily with money; but as soon as you have taken this first action step, you should arrange to work for yourself at a job that gets your hands dirty. In the county of Lancashire in England, which in the past was one of the most wealthy and witchy in the world, this idea is summarized in the proverb, "Where there's muck there's money."

GENE GETS $48,000 PER YEAR FROM A $50 BEGINNING

Gene is a former management executive living in Seattle. He thought his well-paying job was secure; typically, he was keeping up with his fellow executives in spending on luxuries while accumulating little or no cash reserves. This high living led to his downfall when the 1975 recession caught up with his firm and he was laid off. Gene went through all the standard panic moves of a laid-off executive: He wrote resumes; he called friends; he considered moving to Europe—all so he could maintain that fragile high standard of luxury living. A friend of Gene's in Los Angeles had been laid off earlier, in the 1960's aerospace recession, but Bob had made it big by becoming a landscape gardener. Despite Bob's financial success in his new field, Gene and his fellow executives had long ago written Bob off as "kinda weird." After all, he put his hands into soil!

When disaster was staring Gene in the face, when his wife Lila was on the verge of a breakdown, when the specter of unpaid charge accounts was keeping him awake every night, he finally called Bob. Bob invited Gene to come down and see him for a serious talk. If worst came to worst, Bob would give him a position. Moreover, though Bob couldn't spare the time to come to Seattle, he would be happy to help with the expenses of Gene's coming down to visit. Reflecting later, Gene often retells the story of that trip to Los Angeles, shaking his head in wonder at his own naivete.

Bob picked him up at the airport in a battered old pickup truck, one that Gene wouldn't have been caught dead in. Bob was dressed in worn blue jeans and a clean but paint-stained shirt. Not a worry-line showed on his tanned and smiling face. "Had dinner yet?" he inquired of Gene. When Gene mentioned a snack during the flight, Bob replied decisively, "That's usually not enough to keep a bird alive. Let's go eat."

Gene tried to hide his surprise when Bob left the old pickup truck with the doorman of a fashionable Hollywood restaurant. His surprise grew when the maitre d' deferentially escorted them to one of the "right" tables. Surprise turned to amazement when Bob told the waiter he would have his usual, and the usual turned out to be a steak weighing at least two pounds. During the meal, Bob explained how, with no more investment than an ad in the local newspaper, he had been able to become a successful landscape gardener who now employed three helpers.

"In southern California, people want to see their yards being done by oriental-looking types," he commented. "What I need now is a manager so that we can expand into another area of the L.A. Basin. I figure after about a year you would be able to make it your own business."

"But what's in it for you, Bob?" asked Gene.

"Heck, I'm making enough to keep body and soul together," Bob grinned, "and I sure don't want the bother of a big organization. I got enough of that when I was in aerospace."

This attitude flabbergasted Gene. He was so accustomed to the competitive pace of business and the drive to get ahead (even if it meant stepping on someone), that only when he was comfortably settled in Bob's pleasant guestroom did he realize how distorted his own sense of values had become. Always he had taken for granted that "dirty" tasks were done by menial people of low intelligence; that to get ahead required constant competition with and defeating other people.

Gene spent all that next day happily helping Bob with some of his landscaping tasks and meeting Bob's employees; their attitude clearly showed that here was a bunch of guys working together and enjoying it, rather than just putting in time kowtowing to a resented boss. That evening, Gene returned to Seattle after promising Bob he would think about the offer of a managership. Bob's parting comments weighed heavily with Gene:

"Well, you've got an ideal chance to get out of the rat race. Don't fall back into it like a sucker. Even if you don't come down here, at least think about doing something different for yourself and for the family."

Gene returned to Seattle full of enthusiasm; he could not sit still as he told Lila how it had opened his eyes. "That guy's got money to burn," he told her, "and it cost him almost nothing to get into it." But Lila was one of those people who find it hard to think in terms other than those of a regular paycheck for "clean" work. She successfully dampened his spirits with such barbs as, "How are we going to move? We are settled here. Let's wait until Eric is out of school," and "Gardening wouldn't work up here. The season's too short," and "Landscape garden for a living? With your degree?"

When bedtime came, Gene was not only tired from his trip but dispirited by his conversation with Lila as well. He determined, however, that he would follow Bob's suggestion and try to keep away from the pressures of executive life. When he awoke the next morning, he settled down to review what "menial" tasks he could do which would still provide some sort of living wage. Eventually he got it narrowed down to seven opportunities that he could conceivably try. These ranged from "washing cars at home" through "window washing" to "being a chimney sweep." He sealed the description of each opportunity in an envelope and psychometrized the envelopes, holding the idea of peace and prosperity in his mind. "Window washing" won. Without telling the carping Lila, he took out ads in the next day's paper and removed the camper from his luxury truck. With the purchase of a couple of buckets, some sponges, and a new sign, and hauling out his trusty old ladder from the garage, he was ready for his new venture. Gene's Window-Cleaning Service had been born. "It's just a stop-gap, dear," he assured Lila, "till one of those resumes I sent out hits."

The response of his ad was swift and encouraging. Within a month, he had employed two other laid-off executives and eight assistants. Apparently, he had just hit the market at the right time with the right service. In the first year, Gene netted over $48,000 in his business; today he is a contented man who still has his original staff working for him, as well as time to spend with his family.

YOU TOO CAN MAKE MONEY

Gene was lucky, there's no doubt. But you can repeat his experience. People shy away from Tauran "dirty" jobs, yet it is precisely these earth-oriented jobs that can most enrich and "green" your life. The ultimate truth about wealth is that it proceeds from the earth and from man's working with the earth. Granted, there are vast amounts of green dollars to be made by working in support industries such as banking or the stock market, but when you get close to the ultimate source of wealth, the earth, you must succeed.

Pick up your phone book right now; turn to the yellow pages. See whether there is a window-washing service or a gardening service in your city. Nowadays most cities have janitorial services, but this is only a recent phenomenon; for janitorial services seem somehow to be a little higher in status, a little "cleaner," than gardening or window-washing. Recently, too, people are making good incomes in such enterprises as rug shampooing.

None of these businesses costs very much to get into. A few dollars in advertising, a few dollars for uniforms, and a few more for incidentals, and you are set up. Not only can you work with earth emanations in these businesses, but the money you make is all yours. The cost of supplies is very minimal; thus you stop the flow of money right in your own wallet. The money need go no further. It doesn't flow to some absentee boss or to a vast corporation.

In time past, you would naturally have said that the original Tauran pursuit was that of the farmer. But the farmer was able to gain so much material wealth, that both big business and big government became greedy for a share of the profits; today, the small farmer has difficulty retaining on the farm that money which is rightfully his.

MIDA-PSYCHOMETRY POINTS THE WAY

By now, hopefully, you will have developed your psychometric abilities. At the very least, you will be able to feel the emanations from different colors; and, having practiced the exercises in Chapter 1, you can also detect emanating from people such things as ill health and true or false friendship.

Now is the time for you to apply your gift to the detection of money. The simple way to do this is to take six or eight plain envelopes (all exactly alike) and place dollar bills in half of them, and blank pieces of paper of equivalent weight in the other half. Shuffle the envelopes like a pack of cards. Then hold your hand over them as you were instructed to in Chapter 1, and practice detecting which ones have the dollar bills in them. It may take you several hours before you can always detect the ones with the dollar bills; but once you can do it with confidence, make up slips of paper with the various businesses written on them that you have considered for your area and slip these into fresh envelopes. The previous envelopes should not be used because the ones that contained the currency will have picked up the money emanations from it. From your new envelopes, select the two that give you the most powerful money vibrations. Then use your intelligence to decide which of these two businesses you would most like to get into.

In these lists of possible business opportunities, do not be bashful about including one that you favor, whether or not it seems at first thought to have the Tauran or Venusian connections or a vast profit potential. You may find through your Meta-Psychometric technique that one of these businesses would in fact go over very well in your town.

If the business that comes to the surface in your experiment is one which requires a good location, rather than just a post office box or a telephone answering service, get a map of your area and psychometrize *it* to feel out the best possible available location for your business. Notice we include the word "available." It should be included in your thoughtform as well when you are psychometrically analyzing the map; for obviously the very best locations may already be taken in your city or may be beyond your budget, so that you must be satisfied with the best available.

FIFTY-CENT SALE NETS DOROTHY $25 PROFIT

Dorothy, a middle-aged housewife, lives on the outskirts of Pittsburgh. She and her husband Mack, unable to have the children they wanted, had often discussed adopting children, but had held back so long that the adoption agencies now felt that they were too old. Thus Dorothy found the outlet for her love in the breeding of dogs, which normally would be assumed to be a Scorpio/Venusian undertaking, because Scorpio is associated more with reproduction than the Taurus vibrations are. Nonetheless, everything was going fine for Dorothy until a traffic accident took Mack's life; she found that her sales of puppies just did not support herself and the boy she had been employing to clean the kennels.

She wrote to us, asking us what we thought she should do. After some correspondence with her and some psychometric work on our part, we told her that she should extend her business by opening a pet store, and that she should definitely add Tauran emanations to her business by getting involved with all the clean-up work caused by the animals, rather than employing someone else to do it. We were also able to pinpoint two areas for her in Pittsburgh—areas which seemed to have good available locations. One of these was old and inexpensive; the other was in a newly built and relatively high-priced shopping center. We strongly advised Dorothy to rework and rehabilitate the older property because we felt the area would "come up" in the future—and that the rehabilitation activities were Tauran.

Dorothy followed our advice. Today she has a very successful pet store. Contrary to our image of pet stores, though, she sells very few major animals. She tells us that the best possible sale she can make is a fifty-cent goldfish; for through the sale of such a fish, she is able to make upward of $25 profit on all the paraphernalia and accessories that go with the fish. The tank, the aerator, the pump, the filter, the ornaments, the greens, the sand, and the specialized fish food and instruction handbooks are all high-profit-margin items.

Thus with the help of Mida-Psychometry, Dorothy was able to enlarge her modest business into a thriving enterprise. As we had predicted, the old neighborhood into which she moved has now been "discovered." Young couples are moving in and restoring the houses; their children provide an excellent market for small pets and accessories.

MIDA-PSYCHOMETRY GIVES YOU THE EDGE

Each year in the United States thousands of businesses are started—and thousands fail. Most of these businesses require large investments; but there are significant numbers which require minimal investment. With the aid of Mida-Psychometry, you can make one of these minimal-investment businesses successful. You have an edge that most businessmen do not possess. That edge is your developed psychometric ability. Before you ever get involved in a business, you will have psychometrically analyzed it, as well as six or so other businesses. In this way, you have already given yourself a leg up on the competition. If your business is one that requires a special location, you have also found with your talents the best possible location for success in your field. Hold your hand over the yellow pages index, and you can rapidly find with the aid of your Meta-Psychometric powers which businesses in that index are the big money makers. Some of them obviously are not for you; either because they are not suited to your temperament or because you lack investment capital to start them. But you will be surprised at how many small business opportunities are available in which you can be your own boss.

Think of the man who started the Pet Rock craze; and before that, the Hula-Hoop craze. Neither of them had vast capital investment; they just had a good idea. With your talents, you don't even need a brilliant idea. You can simply go into a business that is Tauran or Venusian-connected, and be sure of success.

BE AS RICH AS YOU WANT TO BE

Working for money is just like working for any other goal. You can work at it as hard as you want to. If you possibly can, you should set yourself a fixed goal before you start your effort. When you are poor, you might think, "If only I had $100,000, I'd never worry again." But as you gain in wealth, so you want ever more and more. The gaining of wealth can literally become a treadmill in which you sacrifice your health and all your friends, for it seems that there are always reasons for needing *more* money. When you have that first $100,000 you will find within yourself a desire to make a million! When you have so much money that it is impossible to spend it all, still you will be driven to make more—unless you are willing to step back and say, "Enough."

Set a realistic goal. Make that money as quickly as you know how; then retire. In this way, you will be able to retain your health and your friends, yet be independently wealthy. Making money is much easier than you may think, and only your own imagination limits the ways in which you can make it.

UNCONVENTIONAL SUCCESS STORIES

Do you have $400? You may think that's a paltry amount; or you may think it sounds like the end of the rainbow. $400 is precisely the amount of money Terence had. He decided he would invest it in balloons. Yes, balloons. Difficult to believe, isn't it? That a man would be crazy enough to get out and buy gas tanks, string, and fancy balloons with his entire fortune of $400. Yet, in his first year as a balloon vendor, Terence made over $20,000. Still think he's crazy? He has continued to double that income amount in every single year since; and who cannot help but love a balloon vendor?

The hottest recent success story that we have come across is a business that will cost you as little as $100 to get into. It is called the "ghost dog." You may or may not have seen teen-agers walking down the sidewalk with a dog's leash and collar traveling along just in front of their ankles—but no dog. Sales records of one manufacturer of the "ghost dog" show that in one year he made over $28,000. We sincerely believe that if you have not seen these in your own city, you have a ready-made market available. Sure, it's just a gimmick, just like pet rocks and hula-hoops. Obviously, it is a business that won't last forever. But if you can clean up $20,000 this year in your spare time for an investment of only $100, why aren't you trying it? What is it that you are doing in your life that means you don't have time to try a business like this one?

The strangest business, perhaps, that we have been involved in setting up is worm farming. From the psychometric point of view, location is of prime importance. You need to have a constant flow of sports-bound traffic past your door, and you need a town nearby. When we helped Arthur, a disabled veteran in Missouri, to psychometrize the map of his county, he was able on a $1,000 investment to start a business that we can confidently predict will make him well over $50,000 this year. For not only have his sales of worms to fishermen skyrocketed; but with the present ecological and organic-gardening movement, he is able to sell cartons of live worms both direct and through mail order to thousands of homeowners who are more interested in building their soil than in fishing.

Arthur's operation now includes a rabbit farm, the rabbits producing the necessary compost for the worms to grow in. In winter, Arthur has to feed his breeding rabbits commercial feeds; but of course at that time of year. his need for their compost is low, so he is able to keep his expenses down. In summer, the rabbits thrive mainly on home-grown greens. Arthur figures that with sales of live Easter bunnies, pelts, and cleaned rabbit meat, the rabbit operation pays for itself. This means that he gets his worm compost free. Arthur's final investment was more than the couple of hundred dollars that some worm farmers start with, but for less than $5,000 ultimate investment he now has a comfortable mobile home, a rabbit-and-worm operation, and a very high income, all of which he earns with about four hours' Tauran work a day.

THE MILLIONAIRES' GAME:
COMMODITIES AND STOCK OPTIONS

For those who are unaware of the potentialities inherent in the futures market, we should say that the system whereby an investor can purchase, for example, coffee in the future by paying 10 percent of the contract value today leads to both fantastic gains and losses. For when a trader holds contracts that are gaining in value, he is able to purchase more contracts with the money that he has made from the gain in the value of the contract first purchased (the earlier contract that he holds). Thus traders very often find themselves in the position of making or losing a million dollars for a five-cent per pound change in the price of a commodity. Every day the commodities market is open, millions of dollars are made and lost.

Unfortunately for the small investor, this is a game for the Big Boys. You need a substantial bank account before you are allowed by the market operators to purchase a contract. Recently there have been some cooperative ventures started through which you can get into the market with a group of friends for as little as $1,000 down. You might want to start by joining one of these cooperatives.

A market parallel to the commodities market is the stock-options market, wherein you can purchase stocks at a fixed price by a certain date at some time in the future. This market has a lower potential for risk and for gain than the commodities market; but remember, if you invest and make a mistake, you can lose all of your investment.

BEVY AND THE COFFEE FUTURES

Bevy J. is a well-known psychic in St. Louis. She is an extremely hardworking and dedicated lady. As the saying goes, she couldn't make a fortune because she was too busy earning a living. From the Mida-Psychometry point of view, it is easy to understand that if you are working hard in the gaining of esoteric knowledge, for instance, this pursuit will not increase your output of money-attracting emanations.

Occasionally when Bevy was really strapped, we would offer a little advice or perhaps even attempt to add the necessary Tauran-Venusian emanations to her aura by conducting a ritual for her. But it was through Mida-Psychometry that Bevy finally made it. A businessman, Pete, asked her advice on some investments that he was considering in commodity futures. She psychometrized the coffee option that Pete had open to him. She recommended that Pete invest in coffee that was not even growing on the trees yet. He took her advice, as the report in *The Star* weekly (Figure 12–1) shows.

Pete's investment record has since become a much-discussed textbook case of how to make money in commodities futures. It has even been written up in such prestigious financial publications as *Barrons Magazine*.[1] Over a period of some six months, Bevy worked almost daily with Pete, both pragmatically and psychically analyzing the coffee market. Not only were coffee crops bad in South America, with a record-breaking freeze destroying a large part of the harvest, but the political crisis in Angola also meant that that country's exports for a whole year became almost non-existent. Anyone who drinks coffee knows by now what happened to the price of coffee. It was this increase

---

[1]*Barrons*, May 17, 1976 Page 52. Front page *St. Louis Post-Dispatch*, May 20, 1976.

Psychic is given $60,000 house for helping tycoon make a million

PAGE 19 THE STAR JUNE 29, 1976

By SHIRLEY HOFFMAN

A BUSINESS tycoon has given psychic Beverly Jaegers a luxury home for helping him strike a $600,000 bonanza on the stock market.

Commodities broker John Peter Dixon of St. Louis handed over the keys to Mrs. Jaegers after watching a $24,000 investment in coffee options soar to $1.3 million — a profit of $600,000 after taxes.

"I thought coffee was going up, but might have hedged my bets without Bevvy's encouragement," he told The Star this week.

"With her help, I let it all ride and my coffee investment is still going up."

Now Mrs. Jaegers, her husband and six children have moved into a $60,000 four-bedroom ranch house in Creve Coeur, St. Louis' poshest suburb.

Mrs. Jaegers told The Star that she has helped other clients with stock market predictions.

"I ask them to put the name of the stock on a piece of paper and put it into an envelope," she said.

"I hold the envelope and I get an impression — sometimes I see a graph that goes up or down and other times I just get a yes-or-no impression."

Mr. Dixon, who says he has deep ESP feelings himself, first saw Mrs. Jaegers on a local TV program.

"The minute I saw her I had total belief in her. I started my company on the premise of using ESP in business and I've made myself a paper millionaire in only two years."

Dixon's company, Leverequity, Inc., deals in future, on copper, cotton, platinum, wheat and oats as well as coffee.

Dixon wrote down his hunch about coffee on the last day of 1975, sealed it in an envelope, and gave it to Mrs. Jaegers.

She said: "I ran my left hand — that's the most sensitive one for right-handed people — over the envelope and around the edges while I concentrated.

"I saw a tree, then red berries, then heavy rains and military persons in a place that seemed to be Africa. I saw people carrying empty baskets.

"They should have been full, I felt, but they had only a few berries in the bottom."

That was enough for Dixon, who went ahead with his investment in coffee futures.

"The markets are not really very difficult to determine," he told The Star.

Figure 12-1

The Results of Mida-Psychometry

Bevy used closed-envelope psychometry to make Pete millions.

in price that allowed Pete, with Bevy's constant counseling aid, to make several million dollars. (Pete's account record starts in November 1972 with an investment of $24,000 and ends on April 13, 1976 with a balance of $2,813,000.)

This return on commodities is not unusual. To prove that her success was not a fluke, Bevy next counseled her clients to get into soy beans. Within days of her advice, that market also took off. How many millions of dollars were made by investors in soy bean futures is almost impossible to compute. Our estimate is that it is well over $100,000,000. Bevy's consultant contracts on these investments allowed her to purchase a beautiful home and to fill it with comfortable new furniture in the appropriate green and gold tones that will ensure her future wealth. When the more conventional businessmen scoff at Pete and Bevy with their Mida-Psychometric investments, the only suitable rebuttal is, "I'll see you at the bank."

YOUR KEY TO THE MILLIONAIRES' CLUB

When you have a couple of thousand dollars saved, don't let it stagnate. For as we have said, stagnant money brings with it that aura of clenched suspicion that will ruin your money emanations. Since trade and commerce began, businessmen with capital available have either invested it in other business ventures or have put it into such high-risk areas as commodity futures or stock options. Most commodities, being products of the soil, are intimately connected with the earth and with Taurus-style pursuits. Thus Mida-Psychometrizing the commodities market will reinforce your chances of making riches. Just as you learned in Chapter 1 to detect colors Meta-Psychometrically, and just as you learned in this chapter to detect the Venus-style emanations from dollar bills, so you can detect those market opportunities that will take you from being merely wealthy into the millionaire status.

Your first move will be to subscribe to a newspaper that has in it the daily commodity market quotations. Select two or three specific commodities. Cut out the quotations from the newspaper for the commodities you have selected, and place each quotation in a separate envelope. When one of the selected commodities moves up or down, cut out the new quotations and place these in separate envelopes. Now, Mida-Psychometrizing the pair of envelopes which contains the high and low quotations for any one of the commodities, learn to detect which one is high and which is the low. After a few days of practice you should be able to distinguish high from low.

The next step is to cut out all of the commodities from the newspaper and place each quotation in a separate envelope. Shuffle the envelopes together as you would a deck of cards, and Mida-Psychometrically detect which of the quotations will gain the most in the following weeks. Record your impressions and watch the selected commodity's price for the next week or two. You may find that your detector is in what might be called "negative gear" and what feels to your hand like "up" is in fact telling you "down." If this is the case, try again with another commodity until you are sure you are reading the emanations correctly. Here are you learning to distinguish between your own sensations just as you did when you were learning to detect the various colors psychometrically. It is most important here, of course, for you to spend time every day studying the market and practicing your talents so that when you are ready to invest you won't lose your magically gained wealth. The daily work will ensure that your sensitivity is sustained at a high level.

YOUR SIMPLE STEPS TO WEALTH

Having just read these last two chapters, you may be confused as to what you should do first in order to gain that great wealth or even the key to the millionaires' club that you desire. We have deliberately laid out these chapters in sequential order so that you can start at the beginning of Chapter 11 and follow a systematic approach that will lead you to your goal in easy steps. To summarize those steps:

1. *Money Attracts Money.* The money emanations that you put out will attract money to you. For a sure long-term gain, your first step will be to construct your money lodestone or Midas Bag. If you have insufficient cash on hand to charge this bag and to place in it the appropriate red gold, you should conduct a Venus ritual, either working alone or with a group. This will bring the green emanations into your life.

2. *Balance Ready Green Money and Long-Term Orange Wealth.* To achieve a balance in your life, you should alternate between Tauran and Venusian attractive forces. Remember that during the growing phase of the moon, you should put out attractive vibrations so that the Law of Attraction will work; and during the decreasing phase of the moon, you should use the principle of Attraction of Opposites. This system will allow you to stay healthier and to retain the love of your friends while you gain immense wealth.

3. *The Gods Help Those Who Help Themselves.* You cannot isolate yourself from the world and still expect to become a millionaire. You must get out there and deal with money or with earth-oriented jobs. If you want to make money, deal in the money type that you wish to make. If you wish to become wealthy in the Tauran sense, you must be prepared to get your hands dirty and to work at a Tauran job.

4. *Move Your Money.* Having once been poor, it is easy to cling to the money that you make, or to put it away in a bank account or in a miser's iron box. This attitude creates the wrong field around you, for it brings to the fore Saturnian "secure" emanations of clenching and fear. To become a millionaire, you must keep your money moving and working, and you must recognize that there is a certain degree of risk implied in such ventures. By adequately Mida-Psychometrizing available opportunities, you can avoid the majority of the risks that most businessmen run.

5. *It Won't Drop into Your Lap.* Lastly, we wish to make it clear one more time that gaining great wealth requires diligent work in addition to the aid you get from the Mida-Psychometry system we have outlined. For a time, this diligence will naturally separate you from your friends who are more interested in pleasurable but idle pursuits. That's all right. Having weighed the alternatives, you have made a

rational choice. How many of your pleasure-seeking friends can say the same? How much wealth will they have in ten years' time?

By deciding at the outset the amount of your goal and how much money you intend to make each year, you can balance your life in such a way as to become extremely wealthy and still retain your health and your friends.

13

PUTTING META-PSYCHOMETRY TO WORK EVERY DAY OF YOUR LIFE

PROVE IT TO YOURSELF AGAIN

Throughout this work, we have given you examples of real people and real experiences. In many cases these examples have been documented, but still you may wonder whether the techniques will work for you. We ask you to take just a few moments and conduct one small test. If you conduct this test carefully, you will find it gives very predictable results.

Get a recent photograph of a good friend; place the photo on a small piece of violet velvet. Cover the photograph with salt, and lock it away in a drawer for a few days. Observe the friend's actions closely. One of two things will happen: Either your friend will be persistently thirsty, or he will crave salt. This is the same positive-or-negative psychic result that we described in Chapter 1. Once you know which way your psychic powers work, your results are all predictable. In the case of the salt test, the target person should crave salt; but if your psychic powers are negative, he will crave water instead.

Many, many people have tried this salt test. A very good friend of ours, Bill Finch the exorcist (listed in the Appendix), told us the story of a fellow who tried this on his wife. His supper was so salty that he could not eat it. She didn't know what was wrong with her, the wife admitted, but every time she passed the salt shaker, she felt an urge to salt the cooking supper again.

Once again you have proved to yourself that Meta-Psychometry works. Now go ahead and re-evaluate all of your plans for the future; for you can literally get anything you desire through the use of the techniques we describe in this book.

THE ETHICS OF META-PSYCHOMETRY

Thousands of people write to us every year saying that even though they are absolutely convinced that our techniques would work for them too, still they are afraid of using them because they feel it may be unethical to gain an advantage in this way. The question of ethics is in the forefront today, whether it be the President of the United States, a group of monks running a charity swindle, police forces on the take, or whoever. We are not in any way suggesting that you should emulate these unethical people. We think that you can tell when you do something wrong, and we feel that a psychic crime against an individual is just as bad as a mundane crime. It is true, however, that most people nowadays have some knowledge of psychic phenomena and psychic information. If they wanted to win badly enough, they too could employ these same techniques.

You do not criticize the pole-vaulter for using the latest, lightest, most springy pole he can get when he vaults. Nor do you criticize a football team that comes up with an entirely new play which wins the pennant for them. You don't say that the pole-vaulter is unethical, nor do you accuse the football coach of unethical practices. So we can see no reason why the use of the latest and best psychic techniques should be called unethical. We believe that foreign governments are already using these techniques—against us! It is most important that everyone learn as much as possible about the various means of psychic defense; and since it is well-known that the "best form of defense is attack," you should also know how to perform a psychic attack.

We believe, further, that it is ethical to try to set people on the right path, and to try to prevent people from harming others. Often, as you get involved with curing a person of bad habits or teaching him some lesson, you will skirt the edge of unethical psychic behavior. When you do, you will find that your actions affect your own life. By the immutable Law of Attraction, some of the things that you put out will also be attracted to you; there is thus a safety balancing that occurs in psychic work. If you go overly negative, you will find that your capabilities decrease; because by being negative you attract negative emanations to yourself. In other words, the ethics of Meta-Psychometry are self-adjusting. Do everything you can to solve a problem or to correct a situation, realizing that if you go too negative or you commit some psychic crime unaware, you will in your turn have the same negation visited on yourself by the Law of Attraction.

Somewhere a persistent myth has sprung up to the effect that obtaining money by psychic means is a negative procedure. We ourselves have met many people who had this capability of gathering money psychically; and not one of them, so far as we can tell, ever had a problem because of the procedures they used. On the other hand, we read every day of people who get into terrible situations when trying to get money in the mundane way. They incur ill health and even risk of long terms in prison through their mundane actions. The question you need to ask yourself first is: To what use is the money you gather going to be put? If the answer is a positive good, then go right ahead and use all your psychic talents to aid yourself.

We encourage you to try psychically anything you can dream up—while you carefully monitor your physical and psychic balance; if you see that the work is putting you out of balance, slow down and reconsider the procedures you are using. When you do this, you may find that one or more of the procedures is causing you to have mundane problems.

DON AND THE MERGER

Don L is a New York businessman. Some years ago he started a small specialty clothing concern and built it up until he had some twenty employees working on designs that he and his wife created. Eventually Don was working night and day to keep up with the orders; thus when a large clothing concern, Manchester Linens, offered Don the opportunity of merging his small enterprise with theirs, he carefully considered the offer. He could see that with the cash offered he would be able to afford a new home for himself and his wife, and that since the larger firm wished them to move out of the city to their plant in New Jersey, Don's family would probably have a more pleasant life. He pushed to the back of his mind the thought that all his hard-working employees would probably be laid off, for he knew that what Manchester wanted was his styles and his name, not his workers.

Don pushed ahead with plans for the merger, even though his wife was against it, and even though it came in the middle of getting their fall line of fashions out. Altogether he worked far too hard, and as a result of all this activity he had a mild heart attack. When he returned to work from the hospital, he found that his employees, under his wife's supervision, had been able to fill in for him adequately (if not perfectly) and to get the clothing out.

Often people who have had heart attacks re-evaluate their priorities and their life goals while they lie in hospital in enforced idleness. In Don's case, his re-evaluation convinced him that the merger was not really what he wanted. The fact that his employees had been so loyal and had worked so hard strengthened Don's feeling that he should not go on with the merger. But the papers were already signed, and he could see no easy way of getting out of it without being sued for specific compliance by Manchester. The garment industry is one in which people have to trust one another's word, and it is death even to a well-liked group like Don's to have it said that "you have broken your word."

While he had been in hospital, Don had read one of our books; he decided he would try some Witchcraft to see whether he could get Manchester to abandon their plans for the merger. Don didn't really feel confident in his own ability to undertake the Witchcraft that he supposed would be required to get Manchester to call off the merger, so he wrote asking our advice. We gave him instructions on the building of a pyramid and the charging of documents with astral power. We suggested that he place the merger documents in the pyramid and use a violet Aquarian filter to charge them with Uranian power, which would disrupt the merger.

After thinking about all this, Don went us one better. He drew up a new spring line of fashions, all in very trendy Aquarian styles, and in the line he made great use of violet. He called his whole line "the Violet Aquarians." He charged all the sketches in his pyramid and sent them off for review to Manchester. The Aquarian energy caused the management of Manchester to have second thoughts about the whole deal. Within the week Don had a long telephone call from one of their vice-presidents, asking him whether he was well and whether he thought he was fit enough to become a vice-president with very heavy responsibilities. Don could see that his scheme was working, so he feigned uncertainty about his health condition and about his management ability.

Now Don took yet another step on his own. Having been so successful with his first effort, he felt sure that he could safely use a little more of the power to help in dissolving the merger. From among the literature that he had been given in the early days of negotiations, he cut out photographs of each member of the Board of Directors of Manchester and placed them in his pyramid. He just left them there! Of course *you* know that this would be a tremendous dose of energy, especially for a group of rather older, sedentary businessmen. A week later, Don talked to the same vice-president about what he should be doing about getting the spring line out, and asked whether there shouldn't be some decisions on the sketches he had submitted. The vice-president was extremely cold and formal with him; at the end of the conversation he admitted to feeling under the weather. Don learned that in fact all the people whose pictures he had put in the pyramid had had serious diarrhea, and the chairman of the board had almost died because his ulcer had flared up.

Looking at the Table of Correspondences, you can see how this all happened; for not only does the violet color disrupt friendships, it can also cause disease when it is supplied too generously.

The merger plans were ultimately shelved. Don is still running his small select business in New York. He now has applied his occult knowledge to his fashion line, and you can recognize his styles by the consistencies of color and form.

WHY SHOULDN'T YOU WIN?

Winning the game of life is just as pleasurable as winning any other game. When your favorite football team wins, you don't criticize them. Even if they played somewhat roughly, still you cheer them on. A lot of people will tell you that there are rules in the game; there are certain business ethics which people "must" abide by. You should always ask yourself: Who made the rules? And why? Obviously, many rules are useful and needed. You can't just ignore stop signs and red lights when you're driving, for instance, and expect to survive. Nor can you break contracts or fail to deliver and expect to survive in business.

In the ethical sense, large businesses and governments often completely ignore the rights of individuals. We ourselves left the world of business because of the practices that we saw both between and within firms. Many of the examples that we use in our books are taken from our business life; these are true examples of the things that can happen in real offices. We can also tell you from first-hand knowledge that when the chips are down and the competition is tough between companies, they will do anything to win. The payoff scandals of recent years are just the most recent, blatant examples of this absence of ethical standards.

We would hasten to add that many firms are, in fact, very ethical. You should, therefore, not worry one moment about teaching any firm or any business a lesson by psychic means when you have been defrauded. Strength and power are things that business leaders respect. They react to it positively, and you will find yourself winning.

A question you ought to ask yourself is this: When you win, will you like what you get? Don had a successful small business. He was going to become a vice-president in a large concern, and for a time he reconciled himself to the sacrifice of his employees for the furthering of his own career. If he had not had that heart attack, and had not taken time to re-evaluate himself and his life goals while in hospital, it would have been too late for those people who would have been thrown out of work.

It is not too late for you. You can sit down today and decide whether or not you will be happy with the results of your psychic work. Of course each person is different, and your goals may not be the same goals as those of your next-door neighbor. High on most people's list of goals is the acquisition of money. We personally are more interested in increasing the general awareness of the people we meet than in the gaining of wealth; thus when we get money from our techniques we usually spend it on having pamphlets published and teaching people the first steps in spiritual development. Before you decide to win, therefore, you must decide what game it is you are going to win; because if you play the wrong game, though you win it, you will be no more content than you are today.

SELECTING YOUR FIRST GOAL

Fortunately, Meta-Psychometry can help you in this allocation of priorities. Simply take some slips of paper, write on them a selection from the following list, and place each slip of paper into its own individual new envelope.

Money	Job Improvement
Serenity	Better Health
Friendship	A New Mate
Psychic Balance	

This list includes the most common requests that we get in incoming mail. You personally may have other goals of higher importance, of course. Whatever they are, reduce them to a brief phrase, write them down, and place them in envelopes. Now psychometrize the envelopes, asking for your first-priority goal. Then ask for your second-priority goal, and your third, until you have a complete ranking of the goals that you want to work on. This is your Meta-Psychometric pathway to success. It is the logical progression of fulfillment of your needs. You must now work on each goal in turn. Table 13–1 lists a selection of goals and the chapters in this book wherein you can find the Meta-Psychometric steps that will assure you of success as you tackle each goal in turn. We should say here that if you have been unable to bring serenity into your surroundings, as you were instructed to do in Chapters 1 and 2, then for the completion of this Meta-Psychometric life analysis, you should go away to some quiet motel either at the mountains or at the seacoast where you can spend at least a week alone quietly working on your analysis.

Goal	Chapter
Health	7
Money	11
Mating	9
Psychic Balance	5
Psychic Defense	3
Listening to Others	2
Dominating Others	10
Winning	6
Serenity	3

Table 13–1

Goals and Their Respective Chapters

NELDA'S META-PSYCHOMETRIC PATHWAY TO SUCCESS[1]

Some fifteen years ago, Nelda was employed as a secretary for a St. Louis envelope-manufacturing concern. She was married and had two small children. When her husband was killed in a plane crash, Nelda was snatched from her serene life and placed abruptly in a position where she had to fend for herself. Her parents lived in England, and could provide very little financial help from across the water.

She had some obvious choices. She could go to England, or she could make a new life for herself in the United States. She could take

_____

[1]Nelda is a fictitious person, as is Beth whom you will meet later in this chapter. Though we have been working and telling people about Meta-Psychometry for eight years or more, still we do not have in our files a case history showing the fulfillment of a complete life path. We do have many case histories showing the fulfillment of portions of such a path, however, so we have synthesized two case histories together in the cases of both Nelda and Beth.

the easy way and get married again as soon as possible. She decided instead that she would Meta-Psychometrize her future. Using the envelope technique, she found that her first priority should be to obtain more money, and that this was very closely followed by getting a different job. Immediately following money and a new job came the milestone of improved health; and last, with a very low priority, appeared remarriage.

Nelda was quite surprised by these results, because she had felt that she was reasonably well off money-wise; she liked her job; and her health was in reasonable order, so far as she knew. However, she determined to follow the guidance she had received. Knowing that money attracts money, she looked for a secretarial job in a bank or in a financial institution, and soon found a position with one of the downtown stock brokers. The job she found paid only slightly more than the envelope-manufacturing firm had, and the additional necessary travel was costing her more money; so though her job was putting her into a money-oriented position, her initial step put her at a very slight financial disadvantage. Additionally, the money she had counted on from her husband's insurance was terribly slow in arriving, so she was soon two months behind in her house payments.

At this critical juncture, she had an accident on the freeway and learned to her horror that the car insurance was in her husband's name and did not include coverage on third-party liability for her. Thus she found herself owing almost $1000 for repair of the damage she had admittedly caused in the collision. She reviewed her Meta-Psychometric analysis one more time and realized that she had taken the wrong step first. Her review now told her that she had confused the top two priorities from the envelope technique. Instead of first getting more money and then changing jobs, she had interrelated the two and had changed jobs in order to get more money. In her new situation, she decided to do another complete Meta-Psychometric analysis. In this re-evaluation, the money envelope came out far ahead of any of the others, with health now running a weak second, so she decided to get together with a couple of her occult friends and to perform a Venusian money ritual.

The effect of the ritual was dramatic. What it did was speed up various insurance company actions. The day following the ritual, Nelda got a check in the mail in full settlement for her husband's life insurance. She also received a notification that her house mortgage was fully paid, because her husband had taken out mortgage insurance that Nelda had not been aware of. Within the week, she also got a check from her car insurance agent. Without her knowledge, he had appealed to the company to pay this particular claim; and the Board, having reviewed the case, decided that they should in fact pay it. Thus suddenly she found herself a moderately well-to-do widow.

With the aid of good information from her boss in the brokerage office, she was able to parlay her moderate wealth into a literal fortune. While she was doing this, she started to investigate the matter of her health. Her first move, sensibly, was to go for a full physical checkup. This showed nothing significantly wrong, so she returned to her Meta-Psychometry and used her private rainbow prism to identify the missing color. This work showed her that the turquoise-green element was absent. Her first assumption was that because she was no longer married, this was just a sexual lack, so she started dating several of the fellows from the brokerage office; however, over the next few weeks she could see no appreciable improvement in her ability to perceive turquoise-green in her personal rainbow. Deciding that her lack should be made up more directly, she made herself a green medicine bag. With its help, she was able very quickly to see the full rainbow again. To this day, we still do not know precisely what her health problem was, though in discussing the matter with her we suspect that it was an incipient kidney complaint. Whatever it was, the medicine bag took care of it.

Nelda was now in pretty good shape; she found a small group in St. Louis with whom she could pursue her occult work. Somehow, though, she always seemed to be goofing things up and saying the wrong thing in meetings. On our advice she made herself a blue centaur luck-bringing necklace. At the very first meeting of the occult group to which she wore the necklace, she met Dave, the man she eventually married. Today, some fifteen years later, Nelda is a woman of moderate wealth and total contentment, and lives in Baja California.

FOLLOWING YOUR PATH TO FREEDOM

Let us look at the steps Nelda took. Figure 13–1 shows her pathway to happiness. The positive and negative signs on the graph indicate her state of mind. As you examine her experience, notice how she started off in a negative position just after her husband's death. She continued downward because, after psychometrizing her needs, she made the wrong interpretation and changed her job before getting the money she needed. The debts took her to her lowest ebb, a time when she felt very much inclined to quit this earthly plane. But the Venusian ritual quickly lifted her into the positive realm; the medicine bag

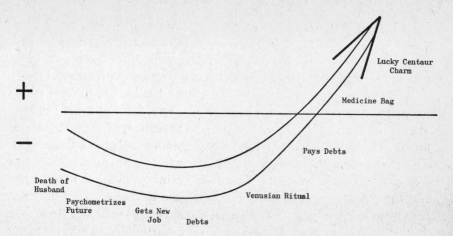

Figure 13-1

Nelda's Pathway to Happiness

further enhanced her happiness and serenity so she could continue on an upward path for the rest of her life. You, too, if you wish, can change your life just as dramatically as Nelda did hers. All it takes is a little effort and a realistic look at the things which may be holding you back.

Every day we get letters asking us to help people define their path to freedom and happiness. Others ask us to do little things for them like hexing their spouse or healing their mother-in-law or making them more beautiful. Our files are full of requests of this type. Only in very exceptional cases do we ever use our powers to grant these wishes. Instead, we try to get people to learn how to do it for themselves; for. in this learning process they discover the importance of first analyzing their whole present and future life.

We can (and often do) help people psychometrize their whole life and establish consecutive logical goals. All goals, of course, are more easily attained when you use psychic techniques to aid you in your path.

Many people seem to be caught in a trap of their own making. Somehow they think in a one-day-at-a-time way; they cannot think in terms of a complete life pathway. A letter we received last year from Bennett W, a 60-year-old gentleman from San Francisco, was typical. He started out by quoting the Judeo-Christian Bible, telling us that we were obviously devils incarnate—and then he closed by saying that he would like us to help him become instantly wealthy. Bennett was trapped. He was trapped in his Christian ethical set; he was trapped in the belief that we were "devils"; yet even within his trap. he knew that we could help him if we wished. However, he was asking us the wrong questions. Quite apart from the insults in the opening paragraph of the letter, he was not giving us sufficient information. Why did he want to be wealthy? What good was it going to do him? What good did he plan to do with his money once he got it?

After we got to know Bennett, we found that he really wasn't a bad sort of a guy and he really didn't want to be wealthy; what he wanted was a secure, comfortable retirement life and someone to argue philosophy with. What he needed was to get a divorce and marry another woman at a compatible mental level. With the aid of our Meta-Psychometric techniques, this is precisely what he did. Both he and his ex-wife are much happier now in serene new environments.

The most deadly trap you can fall into with Meta-Psychometry is the attitude that "it won't work for me." It will always work for you. It will work for you every time you try it, provided of course that you try it with the attitude in mind that it is going to work. Obviously, if you go into it with a negative "it's not going to work" thoughtform in your head, that's exactly what you'll get: nothing.

THE BIRD IN THE GILDED CAGE

Beth W worked as an operations manager of a computer firm in upstate New York. She was a highly successful businesswoman, extremely capable yet all the while maintaining an essential femininity. She was married to an equally successful advertising executive who worked in New York City. They had an "open" marriage; that is, they could each follow their own careers; yet, when they were in the same city, they had a very good time together.

One day, Beth was picked up on a drunk driving charge, and though the offense was relatively minor and caused her little inconvenience, it shocked her into a review of her life. She now admitted for the first time that her life was empty; that is why she had taken to drinking. Even though she was immensely successful, channeling all her energies into her job for some 18 hours a day, she felt that she somehow ought to have a better home life, and perhaps have some children of her own, even at this late stage of her life.

She talked this over with her husband and found that he was violently opposed to any change in their open-marriage situation. It suited him, of course, to have an attractive and well-known woman as his wife—but not to undertake any responsibilities. Beth finally went to the company psychologist with her problems. He told her bluntly that she had diverted her maternal instincts into her work but it was by no means too late for her to consider a change. She went away from his office in a very "up" frame of mind.

Beth was interested in the occult. She decided to use psychometry to replan her life in a logical fashion so she could bring more meaning into it. She used the same envelope technique that we have been teaching you throughout this book. Being of a computer-oriented frame of mind, she started by phrasing all her questions in a yes or no manner. In one envelope she put "drop out of industry, yes" and in another "drop out of industry, no." Other questions that she asked were "relocate, yes" and "relocate, no"; "divorce, yes," "have children, no." Her first tabulation of results looked like Figure 13–2a. The list confused her a little, although in many ways it made her quite happy because it coincided with what she thought she ought to do. The confusion in her mind, of course, was how she should reconcile "divorce" with "children, yes."

Because she was so pleased with this first tabulation, she decided to psychometrize each of the items in greater depth. She attempted, for instance, to ascertain the best time to resign her high-paying job. This second more extensive analysis came out as shown in Figure 13–2b. It told her that she should drop out of industry immediately, relocate then in the southwest high desert, consider earning her livelihood from ski instructing, meet her new mate, and then adopt some children. Now she had a complete new life plan laid out before her eyes, though it meant a tremendous wrenching around of her whole life. Instead of working for a large firm and getting a very healthy paycheck twice each month, she was going to cut herself off from that and rely on ski instructing, of all things, for an income.

Beth couldn't do it. It was a nice dream; it was something she pondered in those quiet, lonely moments she had before dawn; but she

(a)	(b)
1. Drop out Yes	1. Drop out immediately
2. Relocate Yes	2. Relocate Desert southwest
3. Divorce Yes	3. Income ski instructor
4. Children Yes	4. New mate
	5. Children adopt

Figure 13–2

Beth's Psychometric Path

just couldn't quite bring herself to make the break. She did look into the various aspects of a possible new life, and she did subscribe to a couple of sport and travel magazines; and on her vacation she did improve her ski technique. The event that finally made Beth move, was not an executive heart attack like the one Don the fashion designer had; it was another energy-deficiency disease, tuberculosis. As you can see by referring to the Table of Correspondences, this is another of the business-and-commerce diseases, associated with Taurus and an income from the world of commerce and trade. Her firm offered to find her a job at their facility in Tucson, Arizona, but she knew in her heart that if she was ever going to break away from business and drop out, this was the time to do it.

So some seven years ago, Beth took that step. She is now a very popular ski instructor in New Mexico; she married a truck gardener from Taos who, it also happened, was a dropout from a New York stock-brokerage house. Currently they are planning a move to Santa Fe, where they feel the opportunities for his market and landscape gardening will be better. In a recent letter, Beth told us that they have now adopted their third Vietnamese child. Let's listen to Beth's own words:

> Now there is less money—but we need far less. In the past, I may have had a hundred dresses and suits; out here I have four or five pairs of jeans, a couple of ski outfits, and one good frock. Initially, I found it awfully difficult, not just the recuperation from tuber- culosis, but also adjusting to the fact that I was my own boss and that every time I tutored someone, it was money in my pocket. Finally the realization came that things are completely different in New Mexico: that I didn't have to hurry. I am perfectly content. I've had to work at it, but I would recommend to everyone that they seriously consider a full psychometric analysis of their life; not only this, but that they follow the results of that analysis and get themselves a comfortable, rewarding niche in life.

YOU CAN SET YOURSELF FREE

When she dropped out, Beth was earning a salary in the six-figure bracket; that is, more than $100,000 annually. When he dropped out, her new husband had been earning almost that much. These two people now exist on a combined income which is only a tenth of that amount. What is it that binds you to your problems? Is it a salary like Beth's? If it is, surely you could save enough in the next year to retire for the rest of your life and do what you like. Most people, however, are tied to their problems by very mundane things. They stay married even though it is a hell on earth, just because they feel security in that marriage. They have what we refer to as a "death grip" on their partner. Often we see people who are bound together by nothing more or less than hate.

People make continuous excuses as to why they can't move, or why they can't complete a ritual that we've given to them. Some of the excuses are really pitiable. One woman wrote to us in all sincerity expecting us to believe that she could not get ink in her town! Countless other people have complained that they can't get sand or they can't get an aluminum bar. They make for themselves unreal obstacles. They are (and you may be, too) afraid that the ritual *will* in fact work and that they *will* be set free, free of all those problems, free of all those ties, free of all those debts. Why aren't you free of them? Why do you tolerate constant strife when you could walk away from it? Even in times when the jobless rate is high, if you have any kind of training at all, with the aid of your psychometric skills, it is child's play to move from one town to another and get a higher paying job than you had before.

The most common complaint that we get from almost everyone is that they are poor, that they have insufficient money to meet their bills. We ask them always to supply an itemized list of their income and their debts, and in every single case we find that they have purchased luxury items that they could well do without; that if they would take the luxury items out of their life, they would have money to spare. When they protest and claim, "But I need those things," we tell them, then, to do a Venusian ritual as instructed earlier in this book. In most cases, they are too lazy even to get together the elementary necessities for a ritual, so they write again with all their painful excuses and ask us to do it for them.

If you really want to be free, the first thing you must dump out of your life is your work-oriented, sin-oriented ethic. It is not a "sin" to work just one day a week, if in that one day you can make enough money to live on. Once you have slowed down and readjusted your life, you will have time to study the various opportunities that are open to you, and to bring into full play your psychometric ability that will bring serenity and happiness. Why don't you sit down today and analyze your life, and decide which is your major frustration and what steps you should take today to correct that situation? Do you need to get your boss fired? Well, why not do it? Would it be better if your husband washed the dishes while you wrote a book? Well, make him wash the dishes. Or leave him!

Whatever your frustration is, Meta-Psychometry can help you get rid of it. But you must look at the overall picture; you cannot look—or live, for that matter—from minute to minute. You must look at what is best for you in the long term. The procedure is simplicity itself. You know how to do it. So why don't you?

As a final step, if you like, you can take some object that you know you're going to keep for a long time and psychometrize it into the future. First psychometrize it in your present environment, making no changes; then psychometrize it with the colors in the environment that are indicated by possible changes you could make. You will be able to sense the serenity, the peacefulness your future can hold when you change the environment. By carefully adjusting the colors, you should strive for the utmost in future personal serenity, peace, love, and abundance.

YOUR COMPLETE META-PSYCHOMETRIC GUIDE TO A NEW LIFE

This book has brought you a long way. You learned first how to do simple psychometric analyses; how to improve your environment; how to get money; how to become healthy; how to find a new mate. All of these are individually important, but you should now put them all together in a pathway to a new life. Assembling all the parts of the jigsaw and making a full-life picture has been the subject of this last chapter. All you have to do is to follow these steps:

1. Psychometrize your present life. This can often be accomplished with the aid of your private rainbow. Find out what deficiencies you have, and correct them.

2. Now, psychometrically look at your total life circumstances and decide which milestone is the most important and which obstacle you should overcome first. Do this by writing your various needs on slips of paper and placing them in the envelopes. Psychometrize them and place them in a logical order of priority. Then proceed to your next Meta-Psychometric step.

3. Find some possession that you know you will keep with you in your future life; psychometrize it as you let the clock of your life run forward. Bring into its environment the colors appropriate to each of the steps that you plan to take. If your preliminary analysis was correct, as you bring these colors into the environment of the object, so you will psychometrically feel more serenity and happiness. Once you are sure

that you have defined the ultimate in serenity and happiness by these psychometric procedures, you will be ready to proceed to action.

4. Follow the procedures that we have given you in the various chapters of this book to bring your goals into your life in the correct order, so that you will logically move along your path to health, wealth, and happiness. Although we continually say "bring into your life," of course it is equally true that you may have to remove certain people from your environment. Again, we have given you methods to do this.

5. Each time you overcome a major obstacle in your life's path and in your search for happiness, re-evaluate the remaining steps along your way to insure that you have not strayed from your path.

6. In all your undertakings, it is worthwhile carrying with you that extra smoothing of the path that can be obtained from "luck." So, we say, "In good health wear your lucky charm, and win your way to happiness."

A FINAL WORD

As you learn to use your powers and to interpret the actions of other people more surely, so understanding will come into your life. When you have a reasonable share of wealth, health, happiness, and serenity, we urge you to show others your path. For when you teach, you will gain even more understanding and thus bring more fulfillment into your own life.

Appendix

SOURCES OF
MATERIALS AND HELP[1]

Stock and commodity market analysis

Aries Productions
Box 24571
Creve Coeur MO 63141

Send $1 for catalog or $4 for magazine.

Psychic detection squad and general psychometry

Bevy Jaegers Limited
Box 24571
Creve Coeur MO 63141

By police reference only. Send self-addressed stamped envelope for detailed quotation.

Training in meditation and courses in Witchcraft, the Old Religion

Church and School of Wicca
Box 1502
New Bern, North Carolina 28560

Send for free information.

---

[1]Prices and addresses given were correct at press time. We cannot guarantee that they are correct today.

Herbs, fresh and dried

L. W. Estes Company
P.O. Box 365
Alma, Georgia 31510

Amulets and talismans

Magical Child
35 West 19th Street
Manhattan NY 10011

Send $1 for catalog.

Exorcism

William Finch
P. O. Box 1529
Sedona, Arizona 86336

Send self-addressed stamped envelope with details of problem for a quotation.

Light boxes and colored filters

The Fountainhead
P. O. Box 50426
Tucson, Arizona 85703

Light boxes from $50, filters from $10.
Send self-addressed stamped envelope for quotation.

Meta-Psychometry Equipment

Edmund Scientific
Edscorp Building
Barrington, NJ 08007

(Prices and catalog numbers are from their 1976 catalog, and include shipping charges.)

Article	Catalog Number	Price
Pyramid	71617	$21.00
Alnico Magnet	40421	5.25
Prism	801	5.95
Book of colored filters	60403	13.37